LIVING WITH PARADOX
An Introduction to Jungian Psychology

LIVING WITH PARADOX

An Introduction to Jungian Psychology

Anne Singer Harris

California School of Professional Psychology

 Brooks/Cole Publishing Company

I(T)P™ An International Thomson Publishing Company

Albany • Belmont • Bonn • Boston • Cincinnati • Detroit • London • Madrid • Melbourne
Mexico City • New York • Paris • San Francisco • Singapore • Tokyo • Toronto • Washington

 A CLAIREMONT BOOK

Sponsoring Editor: *Claire Verduin*
Marketing Representative: *Cecilia Mantecon*
Editorial Associate: *Patricia Vienneau*
Production Coordinator: *Fiorella Ljunggren*
Production: *George Calmenson,*
  The Book Company
Manuscript Editor: *Elizabeth Judd*

Permissions Editor: *Linda Rill*
Interior Design: *Wendy LaChance*
Cover Design: *Roger Knox*
Indexer: *Madeleine Clarke*
Typesetting: *Bookends Typesetting*
Printing and Binding: *Malloy Lithographing, Inc.*

For more information, contact:

BROOKS/COLE PUBLISHING COMPANY
511 Forest Lodge Road
Pacific Grove, CA 93950
USA

International Thomson Editores
Campos Eliseos 385, Piso 7
Col. Polanco
11560 México D. F. México

International Thomson Publishing Europe
Berkshire House 168–173
High Holborn
London WC1V 7AA
England

International Thomson Publishing GmbH
Königswinterer Strasse 418
53227 Bonn
Germany

Thomas Nelson Australia
102 Dodds Street
South Melbourne, 3205
Victoria, Australia

International Thomson Publishing Asia
221 Henderson Road
#05–10 Henderson Building
Singapore 0315

Nelson Canada
1120 Birchmount Road
Scarborough, Ontario
Canada M1K 5G4

International Thomson Publishing Japan
Hirakawacho Kyowa Building, 3F
2-2-1 Hirakawacho
Chiyoda-ku, Tokyo 102
Japan

Printed in the United States of America

10 9 8 7 6 5 4 3 2 1

Library of Congress Cataloging-in-Publication Data

Harris, Anne Singer [date]
    Living with paradox: an introduction to Jungian psychology / Anne
Singer Harris.
        p.   cm.
    Includes bibliographical references and index.
    ISBN 0-534-21643-9
    1. Psychoanalysis. 2. Jung, C. G. (Carl Gustav), 1875–1961.
I. Title.
BF173.H384 1996
150.19'54—dc20

95-22936
CIP

This book is dedicated to my uncle,
JOSEPH CHAMBERLAIN FURNAS.
A writer all his life,
he dedicated a book to me 40 years ago.
At last I can return the compliment!

CONTENTS

Chapter 5: Personality Types 60

PART TWO:
THEORETICAL COMPONENTS

Chapter 6: Developmental Theory 89

PART THREE:
CLINICAL ISSUES

Chapter 7: Alchemy 107

Chapter 8: Varieties of Jungian Therapy 125

PART FOUR:
INTERVENTION MODES

Chapter 9: Three Major Intervention Modes: Narrative Interpretation, Dream Analysis, and Symbolic Approaches 147

PART FIVE:
CURRENT ISSUES
IN JUNGIAN PSYCHOLOGY

PART SIX:
THE BEGINNING CLINICIAN
AND JUNGIAN THERAPY

PREFACE

Living with Paradox: An Introduction to Jungian Psychology was written to acquaint students of psychology, especially beginning therapists, with Jung's theory in its social and historical context. The book is titled *Living with Paradox* because paradox lies at the heart of all that is best and also most challenging in Jungian theory. Within the state of paradox, we can believe mutually contradictory things with no difficulty; each belief may be true in its own time and setting because timing and circumstances determine all our perceptions. Although many therapists who use Jungian theory are not certified as Jungian analysts, few books on Jung have been directed to Jungians who are not analysts. I have found that clinical students report Jung useful for understanding clients (and themselves) whether or not they practice depth therapy.

This book is addressed to at least two levels of students: those who are learning about Jung in a survey course on psychological theory and those who may wish to go on for specialized Jungian training. It provides a detailed introduction to Jungian concepts, suitable for an honors undergraduate or a first-year graduate-level course in psychology, clinical social work, and related fields.

When organizing a graduate-level introduction to Jung's work, I found no up-to-date short text to orient students to Jungian psychology. One book discussed his life, another his work, and a third took up recent additions to his theory; scattered articles related Jung's concepts to recent scientific developments. This book attempts to summarize these subjects in one easily accessible volume. It gives students an overview of Jung's life, the philosophical roots of his theory, and essential elements of the Jungian approach to depth therapy. In addition, it relates theory to clinical practice and to issues of concern to today's therapists—ecological, scientific, and gender issues, as well as issues raised by the relationship between Jung's personal attributes and the theory he developed. A short section outlines conditions in managed care employment, plus possible approaches to independent practice, including certification as a Jungian analyst.

The vocabulary Jung created for his theory has entered common usage; we all know the terms *introvert* and *extravert, complex* and *archetype.* Jung's personality theory is built around these concepts, and I have relied on John Beebe's generous help to bring them all together within his expansion of Jung's type theory.

Special Topics

Jung treated mostly people in the second half of life. Later Jungians have done extensive work on child development, compatible with the principles of self psychology. This book covers theory and goals of therapy over the entire life span.

Some aspects of Jungian theory have been criticized for their mystical or teleological qualities. Yet, it is just these intuitive descriptions that anticipate recent developments in the physical sciences and in current brain research. Chapter 10 gives an overview of synchronicity, teleology, and archetypes as they relate to the nonlinear equations of chaos theory, fractals, and Lorenz's strange attractor. Holograms provide a bridging metaphor for some of these concepts.

Students are often puzzled about how Jungian theory can be used in a context of increasingly managed public mental health care. Few books talk about the issue of money or about other aspects of the therapeutic frame. I relate the frame to Jung's alchemical *temenos,* address concrete variations in clinical practice, describe current conditions in the field, and suggest ways to operate as a Jungian within that context.

In short, besides covering the basics of Jungian theory, this book should enable students to see how Jungian psychology has grown, where it stands now in relation to other schools of thought, and how it can be incorporated into readers' own lives, whether or not they expect to become Jungian therapists.

Sections are organized to make it easy for the instructor to accent, omit, or rearrange selected portions of the book. The science section and the clinical section are separable from the basic-theory chapters. The developmental diagram in Figure 5.1 is not essential for understanding the fundamentals of Jungian theory but is designed to stimulate the imagination.

Acknowledgments

This book is built on foundations greatly fortified by graduate students at the California School of Professional Psychology whose papers and dissertations I have supervised. As we worked together on their literature reviews, I was able to reassess or discover writings relevant to this book. The experiences of working with them to organize and edit their papers helped me to organize and edit this book.

Some students' papers and dissertations were particularly stimulating. I especially want to mention Hugh Molesworth on Jung's philosophical roots, Lynne Ehlers on the history of alchemy, Roxanna Rutter on counter-transference, and Charles Roth on the use of dreams among both Freudian and Jungian analysts.

Students in my introductory Jung classes, too numerous to mention, pro-vided both stimulation and the challenge to present complex material plainly.

I am indebted to John Beebe's extraordinarily generous editorial and substantive help. He greatly clarified my exposition of his version of type theory in Chapter 5, besides editing and suggesting improvements to my diagram of life development. He refused to accept any credit beyond this brief mention.

A series of talks at the California School of Professional Psychology in the academic year 1993–94 by Donald Sandner (transference-countertransference), Alan Ruskin (dreams), John Beebe (personality types), Michael Reding (money), and other analysts provided up-to-date vignettes of current Jungian theory and practice. I owe special thanks to Donald Sandner and John Beebe for their permission to quote freely from my notes of their lectures. David Tresan, Peter Rutter, and Charles Roth provided suggestions for subjects to include.

Writing an introductory text plunged me into a review of the Jungian literature and of notes I had taken at seminars over the past twenty years. I have tried to connect all the ideas presented in this book to their sources. If the influence of some writers or speakers has surfaced in my words without due acknowledgment, I apologize, and I hope that those individuals will notify me in time to be mentioned in any later editions of this book. The develop-ment of this text was also facilitated by the insightful and valuable comments of the reviewers. I wish to express my appreciation to Mary Howard-Hamilton of the University of Florida, Mel Henderson of Metropolitan State Univer-sity, Kenneth James of Northeastern Illinois University, and Gail Nelson.

I am grateful to my publisher, Claire Verduin, who signed me up on slim evidence that I could produce an acceptable text for Brooks/Cole. I hope that she continues to think that her faith was justified. Elizabeth Judd was my copyeditor; her efforts led to great improvements in the organization and clarity of this book. Finally, all the others who contributed to the production of the book deserve heartfelt thanks for their accuracy and patience.

Anne Singer Harris

LIVING WITH PARADOX
An Introduction to Jungian Psychology

Fundamentals

CHAPTER 1

Introduction

Jungian therapy is growing in popularity (DeAngeles, 1994), and Jungian books, such as *Women Who Run with the Wolves* (Estés, 1992), appear on best-seller lists. A sizable segment of the reading public seems to agree with Jungian therapists that mental health requires acquaintance with our own interior workings, not just successful adaptation to outside demands. We are ready to welcome another professional dimension of psychotherapy besides managed care and short-term intervention. This short book was written to explain major patterns of Jungian theory for those who have had little or no previous exposure to Jung and his followers.

Jungian theory concentrates on universals. Without neglecting current topics such as gender issues and cultural diversity, it still focuses mainly on the individual quest for meaning. Symbols and myths play a prominent part in Jung's theory, so perhaps a folktale will best introduce his thinking.

INSCRUTABLE FATE

Nasrudin was walking along an alleyway when a man fell from a roof and landed on his neck. The man was unhurt; the Mulla was taken to hospital.

Some disciples went to visit him. "What wisdom do you see in this happening, Mulla?"

"Avoid any belief in the inevitability of cause and effect! He falls off the roof—but *my* neck is broken! Shun reliance upon theoretical questions such as: 'If a man falls off a roof, will his neck be broken?'" (Shah, 1971, p. 26).

The Heart of Jung's Work

Both Nasrudin and Jung avoided abstract, statistical statements about what one should expect to happen, concentrating instead on the unexpected and never-repeated particular event. Jungian psychology studies individuals.

Jung's theoretical approach parallels recent scientific findings in chaos theory to a surprising extent (see Chapter 10). For example, like the cycles in a chaotic system, each life trajectory is unique, but together trajectories form collective patterns. They spiral around a common center, which Jung called the *self*.

Paradoxical Perspective

Jung's theories are founded on the principle of paradox. The meaning of the term *paradox* will become clearer as we continue, but a dictionary definition followed by a few comments will start the process. *Chambers Concise 20th Century Dictionary* defines *paradox* as "that which is contrary to received opinion: that which is apparently absurd but is or may be really true: a self-contradictory statement." In Jungian usage, this term has a broader meaning. To Jungians, *paradox* need not mean absolute contradiction or inconsistency, but includes ambiguity, a puzzle or dilemma, a tension between opposite poles of an issue, even incongruity between elements of a larger whole.

Some of these ambiguities are purposeful, and some are accidental. Jungian theories display an assortment of inconsistencies. Jung's own approaches gradually developed over almost 60 years and have been modified and supplemented by other people in different times and contexts. Jungian subschools have developed. The accumulation of Jung's writings, plus the additions and later comments by other writers, can be confusing.

However, this state of affairs is not necessarily unfortunate. I doubt that any analyst would say of Jungian therapy, "It has to be done exactly the way Jung did it." Analytical psychologists would worry if Jung's work were taken as gospel, since most believe that it is never advisable to copy a leader exactly, no matter how talented the leader may be. Jungian analyst James Yandell (1977, p. 37) quotes Basho, a 17th-century Japanese poet: " 'I do not seek to follow in the footsteps of the men of old; I seek the things they sought.' "

This introduces our first paradox. To be a Jungian means to develop your singular temperament, not slavishly conform to a set of rules invented by Jung or his successors; at the same time, to be a Jungian practitioner you need to know, and guide yourself by, the basic tenets of Jungian theory. As Basho implied, disciples of a great leader can attain the leader's objective only if they value the goal over the technique. Jungian practitioners retain a primary confidence in the truth of this first paradox.

The title of this book, *Living with Paradox*, is itself meant as a signal to the reader that there are no simple yes or no answers in Jungian psychology. Everything depends on the particular situation, and one part of any answer may seem diametrically opposed to some other part. Jung emphasized the role of the "tension of the opposites" in attaining an archetypal balanced wholeness. If you follow Jung's way of psychotherapy, you must not only tolerate but actively seek out the painful and maddening opposites in your life, and in the lives of your clients, to arrive at creative new solutions to old problems.

ENANTIODROMIA. A central feature of the Jungian paradox of opposites is that any action or trait taken to an extreme will become its antithesis. The term for this is *enantiodromia*. Take the example of a woman who always insists that her husband decide how to spend their money. Her insistence compels him to be the decision maker. However, her refusal to decide is itself a most powerful decision.

Unlike this example, many paradoxes have positive effects. Happy outcomes result from the ability of paradox to rescue people from polarizing conflicts, and heightened conflict between elements can lead to a creative transcendence of an issue. (These matters are pursued further in Chapter 3.)

There are other aspects to paradox. We will approach paradox from various directions throughout this book.

A Complex Domain of Meanings

Jungian theory is less than straightforward partly because of its structure, which is symbolic-hermeneutic (interpretive) rather than causal-mechanistic, like Freud's. As J. J. Clarke (1992, p. 9) says, it is "not a causal network but a domain of meanings and purposes." Hermeneutic systems interpret events multidimensionally, whereas causal-mechanistic systems seek to develop immutable meanings and laws.

Both/And, Not Either/Or

A hermeneutic system creates the freedom to see issues as conglomerates of contradictory elements—that is, as both/and rather than either/or predicaments. For example, if you really are convinced of the Jungian tenet that every conscious attitude is compensated by an opposite and equally powerful unconscious attitude, your picture of yourself must inevitably include both positive and negative elements. Consequently, no matter how short of your ideals you may fall, you can't possibly think you are all bad. Neither will you struggle endlessly to become perfect. The paradoxical theory of compensation assures you that you are capable of neither total evil nor total perfection.

Thus Jungian theory advocates *individuation,* the constant development of all one's possibilities, but never *perfection.* Like the pot of gold at the end of the rainbow, the goal keeps running ahead as you chase it. Further, each step opens up possibilities you could never anticipate.

Jung knew that each of us is unique, in both our limitations and our talents. This belief receives support from the findings of recent basic biological research. For instance, neuronal development diverges as a result of experience even between the brains of identical twins (Crick, 1994, p. 236).

The Plural Psyche

Individual differences are further influenced by the setting of events. As we will see in more detail in Chapter 3, your psyche is composed of a collection of divergent bipolar impulses (that's why we call it plural), and so your actions depend on which aspects are being mobilized by your surroundings—that is, by the context. Thus, your personality is made up of many subpersonalities, and their salience shifts as one or another takes the stage. Your ego is rather like a committee, whose elements take turns acting as chair (Booth, 1990). We all learn this early in life: Even very small children know that they can get more stories from Mama-at-bedtime than from Mama-cooking-dinner.

All of these considerations make it hard to create rules of behavior that will apply to anyone in every situation. Jungian theory hardly tries but instead presents a set of principles and a kit of dynamic tools with which to assemble a unique explanation of each life as it develops.

The Jungian Approach

Students often ask about Jungian therapy, "How is it done?" and some are disappointed when I reply, "I can't say it's really *done* at all; it's more a habitual way of relating to your client and to the world in general." One particularly quick student thought a moment and then asked, "In that case, what does Jungian psychology offer that religious systems do not?"

When looked at in detail, analytical psychology is different from religion—or Freudian analysis or object relations or science—and also includes elements of each. Some comparisons of these subjects are given in Chapters 6, 8, and 10.

THE TRANSPERSONAL. Transpersonal theory asserts that we are affected in unknown ways by events beyond our bodies and beyond our immediate surroundings. It usually includes the concept of a grand design of the universe. Jungian psychology leaves more room for the transpersonal than other psychological theories do and has been criticized for being mystical as a result. As scientists push farther into the secrets of the mind and brain, the unanswerable questions of psychology, religion, philosophy, and now physics and mathematics, seem to draw closer to one another.

Relevance of Jung to Contemporary Issues

Much of Jung's thought can be applied with surprisingly little alteration to issues that concern us today, such as world peace, ecology, gender, and attitudes about mental illness. This book attempts to familiarize you with the links between Jungian analytic psychology and some of these issues.

The Shadow and World Peace

Jung believed that aggression on the collective level results from a failure to take responsibility for it at the personal level. He related this aggression to a refusal to recognize our own shadow aspects. In Jungian language, the shadow is "the thing a person has no wish to be" (CW 16; para. 470).[1] When we *project* (see Chapter 7) our deepest *shadow* (Chapter 4) onto another person or nation, we see that person or nation as the cause of all our ills and disappointments. If the other does the same, soon we may be attacking each other in the name of making the world better.

On the other hand, if each person learned to recognize and take responsibility for his or her own aggressive urges (among others), the outside world would get less of the blame. Thus many Jungian therapists believe that individual psychotherapy acts at a primary level to lessen the threat of local, national, or even global conflict. Because society is made up of individuals making their thousands of individual decisions, if the majority of us favored peaceful solutions to problems, conflict would decrease. It could be as simple as that.

Ecology

Jung himself was happiest when close to nature and spent much time sailing on Lake Zurich or walking in the Swiss mountains. The end of his life was

[1]Citations to Jung's *Collected Works* (CW) will generally take this form throughout the book. Here "18" is the volume number and "1584" is the paragraph number.

darkened by a fear that humankind might destroy itself and the world through nuclear war. Jung's Gnostic position that we are all part of a larger whole (what he called the *pleroma*) leads to a concern for the world as a small part of the *creatura*, the embodiment of the pleroma's underlying unifying principle (see Chapter 5). Neither philosophy nor science can document the existence of such a whole—either you believe there is such a thing or you don't—but it's a useful hypothesis. This unified view specifically implies that when we harm or exterminate animals, trees, water, air, or any other aspect of the natural world, we are harming a part of our larger selves.

Jungian therapists devote their lives to the appreciation and tracking of human consciousness, while exploring the meaning (or lack of it) that life provides us. The practice of Jung's psychology does not require that we believe in a unitary principle, but it does require a respect for aspects of the universe beyond the merely human ones.

Gender Issues

Many people are moving toward the belief that traditional political structures, based on ambition and power struggles, have been the cause of injustice to human and nonhuman entities alike both on a global level and within each society. One aspect of this injustice has been that women were often considered to be property, and women's modes of thinking and feeling were denigrated in favor of traditionally "masculine" modalities.

These *gender roles* are to a great degree culturally established, and the cultures holding world power and resources in the last few hundred years have mostly been androcentric (male-oriented). Jung was biased by his own culture; the conditions of his birth and upbringing influenced both his personal conduct and his thoughts about women's psyches in ways for which he has been justly criticized. Jungian psychology is just beginning to address problems of racial inequality and other similar concerns. Gender, though, is integrally implicated in discussions of the anima/animus archetype, and Jung was ahead of his time in positing both male and female elements within each person. We further discuss gender issues in Chapters 6 and 11.

Psychopathology

Jung's theories of psychology were always more open, fluid, and intuitive than Freud's, and certainly more so than later behavioral theories based on pure stimulus-response causal events. In recent years authors such as Barbara Stevens Sullivan (1989) have increasingly deemphasized the pathology of mental disorder, saying that we rely for optimal mental health on all the multiple levels of our psyches, from primitive to developed.

In this view the difference between sanity and insanity appears to depend on our ego strength, our ability to contain turbulent energies within a sense of selfhood. This requires a flexible, not a rigid, sense of identity and a tolerance for ambiguity.

Almost every section of this book, on both theory and practice, develops aspects of the Jungian attitude toward the origin and treatment of emotional disorder. Jung's personality theory provides an excellent basis for an understanding of the infinitely variable relationships among our psychic processes—conscious and unconscious, ego-centered and archetypal. The work with infants by Michael Fordham's (1957, 1963) group in England tracks the origins of emotional problems during early ego development (see the section on Fordham in Chapter 6).

READINGS

Samuels, A., Shorter, B., & Plaut, F. (1986). *A critical dictionary of Jungian analysis.* London: Routledge.

CHAPTER 2

Origins of Jung's Thought: Personal and Philosophical

Jung's thought grew out of his surroundings, both personal and academic. This chapter looks briefly at his personal background and intellectual origins to provide a framework for the discussion of Jungian theory in later chapters.

A Biographical Sketch

Carl Gustav Jung was born July 26, 1875, to Emilie Preiswerk Jung and the Reverend Johann Paul Jung, a pastor in the Swiss Reformed Church. The professions of both religion and medicine were traditional in Jung's family: His paternal grandfather was a physician, and eight of his uncles were pastors. The family was cultured but impoverished.

Jung's mother's family was very involved in spiritualism; Jung's medical dissertation, *On the Psychology and Pathology of So-Called Occult Phenomena*, published in 1902, was based on séances conducted with his cousin Helene Preiswerk. The dissertation investigated the emergence of "alternate personalities" under hypnosis and created a foundation for Jung's subsequent work on archetypes and complexes.

Jung later described his mother, who had participated in these sessions, as displaying two distinct personalities in daily life. Jung (1961a, pp. 33–34) saw himself as having two natures as well. One was prosaic and involved his everyday existence. The other was archetypal; it was first represented by a childhood vision of an 18th-century man of authority. He called the two

natures his "No. 1 personality" and "No. 2 personality," respectively (p. 68).
Jung's experience of the multiplicity of his personality, later supported by his
readings in philosophy (Clarke, 1992, p. 14), was less pathological than has
been implied by writers such as John Kerr (1993) (see below).

Jung's childhood was largely solitary and troubled. Corinna Peterson (1989,
p. 302) has summarized some of the stresses of that period:

> [He experienced] comparative poverty, tension between his parents, a sense
> of isolation, and the disillusionment evoked at this stage by religion. . . .
> Looking back at himself at the age of nineteen, Jung later emphasized this
> sense of being torn between two poles: "In science I missed the factor of
> meaning, and in religion, that of empiricism."

In his critical review of analytical theories, the psychologist John Kerr
(1993, pp. 45–60) has given an unfriendly psychological interpretation of Jung's
early development, saying, for instance, that "the child was not well adapted
to polite, or even juvenile, society. A lifelong friend . . . remembers . . . 'I had
never come across such an asocial monster before' " (p. 46). What Kerr does
not mention is that the reporter and Jung were both 3 or 4 years old at the
time of this first encounter, and that Jung's sin was that of ignoring his young
guest (Hannah, 1976, pp. 29–30). Other writers have been less critical (see
Clarke, 1992, and Carotenuto, 1982). It is worth noting that Jung's interest
in the interior life of the psyche, which appears to have begun in his difficult
childhood, later developed into the positive guiding force behind the evolution of his psychological theories.

Certainly Jung mastered the intellectual tasks of growing up. He attended
a local school until he transferred at age 11 to the Gymnasium in Basel. He
was a medical student at the University of Basel from 1895 to 1900, when
he was appointed to a position with the Swiss psychiatrist and neurologist
Eugen Bleuler at the Burghölzli Psychiatric Hospital in Zurich. In 1902 his
medical dissertation appeared, and during the winter of 1902–1903 Jung took
a leave to study hypnosis with Pierre Janet, a French physician and psychologist,
at the Salpêtrière in Paris. Returning to Zurich, he resumed his hospital duties
and also served as a lecturer at the University of Zurich from 1905 to 1913.

A decade earlier, in 1903, Jung had married Emma Rauschenbach, the
daughter of a prosperous businessman. They eventually had one son and four
daughters. Emma served as a subject for her husband's early research on word
association (Kerr, 1993, p. 70). She was aware that Jung was subject to in-
fatuations with other women and for many years tolerated the presence of
Toni Wolff, his inspiration, assistant, and lover. Emma became a Jungian writer
and analyst and was especially interested in the Grail legend (Jung & von Franz,
1970). She died in 1955.

Jung gave his own version of these events—sketched by Storr (1983) and many other authors—in the autobiographical *Memories, Dreams, Reflections* (1961a). He describes a lonely and fantasy-filled childhood, but of course not a "pathological" or "monstrous" one. He tends to skip over aspects of his later life that have provoked criticism. But as with any great innovator, criticism of Jung's personal foibles should be distinguished from evaluation of his intellectual achievement. Clarke (1992) reminds us that Jung himself believed that a theory proved itself by being useful. He quotes Jung as saying that even philosophy " 'still has to learn that it is *made by human beings* and depends to an alarming degree on their psychic constitution' " (p. 26; Jung's italics).

Jung and Freud

From 1907 to 1912 Jung worked closely with Sigmund Freud, founder of psychoanalysis. Freud was 19 years older than Jung, and his infant theory of psychoanalysis was struggling to emerge as a treatment method in Vienna in 1906, when Jung first read about it. By that time Jung was established as a lecturer at Zurich University and was a senior staff physician at the Burghölzli mental hospital. He was also conducting, with Franz Riklin, his pioneering experiments with the Word Association Test. Freud's ideas paralleled the results of Jung's research, and Jung became an enthusiastic advocate of psychoanalytic theory and techniques. Jung's position in Zurich helped to establish Freud as a major figure in the medical circles of the time.

The two men collaborated to disseminate and promote psychoanalytic theory through meetings and publications. A considerable rivalry developed. They were often thrown together at meetings; in 1909 they traveled together to the United States to speak at Clark University, and they both appeared at meetings of the International Psychoanalytic Congress from 1909 until Jung's "defection" in 1913.

Personal relations between Jung and Freud were also complicated by the early analysts' practice of interpreting each other's dreams. This led to mutual distrust. The dangers of playing the overlapping roles of both friend and analyst had not yet been recognized.

Early analysts were also less than cautious in another arena: They often sustained love affairs with patients or former patients. We know that Jung became emotionally embroiled with three of his women patients: his cousin Helene Preiswerk (the subject of his doctoral dissertation); then Sabina Spielrein, who may have been the inspiration for his concept of the anima; and Toni Wolff, who became both his professional associate and his acknowledged lover for many years. Some of the implications of these events are taken up in Chapter 7, in our discussion of countertransference, as well as in Chapter 11, on three major problems with Jungian theory.

When Freud and Jung met, Jung was the more powerful figure. Contrary to some published statements, he was never Freud's apprentice (Clarke, 1992, p. 5; Kerr, 1993, p. 9). The two men did, however, adopt a symbolic father/son relationship marked by an emotional attraction frightening to Jung. Freud wanted to groom Jung as his heir apparent, and Jung saw in Freud a father figure stronger than his own ineffectual biological father. The dynamics of this mutual *projection* added complexity to their relationship, and bitterness to their eventual split.

THE SPLIT WITH FREUD. By 1912, after several years of collaboration, Jung's ideas had diverged significantly from Freud's. Freud's insistence on the specifically sexual origin of psychic energy, known to psychoanalysts as the libido, was a major problem for Jung, who defined it in much more general, symbolic terms.

For various reasons, both personal and theoretical, Jung defined the libido as psychic energy with multiple, not solely sexual, origins. He saw it as arising from the tension between the many polar opposites in the psyche, such as male/female, good/bad, or conscious/unconscious (see Chapter 3).

Because Jung's and Freud's differing personalities were intertwined with their theories, the breach between them was a crisis of personal friendship as well as a philosophical severance. Freud saw his method as scientific but soon elevated his theory of infantile sexuality to a dogma. Jung not only avoided creating a tight system of rules but was highly critical of all dogmatic statements. Clarke (1992, p. 13) comments that Jung was shocked by Freud's dogmatic stance. Jung's method was conjectural and pragmatic, and he saw his own work as subject to continual revision and as a personal confession or personal myth, never as a closed system.

Freud's work did influence Jung's approach to the interpretation of dreams (Clarke, 1992, p. 6). Jung, using data from his Word Association Test, described resemblances between the response-time disturbances emerging in his own work and Freud's account of repression in dreams. He extensively acknowledged (and validated) Freud's supposition that concepts can be pushed from the conscious mind into the unconscious, where they continue to affect individual psychology.

THE ORIGINS OF JUNG'S NEW IDEAS. Others besides Freud who influenced Jung included philosophers who had been writing about the human mind long before psychology was invented. Later in the chapter we will see that Kant's work was central to Jung's theories. Another source of influence was the

Romantic philosopher Carus. Jung adopted Carus's definition of the psyche as "the total interacting field that embraces both the conscious and unconscious realms" as well as Carus's opinions that dreams perform "a restorative function for conscious life, and . . . consciousness and unconsciousness [have] mutually compensatory functions" [Clarke, 1992, p. 73). (For more on Jungian dream theory, see Chapter 9.)

TWO OTHER MAJOR DIFFERENCES BETWEEN JUNG AND FREUD. Although Jung had repudiated his father's church, early religious training may have lingered in his search for something *transpersonal* in life. Freud's goal, in contrast, was to discover purely biological motives for human behavior.

Jung retained a belief in the usefulness, under some circumstances, of Freud's "reductive" approach, but he thought that motivation was also "prospective" or forward-looking and directed toward valuable goals unknown to the ego. Partly because of the influence of Sabina Spielrein, Jung came to believe that human development was teleological—that is, directed to an end and governed by purpose.

The preceding points constitute two of Jung's major contributions to psychology, achieved only through the sacrifice of his ties with Freud.

"THE REST IS SILENCE." After the theoretical split between the two men was made public by Jung's publication in 1912 of "On the Psychology of the Unconscious" (Jung, 1969e), Freud and Jung exchanged increasingly acrimonious letters. The last was in January 1913, after which Jung wrote a postcard to Freud:

> Kusnacht-Zurich, 6 January 1913
>
> Dear Professor Freud,
>   I accede to your wish that we abandon our personal relations, for I never thrust my friendship on anyone. You yourself are the best judge of what this moment means to you. "The rest is silence."
>   Thank you for accepting Burrow's paper.
>
> Yours sincerely,
> JUNG

(McGuire, 1974, letter 344J, p. 540)

The two men never reconciled.

Jung's Midlife Crisis

Occurring as it did halfway through his career—during what Jung later characterized as "midlife"—the split with Freud was a turning point for Jung, and it cast him into a deeply troubled psychic state. When he coined the term *midlife crisis*, Jung was describing his own experience.

The essential notion is that at the middle of the life span, around the age of 35 to 40 (later for some), many men and women reach a point at which they stop, catch their breath after their first attempts to establish a career and family, and ask themselves if this is all there is to life. Previous activities seem drab and pointless, and they feel deprived of joy. If all goes well, their assessment goads them to develop some previously neglected parts of their life and to progress toward the goal of balanced individuation.

Jung's break with Freud caught him at exactly such a midpoint. This was also the time when he decided to admit Toni Wolff into his intimate life. These events hurled him into the depths of his own psyche and evoked a painful self-analysis.

In 1913 he gave a series of lectures at Fordham University on the theory of psychoanalysis, but by the end of 1914 he had given up regular teaching, as well as his academic position at the University of Zurich, to work full time at writing and psychotherapy.

During this inward-turning period Jung spent hours on the shores of Lake Zurich, playing with rocks, mud, and water, building himself first a miniature village and eventually a full-sized retreat at Bollingen. In later life he spent many hours alone in what represented his true psychic home.

Jung emerged from this prolonged crisis with renewed energy, and much of his most innovative work grew out of the introspective efforts of those years. Some aspects of this work are discussed in the section on active imagination in Chapter 9.

Jung's Later Life

The rest of Jung's life was long and increasingly full of recognition. The Psychology Club in Zurich was founded in 1916 to provide a forum where the growing number of Jungian students could meet for instruction and informal socializing. Toni Wolff, Jung's right-hand assistant, was its president during its heyday, from 1928 to the end of World War II (Hannah, 1976, pp. 197, 286).

Jung gave his first seminars in England in 1920 in Cornwall, and he lectured in Zurich almost continuously from 1928 to 1939. In the 1930s he received honorary degrees from Harvard and Oxford (Tresan, 1994).

Jung traveled to New Mexico, Tanganyika, and India, seeking evidence for his theory that all cultures share common archetypal influences. He showed considerable respect for indigenous cultures, even learning Swahili for his African trip. Although ahead of his time in many ways, Jung's sensitivity to people of color was severely limited by his era and his Swiss culture. In the film *Matter of Heart*, some amusing—although inappropriate—old movie footage shows him affectionately pinching the cheek of an apprehensive African boy.

Jung long resisted the urging of his students and colleagues to formalize his teachings, but in 1948, toward the end of his life, he helped to establish the first Jung Institute in Zurich. Classes there focused on cultural and symbolic subjects, giving only limited attention to conventional clinical applications. The emphasis on dreams and the archetypal continues to this day.

Jung died on June 6, 1961, in his 86th year.

Current Jungian Psychology

In 1946 a Jungian Institute was founded in London, followed in 1947 by the San Francisco Institute. Today there are 13 Jungian training institutes in the United States as well as others throughout the world. The International Association for Analytical Psychology counts more than 2000 qualified Jungian analysts among its members. Note that, in the United States, Jungian institutes are clinically focused and have never required applicants to possess a medical degree, as the Freudian centers did until recently.

The English translation of Jung's *Collected Works* comprises 20 volumes, available in both hardcover and paperback as Bollingen Series XX from Princeton University Press. Jungian articles appear in such journals as *Anima*, the *San Francisco C. G. Jung Institute Library Journal*, the *Journal of Analytical Psychology*, *Parabola*, *Psychological Perspectives*, and *Spring*.

The Philosophical Origins of Jung's Theories

Philosophy represents an essential foundation of Jung's thought. We have mentioned that some ideas from Kant and Carus were central to aspects of Jung's theories relevant to his eventual split from Freud. The following section provides more detail.

Jung's Use of German Philosophical Idealism

Two related features distinguish the philosophy adopted by Jung. One is the subject of our dual self; like Kant, Jung believed our mental and physical aspects to be mutually dependent. Then, like Kant, Jung applied this dual philosophy to nature, seeing it as composed of both the world of matter and the world of spirit. This latter feature led Jung to the vision of an underlying *unus mundus* or unitary world (Clarke, 1992, pp. 60–61) having wide ecological implications:

From the German Romantic philosophers Jung derived his emphasis on the dynamic force of opposites [in the psyche], the recognition of the essential role of darker, negative aspects of experience, the central role of intuition, and . . . an organic outlook which seeks to unify spirit and nature. (p. 64)

We can divide philosophers into those who focus on building a comprehensive system and those who focus on resolving problems. Jung was a problem thinker, along with Plato, Kierkegaard, Nietzsche, and later Wittgenstein (Clarke, 1992, pp. 18–19). Like these philosophers, Jung declared experience to be more important than theory (p. 70).

As we saw in the section on the split with Freud, Jung's more individual approach was fundamentally incompatible with Freud's effort to build a tight system of psychological rules.

Philosophical Roots of the Archetypes

Jung can be classified as an idealist, of whom Plato was the first. Plato posited the existence of a system of eternal realities entirely separate from our world of matter and known only through the intellect, not the senses. Jung (1933, p. 190) expressed this idealism when he wrote:

All that I experience is psychic. . . . My sense-impressions . . . are psychic images, and these alone are my immediate experience. . . . We are in all truth so enclosed by psychic images that we cannot penetrate to the essence of things external to ourselves. All our knowledge is conditioned by the psyche which, because it alone is immediate, is superlatively real.

This is Kantian philosophy par excellence. Jung assumed that categories exist a priori in the mind and constitute a set of rules governing the way we experience the world. For Jung, mental "structure" was the product of an active psychic process. The psyche's job is to integrate our perceptions; in Jung's terms, we are mentally disposed to organize our perceptions.

Jung did believe that "we are locked into the *common* world of the human psyche. To speculate about what may be *really* out there is fruitless" (Clarke, 1992, pp. 32–33). In this way Jung was not a classical Kantian, but a *neo*-Kantian. One writer has said of the neo-Kantian outlook:

Reality is covered, as it were, with a veil of language, symbol, and myth, and it is only through the mediation of these that knowledge is possible at all. Furthermore, this veil is not static and timeless, but is itself the product of history and cultural evolution. (Avens, 1980, p. 19)

Though these remarks refer specifically to the perspective of the philosopher Ernst Cassirer, they could also describe Jung's outlook. This outlook helped Jung explain why cultures differ in their worldviews.

As Jung documented personal experience and searched for parallels with experiences of people in other cultures, he paid particular attention to the relative nature of the beliefs he derived. He wrote: "If I call something true, it does not mean that it is absolutely true. It merely seems to be true to myself and/or to other people" (CW 18; para. 1584).

Social-constructivist psychoanalysts—those who emphasize the subjective nature of reality—have recently taken up this relativistic approach. Irwin Z. Hoffman (1992, p. 293) writes: "As conviction based upon objective knowledge is reduced, conviction based upon the analyst's subjective experience is increased." Jung's phenomenological approach anticipated such social-constructivist theory.

Jung said that the function of the mind is to construct models. His theory is itself a model, a projection on nature, modifiable by inputs of knowledge. Jung saw the projection of a model maker's ideas onto nature as a normal function rather than an aberration, since no one can know objective truth.

Models are all hermeneutic; that is, they interpret events multidimensionally. They are not *causal* networks but domains of meanings and purposes that shift between events and their context, much like modern "grounded" theory. When carefully applied, models are self-correcting. They are also very individual and need careful interpretation. The interpretations will vary over time, depending on context. In fact, the development of a good model closely parallels the neuronal development of the brain (see Edelman, 1992).

Jung based much of his psychology on immediate experience and sometimes seems to want to throw out theory altogether. At other times, like some modern writers, he sees all experience as "theory-laden," making it impossible to separate the data from the theory behind their collection. Clarke (1992, p. 15) explains it this way: "I can never completely abandon my own outlook and view the world from inside another's. . . . There can, therefore, be no single authentic Jung awaiting disclosure."

READINGS

Clarke, J. J. (1992). *In search of Jung*. London: Routledge.

Hannah, B. (1976). *Jung: His life and work—A biographical memoir*. New York: Putnam.

Jung, C. G. (1933). *Modern man in search of a soul*. New York: Harcourt Brace Jovanovich.

Jung, C. G. (1961a). *Memories, dreams, reflections* (A. Jaffé, Ed.). New York: Random House.

Jung, C. G. (1994). *Collected works* (2nd ed., 20 vols.). H. Read, M. Fordham, G. Adler, & W. McGuire, Eds.). Bollingen Series XX. Princeton, NJ: Princeton University Press.

Storr, A. (1983). *The essential Jung.* Princeton, NJ: Princeton University Press.

CHAPTER 3

Basic Theory

This chapter reviews basic tenets of Jungian theory and the associated terminology to provide background for later chapters on personality type and the schools of therapeutic intervention.

Several sets of concepts and terms will concern us here. To begin, most therapists will recognize as "Jungian" certain general concepts such as *archetypes*, the *collective unconscious*, and the therapeutic technique known as *amplification*.

Other terms have entered our vocabulary so completely that Jung is seldom remembered as their author. Examples include *personality complex*, *synchronicity* (meaningful coincidence), and *introversion* and *extraversion* as personality descriptors.

A third group of terms is shared by Jungians, Freudians, and other theorists using a dynamic model of the psyche. Many of these terms emerged from dialogue among early (or later) analytical writers. Typical themes include the role of *unconscious* factors in our personalities, the importance of *dreams* as clues to the unconscious, and the operation of the clinical phenomena of *projection*, including *transference* and *countertransference*.

The definitions of the central Jungian ideas taken up here are only first approximations, since a thorough understanding requires a lifetime of working with them. It is less important to memorize definitions than to accumulate clinical insights associated with their use. Jung himself is quoted as saying, "Thank God I'm not a Jungian!" (Clarke, 1992, p. 20).

Paradox Revisited

Chapter 1 discussed the concept of paradox. We now turn to some of the origins and effects of paradoxical oppositions in Jungian theory.

Jung's writings took shape over a period of nearly 60 years (1902–1961), and his theories evolved over time. He never pulled his papers into a tight, harmonious system, even when revising for his *Collected Works*. Thus some find his ideas hard to pin down, even mutually contradictory. Jung's dense writing style also contributes to these difficulties.

The Focus on Individuals, Not Averages

Jung's focus on the individual also makes it hard to systematize thinking. In 1956 he wrote:

> Since self-knowledge is a matter of getting to know the individual facts, theories are of very little help. For the more a theory lays claim to universal validity, the less capable it is of doing justice to the individual facts. Any theory based on experience is necessarily *statistical*; it formulates an *ideal average* which abolishes all exceptions at either end of the scale and replaces them by an abstract mean.
>
> Not to put too fine a point on it, one could say that the real picture consists of nothing but exceptions to the rule, and thus, in consequence, absolute reality has predominantly the character of *irregularity*. (CW 10, para. 493–494)

Jung distinguished the task of understanding an individual from that of building knowledge about humankind. He elaborates on the preceding quotation as follows:

> If I want to understand an individual human being, I must lay aside all scientific knowledge of the average man and discard all theories in order to adopt a completely new and unprejudiced attitude. I can only approach the task of *understanding* with a free and open mind, whereas *knowledge* of man, or insight into human character, presupposes all sorts of knowledge about mankind in general. (CW 10, para. 495)

Since Jung, unlike Freud, never attempted to create a unitary system of thought, his statements vary with their *context*. If we place them next to each other, some of the apparent contradictions look absurd, although within its setting each statement is perfectly "true." For Jungians, truth is usually relative, not absolute. In this way, *paradox* emerges from the core of Jungian theory.

Archetypal Polarities, Libido, and Paradox

Another kind of paradox results from the complex system of checks and balances in Jungian theory, where every attribute implies its opposite. Unconscious factors balance conscious factors, dreams balance waking life, one pole of an archetype balances the other—and we operate out of all of them simultaneously. The pervasiveness of the opposites will become clearer from the details of individual archetypes in Chapter 4.

Each element of the psyche is assumed to consist of a pair of conceptual poles connected by an axis or field of force. Our psychic energy, called *libido*, is generated by the tension—the field of force—between each pair (and among multiple pairs) of these poles.

These poles can symbolize any sort of dichotomy: old/young, dark/light, good/bad, and so on. They are all contained in the larger setting of the psyche, where life events create constant shiftings and adjustments of all the polarities. These life events may appear to be located in either the inner or outer realm; they may involve things that develop within the psyche or impinge on it from outside.

Enantiodromia and Transcendence

Since psychic events occur in pairs of opposites, when we are concerned with one pole, the other is by definition also involved. If I am extremely concerned about being "good," I must also be fighting my naturally powerful tendencies to be "bad," and so on. In fact, any extreme, when pushed to the limit, is transformed into its polar opposite. As we saw in Chapter 1, the process of switching poles is called *enantiodromia*. For another example of this, consider a mother who is so "good," so devoted to her child, that she becomes a "devouring" mother and gobbles up the child's individuality.

If we can maintain the tension between opposites without either fleeing the field or flipping into an enantiodromia, we may become aware of some new concept *transcending* the opposites. This sequence parallels the philosopher Hegel's system of "thesis, antithesis, synthesis." Hegel argued that one concept (thesis) inevitably produces its opposite (antithesis); their interaction yields a new concept (synthesis), which then becomes the thesis in a new process.

Keeping in mind the complexities of Jung's thought and the difficulty of systematizing it, what concepts can we identify under the "Jungian" rubric?

Basic Concepts: The Self

Samuels, Shorter, & Plant (1986, p. 135) define the Jungian Self as "an archetypal image of man's fullest potential and the unity of the personality as a whole." The image of the Self is *archetypal*. We will return to the topic of archetypes in Chapter 4; for now, we should note that in Jungian theory, the idea of the Self as an archetypal image implies the presence of a tendency to organize psychic events that lies beyond the field of human possibility.

If you compare Jung's Self (capital S) with the "self" (small s) of Heinz Kohut and others dealing with object relations or self psychology, you will find that they overlap, but not completely, and that Kohut's self is more like Jung's ego than like Jung's Self. Object relations deals with the way we learn as a child to relate to others, and how we carry impressions of those early objects of our interactions into later life. In that theory, our self is what relates to the objects; it is personal to us, not transcendent in any way.

Primal and Ultimate Self

In a careful clarification of Jung's theory, Joseph Henderson (1984, pp. 86–87) distinguishes two aspects of the self, primal and ultimate:

> My idea is that the Self is there as the given condition of the archetypal background of all consciousness, and of course we can know nothing about its intrinsic nature, as Jung has told us. But, as individuals with a psychological attitude, we can orient and reorient ourselves to the primal Self and its "eternal recurrence of all things," or to the ultimate Self and its presentiment of final things in a mystery to be revealed beyond imagining.

(The last sentence means that an archetype points to phenomena that we hypothesize to lie beyond the capacity of our brains to comprehend.) The personal self or Ego occurs as a complex and is just one part of the two aspects of the larger Self discussed by Henderson.

The present text capitalizes the archetypal term *Self* in Jungian theory to distinguish it from the Jungian personal *self* (or Ego), and from the *self* of object relations theory, but relies solely on context to differentiate the primal and ultimate Self.

Ego and Self

The Self is an archetype (a patterned innate predisposition for dealing with tensions of opposites). It may be useful to visualize it as a vortex of energy like a whirlpool, and to picture the changing tensions among its internal elements as producing eddies or subvortices (complexes) that enlarge and shrink here and there, and over time. In this metaphor,the ego is one eddy among many and may "shrink" or "enlarge" in an individual's psychic whirlpool.

Jung clarified the relationship between Self and ego as follows (the editors of the *Collected Works* chose not to use the uppercase S): "The self is not only the centre, but also the whole circumference which embraces both conscious and unconscious; it is the centre of this totality, just as the ego is the centre of consciousness" (CW 12, para. 44). "The self, in its efforts at self-realization," Jung said elsewhere,

> reaches out beyond the ego-personality on all sides; because of its all-encompassing nature it is brighter and darker than the ego, and accordingly confronts it with problems which it would like to avoid. Either one's moral courage fails, or one's insight, or both, until in the end fate decides. . . . You have become the victim of a decision made over your head or in defiance of the heart. From this we can see the numinous power of the self, which can hardly be experienced in any other way. For this reason *the experience of the self is always a defeat for the ego.* (CW 14, para. 778; Jung's italics)

In short, the ego, being only part of the Self, is not autonomous. This fact seldom sinks in before you reach middle age.

By focusing on the "defeat" and forgetting that the ego's outlook is relatively limited, you might conclude that the "defeat for the ego" is a wholly negative experience. Moving beyond the ego complex usually does involve a painful crisis of "letting go," as described by William James in *Varieties of Religious Experience* (1902, pp. 212, 272–274). But it opens up the wider, non-ego perspective and represents a major step in personal growth. Once you are reconciled to giving up the old ego perspective's illusion of power, you experience the authority of the Self as pivotal.

The Self in Child Development

Jungian developmental theorists, especially Michael Fordham and other writers in England, dispute Jung's description of the primary Self in the newborn infant. An important issue concerns the mutability or changeability of the primary Self. Jung thought that the primary Self was an innate potential wholeness, unconscious at birth, an integrating and organizing archetype that emerged in expanding islands of consciousness during childhood. But in modifying Jung's theory, Fordham (1957, 1961) argues that rather than gradually emerging whole, the primary Self passes through regular cycles of integration and deintegration, starting at birth.

Edward Edinger (1972, p. 5) speaks of the process of ego-self union and separation, which describes a spiral, rather than the repetitive cycle of Fordham's Self-ego integration-deintegration:

> The process of alternation between ego-Self union and ego-Self separation seems to occur repeatedly throughout the life of the individual both in childhood and in maturity. Indeed, this cyclic (or better, spiral) formula seems to express the basic process of psychological development from birth to death.

These additions to Jung's theory imply that although the Self is all-inclusive, the cohesive organization of the Self is mutable, so that the relationships among elements within the Self shift as the elements themselves are altered.

The Self and the Collective

Jung repeatedly contrasted the individual responsibility to one's Self with the responsibility to a social collective, such as a creed or social system:

> To be the adherent of a creed . . . is not always a religious matter, but more often a social one, and, as such, it does nothing to give the individual any foundation. For this he has to depend exclusively on his relation to an authority which is not of this world. (CW 10, para. 509)

He believed that individuals lacking a strong personal connection to the Self would be at the mercy of demagogues. He also connected the ego-Self relationship to moral and spiritual values. In his essay "The Undiscovered Self (Present and Future)," for example, he says that "the value of a community depends on the spiritual and moral stature of the individuals composing it" (CW 10, para. 516).

The Self and the Transpersonal

The Self is by definition transpersonal, or more than the sum of the individual. The transpersonal aspects of the Self have attracted criticism from hardheaded scientists, who call them "mystical" and "unscientific." One critic even goes so far as to allege that Jung knowingly founded a charismatic religious cult (Noll, 1994).

Jung did characterize the Self in terms that paralleled descriptions of the "ineffable" or indescribable deity of early theologians and philosophers. Some Jungians also like to point out that Jung's concept of the Self is remarkably like a nonsectarian God image, akin to the Quakers' "Inner Light"—an immanent portion of God implying the whole and steering one's conduct and emotional life (Kelpius, 1951, p. 72). In fact, many Quakers have taken a great interest in Jungian psychology; Quaker groups have met to discuss Jung since 1943 ("Quakers and Jung," 1993). The spiritual implications of Jung's approach are attractive to therapists and others who see a need for a transpersonal dimension to complement personal psychology. Others prefer to construe the concept of Self as philosophical rather than religious.

Basic Concepts:
Elements (Processes) of the Psyche

Jung defined the psyche as "the totality of all psychic processes, conscious as well as unconscious" (CW 6, para. 797). Here, as always, the unconscious includes both personal and collective aspects.

The Psyche Organizes the Self

For Jung, the Self and the Psyche had much in common; you may find it difficult, even unnecessary, to puzzle out their differences. Samuels et al. (1986, p. 116) say about this:

> The conceptual overlap between the psyche and the self may be resolved as follows. Though the self refers to the totality of the personality, as a transcendent concept it also enjoys the paradoxical capacity to relate to its various components, for example, the ego. . . . The psyche encompasses these relationships and may even be said to be made up of such dynamics.

These matters are complex and involve several Jungian terms. The *Self* is the whole structure but can relate to its parts, somewhat as my neurological system can send signals to my arm or leg. The *Psyche* seems to be like the neurochemical reactions of the system, and carries out the operations among the parts of the *Self* (with which it completely overlaps). This, although less than crystal clear, seems to mean that the psyche consists of the *relationships* among the dynamic parts of the Self. The Self and its parts are treated as more reified or "thinglike"; the components of the personality are what "have" the relationships, by means of the processes of the Psyche.

If the psyche consists of the dynamic relationships of the Self and its elements (as defined by Samuels et al. above), exactly how is the psyche "different from" the Self? That question has no concrete answer, but here we will call the psyche the *active* principle of the Self, even though the words *psyche* and *Self* are both metaphors or symbols that resist being pinned down by the linearities of language.

The Unconscious

The concept of unconscious mental functions had existed in philosophy and psychology for some years when Freud and Jung adapted it to their own purposes. Freud was the first to describe in detail the hypothetical origins of our personal unconscious. He influenced Jung's thoughts on the subject, although as we saw in Chapter 2, Jung was not a "disciple" of Freud but a rival theorist, especially in his view of the unconscious, which departed radically from Freud's.

The following brief review of Freud's position should help clarify the differences between the two theories.

FREUD'S VIEW OF THE UNCONSCIOUS. Freud took a hardheaded "scientific" view of theory, omitting any favorable reference to spiritual topics. His concept of the unconscious was roughly comparable to Jung's personal unconscious. Freud believed that the unconscious housed all the events, thoughts, and feelings repressed by the ego at the prompting of the conscience (a part of the *superego*). He saw the unconscious as the dark basement of the psyche and the superego as a strong unconscious inhibitory mechanism that criticizes the ego. Civilized life is possible, said Freud, only because the civilizing process makes us repress our most primitive urges and extravagant potential for wrong doing (see Freud, 1930/1961).

Freud believed that the instincts in the unconscious, collectively composing the *id*, were all based on the generalized generative force of the sexual drive. He called this drive the *libido*. The libido becomes channeled, he said, into forms of expression acceptable to society by a refining process he called *sublimation*. Freud hypothesized a conflict between the libido (Eros) and the death instinct (Thanatos). Jung set up a different dichotomy, of Eros opposite the will to power (CW 7, para. 78). Analyst James Hillman (1972, p. 81) proposes yet another plausible opposition, between Eros and Phobos (Fear). Paradox in Jungian theory is heightened by such conflicting but plausible theoretical positions.

For more detail about Freud's theories, see his *Basic Writings* (1938). You may want to keep in mind that contemporary Freudians have modified Freud's original theory of psychoanalysis. Today Freudian and Jungian theories are in many ways more similar than they once were, especially in their shared use of self psychology and object relations theories.

Jung, unlike Freud, divided the unconscious into two parts: personal and collective. Freud's entire "unconscious" is roughly comparable to Jung's "personal unconscious." The collective unconscious contents have never been and theoretically never can be conscious. They consist of ancient, probably neurologically determined tendencies to structure our perceptions in certain ways.

Ego consciousness plays a relatively small role in the individual psyche. "Reality," as we tend to perceive it, also plays a minor role. Our subjective, largely unconscious psychic reality is at least as important as the "objective" world. Jung said:

> We must never forget that the world is, in the first place, a subjective phenomenon. The impressions we receive from these accidental happenings are also our own doing. It is not true that the impressions are forced on us unconditionally; our own predispositions condition the impression. (CW 4, para. 400)

Jung's concept of *predisposition* has been confirmed in several ways. Linguist Noam Chomsky (1957) has argued that we have something analogous to innate "templates" in our brain that let some perceptions enter consciousness while screening out others. Recent developments in neuroscience modify this notion, but they still suggest that we have evolved brain structures that actively process our perceptions and predispose us to learn specific types of behavior.

We have also evolved the capacity to react selectively to dangerous stimuli even before we have identified them as such (LeDoux, 1994). This is an excellent scientific demonstration of the operation of the unconscious. Here William James (1890/1950, pp. 449–450) anticipated both Jung and neuroscience when he wrote, "Common-sense says, . . . we meet a bear, are frightened, and run. . . . This order of sequence is incorrect. . . . The more rational statement is that we feel afraid because we tremble."

Selective inattention is another aspect of predisposition. Depending on our varying internal needs, we effectively but unconsciously ignore certain phenomena. An example would be our failure to notice an accidental injury until the crisis is over. More purely psychological examples can be vexatious. When we fall in love we are likely to ignore large faults in our partner. Our selective inattention in this case shuts out unwelcome psychological information.

To tie the discussion together, the processes in the psyche are seen as including:

1. The *ego*, which is the center of consciousness.
2. The *personal unconscious*, containing material forgotten, repressed, or too faint ever to have registered in consciousness
3. The *cultural unconscious*, made up of socially derived material
4. The *collective unconscious*, consisting of *archetypes*, which manifest themselves, through symbols, as complexes of the individual

Remember that these are *processes*, not concrete *things* located somewhere in time and space. We now elaborate on each process in turn.

The Ego: The Conscious Part of the Psyche

The ego is the part of the self usually thought of as "I" when we say things like "I'm hungry" or "I hate it when you do that."

JUNG'S DEFINITION OF THE EGO. Jung, like Freud, called the ego the center of consciousness, but Jung saw it as less of a dungeon-keeper of the instincts than Freud did. Freud said that the ego represses impulses from the id. The id includes all of our most "primitive" instincts, and Freud's ego serves as their jailer and parole officer. Jung described the ego as follows:

> We understand the ego as the complex factor to which all conscious contents are related. It forms, as it were, the centre of the field of consciousness; and, in so far as this comprises the empirical personality, the ego is the subject of all personal acts of consciousness. (CW 9ii, para. 1)

Jung also noted that

> the ego is, by definition, subordinate to the self and is related to it like a part to a whole. . . . Just as our free will clashes with necessity in the outside world, so also it finds its limits . . . in the subjective inner world, where it comes into conflict with the facts of the self. . . . So the self acts upon the ego like an *objective occurrence*. (CW 9ii, para. 9)

RELATIVIZATION OF THE EGO. The unexpected realization that there is more to our personality than just our ego brings about what Jung called the *relativization of the ego*. He said that with the discovery of a psyche outside consciousness, "the position of the ego, till then absolute, became relativized; that is to say, though it retains its quality as the centre of the field of consciousness, it is questionable whether it is the centre of the personality" (CW 9ii, para. 11). This is a desirable event through which you come to realize that you cannot control every aspect of your life.

INFLATION OF THE EGO. *Inflation* occurs when you identify with an archetype; you may become arrogant, feeling that you possess superhuman characteristics. The connection between ego and Self thus has its shadow side; Samuels et al. (1986, p. 135) remind us that

> the relationship of ego to self is a never-ending process. The process carries with it a danger of inflation unless the ego is both flexible and capable of setting individual and conscious (as opposed to archetypal and unconscious) boundaries.

To avert inflation, it helps to remember (for instance) that you can never be an embodiment of the whole Hero archetype. The archetype may sweep you into most impressive acts of heroism, but you must drop the heroics once the crisis has passed to avoid being trapped in an inflated Persona.

Inflation can also be *negative*. You are in the grip of this type of inflation if you become extremely depressed and identify with the archetype of Saturn. Possession by archetypal inflation can be associated with the wider swings of manic depression (Bipolar Disorder in the *DSM-III-R*).

FUNCTIONS OF THE EGO. Jung said that the elements of the ego are always the same but vary infinitely in "clarity, emotional coloring, and scope" (CW 9ii, para. 10). Or to put it differently, each of us has a sense of identity (unless we are seriously mentally disturbed), but our identities are more or less diffuse, make us more or less happy, and include various components, depending on our individual personalities. To take a simple analogy, this reminds me of one mail-order catalog that shows a basic dress pattern rendered in various sizes, with a choice of several colors, in print or solid fabrics.

What functions does Jungian theory assign to the ego? The ego *mediates* between the unconscious and the outside world. Whether it does this effectively depends on whether you enjoyed a relatively normal childhood development. If you are psychologically healthy, you will possess a distinct *ego identity*, which implies that you experience yourself as having continuity, sameness, individuality, and autonomy over time. Your inner and outer *ego boundaries* will be strong, flexible, and relatively permeable when appropriate. Relative to outer events and other people, you will feel that you can contain and locate what is "inside" as distinct from what is "outside" (Maduro & Wheelwright, 1983, p. 137).

The ego also fortifies your *sense of identity* against the intrusion of complexes from the unconscious, against stress, and against various other catastrophes. As with all the elements of the psyche, the ego's strengths and weaknesses vary among individuals and with the context of events.

The Personal Unconscious

Jung based some of his ideas about the personal unconscious on the earlier work of Austrian physician and physiologist Josef Breuer and German physician Emil Kraepelin. Breuer's cathartic method of therapy and theory of hysteria formed the basis of psychoanalysis. Kraepelin argued that all mental illness is due to organic brain dysfunction. In 1893 he was the first to define *dementia praecox*, calling it a degenerative disorder. This was renamed *schizophrenia* by Bleuler in 1908. Bleuler demonstrated that some schizophrenics get better, ruling out a "degenerative" disease diagnosis for them. Besides having been influenced by these physicians, Jung is also known to have read extensively in Plato, the Neoplatonists, Nietzsche, Bergson, and other philosophers concerned with the unconscious part of the human mind (Clarke, 1992).

Jung's three categories of the personal unconscious are: (1) elements forgotten by an individual (such as the location of your misplaced car keys), (2) elements repressed and then expressed (like the lyrics of a popular song that you haven't thought of for years and suddenly remember), and (3) elements that have never reached consciousness at all (naturally, we can't begin to describe what these might be) (CW 9ii, para. 4). Like Freud, Jung thought that elements unacceptable to the ego were held in the personal unconscious, but Jung disputed Freud's belief that they were its only contents. In Jung's view the personal unconscious could also be a source of unsuspected strengths, which might be brought to consciousness and further evolved either through a natural developmental process or with therapeutic help.

The Cultural Unconscious

The cultural unconscious is more general than the personal unconscious but is not impersonal like the collective unconscious. Though it was foreshadowed in Jung's writings, the concept of the cultural unconscious was defined and codified by Joseph Henderson (1964, 1990). Henderson described cultural consciousness as emerging from the collective unconscious, much as individual consciousness does. Cultural consciousness comprises the elements that all members of a culture carry in their psyches as a result of experiences and genetic tendencies unique to their group. These elements become attenuated and mingled over time, as cultural distinctions become blurred.

Jung had persuasively argued that under certain conditions archetypes (universal tendencies to organize our perceptions in certain ways), though culture-transcendent, may be ignored or forgotten: Archetypes are

> like riverbeds which dry up when the water deserts them, but which it can find again at any time. An archetype is like an old watercourse along which the water of life has flowed for centuries, digging a deep channel for itself. The longer it has flowed in this channel the more likely it is that sooner or later the water will return to its old bed. (CW 10, para. 395)

Thus, although archetypes are transcultural, Jung implied that they can lose their meaning for us, becoming dry and empty forms. Under favorable conditions they can refill with meaning. This makes it plausible to say that, like individuals, cultures can repress or forget some archetypes and that different archetypes may "flow" well in different cultures, just as they can in individual psyches.

These different versions of the cultural unconscious—or of culturally "irrigated" reality—give countries what seem to be their distinctive national characteristics. On a humorous note, the following joke is attributed to Roy Fairchild of the San Francisco Theological Seminary: "Speaking typologically, in Heaven one will find French chefs, English police, German mechanics, Swiss managers, and Italian lovers. In Hell one will encounter French mechanics, English chefs, German police, Italian managers, and Swiss lovers" (Beebe, 1991). Caution is advisable, however, since beliefs about national personality types can become important sources of culturally based misunderstanding and conflict. World War II provided a tragic illustration.

HENDERSON'S DEVELOPMENT OF THE CULTURAL UNCONSCIOUS. Joseph Henderson (1990a, 1990b) elaborated on the concept of the cultural unconscious after Jung's death. He departed from Jung's approach because he gradually saw that "much of what Jung called *personal unconscious* was not personal but cultural" (1990b, p. 117).

For Henderson, the cultural unconscious is

> an area of historical memory that lies between the collective unconscious and the manifest pattern of the culture. It may include both of these modalities, conscious and unconscious, but it has some kind of identity arising from the archetypes of the collective unconscious, which assists in the formation of myth and ritual and also promotes the process of development in individuals. (p. 103)

He goes on to explain that although archetypes are changeless, the *forms* they assume are mutable, and so they vary among both individuals and cultures. In addition, the changes and transformations are not random, because they also are archetypally determined (p. 104). He gives the Oedipus complex as an example; it can only develop in a child exposed to a cultural pattern similar to the one described in the Greek play.

Henderson notes that the cultural unconscious most often manifests itself in dreams. As an illustration, he mentions the Australian aborigines' concept of the *Dreaming* (sometimes called *Dreamtime*), which is a world of images outside the time and space of ordinary existence. He writes:

> In this reflective world of the Dreaming, we may find forms that connect us with real events or people in history, but we may also find that this form may suddenly fade into a world where archetypal imagery is found at its place of emergence, where it is elemental and represented merely as earth, air, fire, and water, and sometimes associated with animals or plants. If these in turn become humanized, we have the beginnings of culture, with the invention of numbers and number games, music, ceremonial art, and religion. In due course we then have a culture that transcends the archetypal world, and the first threshold of cultural consciousness has been reached. (1990a, p. 107)

One version of cultural consciousness can be viewed in Figure 5.1, where it occupies the middle ground shown as the wavy band in the diagram.

THE PERSONAL SHADOW AND THE CULTURAL UNCONSCIOUS. Since unconscious processes lie at depths varying from personal to archetypal, and the Shadow is associated with the unconscious side of our personalities, it follows that the Shadow must have several aspects. These will differ depending on the circumstances. Even the personal Shadow will have cultural overtones. As Henderson puts it:

> Insofar as the personal shadow is the opposite, *not of the whole ego but only of the persona*, it always has a social (and therefore cultural) aspect, since the persona embodies our need for appropriate social interaction. Therefore, a study of unconscious cultural conditioning may become an absolute necessity in order to understand certain projections that people make upon each other. (p. 112; Henderson's italics)

A greater appreciation of the concept of unconscious cultural conditioning among debaters of gender issues and other social issues would go far to clarify current debates.

The Collective Unconscious

Jung was struck by his discovery that myths and fairy tales from widely separated cultures reflected similar themes. He eventually concluded that these themes spring from deeply human tendencies to organize experience along certain lines. He called the tendencies *archetypes* and said that together they made up a generalized human substrate called the *collective unconscious*. Jung distinguished between our personal psychology and a collective psychology as follows:

> Our personal psychology is just a thin skin, a ripple on the ocean of collective psychology. The powerful factor, the factor which changes our whole life, which changes the surface of our known world, which makes history, is collective psychology, and collective psychology moves according to laws entirely different from those of our consciousness. The archetypes are the great decisive forces, they bring about the real events, and not our personal reasoning and practical intellect. . . .The archetypal images decide the fate of man. (CW 18, para. 371)

ARCHETYPES. A few additional comments on archetypes will help to clarify the idea of the collective unconscious. Early in his thinking, Jung came to the conclusion that no single drive, including the sexual, could adequately explain the whole range of human activity. Thus he broadened the definition of the *libido*, which for Freud meant the polymorphous sexual drive, to encompass a larger category of *energy*. Jung attributed the source of this libidinal energy to tensions between the poles of many *opposites* in the psyche, eventually naming these opposites archetypes. Briefly, "The archetype is a psychosomatic concept, linking body and psyche, instinct and image" (Samuels et al., 1986, p. 26). Together the archetypes constitute the collective unconscious.

Jung hypothesized that the archetypes form "an omnipresent, unchanging, and everywhere identical *quality or substrate of the psyche per se*" (CW 9ii, para. 12) and that "the ego rests on the *total field of consciousness* and [also] . . . on the *sum total of unconscious contents*" (CW 9ii, 4; Jung's italics). He also said:

> Archetypes are, by definition, factors and motifs that arrange the psychic elements into certain images, characterized as archetypal, but in such a way that they can be recognized only from the effects they produce. They exist preconsciously, and presumably they form the structural dominants of the psyche in general. (CW 11; para. 222n)

Thus, although we can talk about the archetypal symbols of our dreams and personalities, we cannot be aware of archetypes themselves, but only of the ways in which their symbolic patterns appear in our lives. This underlines an important point: No processes of the collective unconscious (unlike some processes of the personal unconscious) have ever been conscious; in Jungian theory, the collective unconscious is made up of "prerational" archetypes.

Archetypes, like mathematical infinities, come in different sizes. Like the earlier concept of the Self interacting with its parts, this is a paradox difficult to grasp. Theory says that the infinite size of the Self is larger than the infinite size of any of its parts. "Smaller" activated archetypes are expressed through the "larger" Self, which is itself an archetype.

Archetypes have another paradoxical quality: Although each archetype is absolute, and our whole world can be organized by a single archetype, the number of archetypes is infinite. As a result, driven by personal experience, we will shift among worldviews as if we were looking through the different colors of a stained glass window. Artists and poets know about this; the following lines from "Adonais," by 19th-century British poet Percy Bysshe Shelley (1925, p. 438), provide an example:

> The one remains, the many change and pass;
> Heaven's light forever shines, earth's shadows fly;
> Life, like a dome of many-colored glass,
> Stains the white radiance of eternity.

In one (less poetic) passage, Jung said that the archetypes are,

> so to speak, organs of the prerational psyche. They are inherited forms and ideas which have at first no specific content. Their specific content only appears in the course of the individual's life, when personal experience is taken up in precisely these forms. (CW 11, para. 845)

For archetypal material from the unconscious to manifest itself in daily life, processes of the collective unconscious must first move the material into the personal unconscious. Since the two types of unconscious process (personal and collective) are both psychic phenomena, they are separable only in theory.

Edward Whitmont (1969, pp. 41–56) uses the term *objective psyche* to describe the sum of the personal, cultural, and collective unconscious. This can be confusing, since Jung sometimes used *objective psyche* to denote the collective unconscious alone. He viewed the collective unconscious as "objective" because it seemed to be unaffected by personal bias. When you read because it seemed to be unaffected by personal bias. When you read contemporary Jungian writers, you may need to discern their meaning from the context.

ORIGIN OF THE CONCEPT OF THE COLLECTIVE UNCONSCIOUS AND ITS ARCHE-TYPES. Until lately, few non-Jungian therapists realized that Jung did not originate the notion of the collective unconscious. Several books have corrected this view, tracing the origins of the concept to Gnostic writings of the early Christian era, and before that, through the writing of the Neo-platonists to Plato himself. Jung often referred to these early sources; the following statement provides a typical example: "There are present in every psyche forms which are unconscious but nevertheless active—living dispositions, *ideas in the Platonic sense,* that preform and continually influence our thoughts and feelings and actions" (CW 9i, para. 154; my italics).

Jung was also aware that writers in other areas of the social sciences had evolved concepts similar to the notion of cross-cultural archetypes:

> Mythological research calls them "motifs"; in the psychology of primitives they correspond to Lévy-Bruhl's concept of "représentations collectives," and in the field of comparative religion they have been defined by Hubert and Mauss as "categories of the imagination." Adolf Bastian long ago called them "elementary" or "primordial thoughts." From these references it should be clear that my idea of the archetype—literally a pre-existent form—does not stand alone but is something that is recognized and named in other fields of knowledge. (CW 9i, para. 89)

Although Jung based many of his concepts on ancient sources, some aspects of his ideas about archetypes were ahead of their time, even anticipating scientific developments of the late 20th century.

Basic Concepts:
Synchronicity and the Psychoid Archetype

The concept of synchronicity is touched on here, then taken up again in Chapter 10 as it relates to modern physics. F. David Peat (1987) calls synchronicity the "bridge between matter and mind," explaining that meaning expresses itself in daily life through synchronicity in the same way that archetypes express themselves through symbols. He offers this example of synchronicity in action:

SYNCHRONICITY

A certain Monsieur Deschamps, while A boy in Orleans, was given a piece of plum pudding by a certain Monsieur de Fortgibu. Ten years later he discovered another plum pudding in a Paris restaurant and asked if he could have a piece. He was told, however, that the pudding had already been ordered—by M. de Fortgibu. Many years afterward M. Deschamps was invited to partake of a plum pudding as a special rarity. While he was eating it he remarked to his friends that the only thing lacking was M. de Fortgibu. At that moment the door opened and an extremely old man, in the last stages of disintegration, walked in. It was M. de Fortgibu, who had got hold of the wrong address and had burst in on the party by mistake. (Peat, 1987, p. 8)

Jung called this kind of arresting coincidence *synchronicity:* Synchronistic events are connected only by the meaning they carry for the observer, not by normal cause-and-effect relationships.

A contemporary instance of synchronicity was described in the *San Francisco Chronicle* (Martin, 1994). The narrator was riding down a mountain road to go salmon fishing when he remembered he had left his soft drinks at home. At a bend in the road, he almost ran into his dog, who was holding in her mouth an ice-cold six-pack of his favorite soda. He took the sodas and sent the dog home but never did find out where the six-pack came from. His own drinks were still in the refrigerator when he got back. He called the story "Hand of Dog"[1] as a reversed takeoff on the cliché, "hand of God."

This chapter has covered some basic Jungian concepts, including enantiodromia and transcendence, major components of the Self (the conscious ego and the three levels of the unconscious),and the notion of synchronicity. Next we will consider archetypes, the organizing tendencies underlying all our mental processes.

READINGS

Clarke, J. J. (1992). *In search of Jung.* New York: Routledge.

Edinger, E. (1972). *Ego and archetype: Individuation and the religious function of the psyche.* New York: Putnam.

[1]*Hand of Dog.* Copyright © San Francisco Chronicle. Reprinted by permission.

Freud, S. (1938). *The basic writings of Sigmund Freud* (A. A. Brill, Ed.). New York: Random House.

Henderson, J. L. (1990a). The cultural unconscious. In *Shadow and Self: Selected papers in analytical psychology* (pp 103–113). Wilmette, IL: Chiron.

Henderson, J. L. (1990b). The origins of a theory of cultural attitudes. In *Shadow and Self: Selected papers in analytical psychology* (pp. 114–123). Wilmette, IL: Chiron.

Whitmont, E. C. (1969). *The symbolic quest.* Princeton, NJ: Princeton University Press.

CHAPTER 4

Some Major Archetypes

Archetypes are anchored in our brain structure. Recent brain research indicates that our present neuronal configurations arose through evolutionary means, rather than existing a priori, and predispose us to organize experience in certain ways identifiable as human. Presumably, nonhuman entities (say Martians) would be equipped with neuronal patterns and corresponding archetypes different from ours, structuring their alien experience in accordance with their alien biology. We could imagine that their "eyes" might "see" ultraviolet radiation, for instance, and cause them to pattern this experience through symbols derived from an associated archetype.

To give a non-Martian example of predisposition: Very young children have an innate notion of what a plural noun form should be and have no trouble pluralizing made-up words without going through any process of trial and error (Singer & Singer, 1969, pp. 134–138). Similarly, children readily understand and respond to archetypal images in fairy tales and can symbolically see themselves in the stories.

In Jungian theory, archetypes occupy the middle ground between mind and matter. On the one hand, they are conceptually related to Plato's ideal forms, and, on the other, they are said to arise from neurological characteristics of the human brain. To highlight their dual nature, Jung called them *psychoid*.

Jung spoke of the *Pleroma*, a region outside space and time, which precipitates itself through the agency of human consciousness into the *Creatura*, the world of our experiences. The archetypes occupy the Pleroma, but our experience of them emerges in the Creatura, where they are clothed in symbols.

Our perceptions of the world are ordered by the archetype dominant in our psyche at a particular time and place. Both the selection of archetypes to appear "on stage" and the variety and frequency of their appearance differ among individuals, creating an endless series of permutations, so that, like snowflakes, no two perceptual fields are identical. This realization underlies Jung's distrust of dogma in psychology as well as his insistence on addressing individual cases.

Hillman (1972) eloquently supports Jung's view. He says, for instance, that a truly therapeutic attitude must include a personal, individual involvement, rather than a patronizing, "objective" psychological attitude (pp. 88–90).

Bipolarity of Archetypes: The Syzygies

What do we mean by the term *syzygy*? The compact edition of the *Oxford English Dictionary* provides a preliminary definition: "a pair of connected or correlative things; in Gnostic theology, a couple or pair of opposites." Jung's psychology is founded on the existence of syzygies or opposites in the psyche. In this book the term *syzygy* is shorthand for any pair of psychic opposites. Some definitions follow.

BASIC BIPOLARITY: CONSCIOUS/UNCONSCIOUS. Hillman (1979, p. 12) asserts that the most basic polarity in the psyche is between conscious and unconscious. This polarity is itself archetypal, and all other archetypes partake of that fundamental duality. However, it is only one of several coexisting syzygies, making archetypes complicated indeed.

POSITIVE/NEGATIVE POLARITY. Jungians also define each archetype as having a positive and a negative aspect, so this is a second way that archetypes are bipolar, although they are not dichotomous:

> The archetype is perceived as containing an inherent and opposed duality which can be expressed as a spectrum (for example, considering the archetype of the Great Mother, the good or nourishing mother would be at one end of the spectrum and the bad or devouring mother at the other end). Analytically speaking, an archetypal content can be said to be integrated only when the full range of its spectrum has been made conscious. (Samuels et al., 1986, p. 103)

Thus archetypal effects can be more or less conscious and experienced in various proportions of their positive or negative aspects. In ordinary life, most of us occupy one end of the spectrum on which our various polarities fall, which tends to inhibit consciousness of the other ends.

Thus clients in Jungian analysis have not completely understood and incorporated an archetype until they consciously recognize all aspects of it as it appears within the psyche. When this happens, a third, *transcendent* option may appear, uniting the opposing qualities of any spectrum.

Shape Shifting Among Archetypes

Archetypes tend to shift shape and flow into each other like the Greeks' Old Man of the Sea, who changed into a slippery and elusive series of creatures in the hands of anyone attempting to capture him. This is because archetypes are content-free, patterned tendencies of thought; their qualities overlap, they are not hierarchical, and their symbolic expression is complexly layered.

This is a messy and unpredictable realm in which to wander, and its shiftiness annoys people who like to call a spade a spade and never a shovel. Murray Stein (1983) calls this space "liminality"; it is the domain of Hermes, the trickster guide. To tolerate these conditions, a person must tolerate ambiguity.

Paradoxically, Jungian writers have a habit of defining these shifty archetypes, as summarized below. Keeping in mind the archetypes' tendency to melt into each other, their *general* characteristics can provide the background for specific "figures" of their symbolic enactments in real time.

Major Jungian Archetypes

Definitions of some major archetypal symbols and John Beebe's version of their less-conscious polar opposites are given in the following pages (see Beebe, 1984a, 1986, 1988a, 1993c). As explained above, some archetypal pairs are "opposites" of each other in addition to having internal positive/negative polarity. The resulting relationships among elements are intricate.

I have adopted Beebe's explanation of personality type, and so in this chapter the pairs of archetypes first described are those that occur in his type system, to be elaborated on in Chapter 5. The "Opposing Personality" (the fifth archetype, below) is Beebe's own concept, not a classic archetype like the others. Each of the following groups is arranged on a (roughly) positive/negative seesaw, with the term *versus* as the fulcrum.

Persona or Hero Versus Shadow or Opposing Personality

In mythology, the hero often stands for the aspect of personality with which we meet the expectations of the outside world of our parents, and more generally for socially recognized achievement. Jung's term for that outside world was the *Collective*.

PERSONA. The Persona is the face with which we meet the world. The word *Persona* is derived from the Greek term for the masks of comedy and tragedy worn by early dramatic actors to indicate their roles (Napier, 1986). We hide our less socially acceptable aspects behind a mask of adaptation created to face the demands of our parents and the Collective.

The Persona is a function of the ego and is largely conscious; it may be constant or changeable. A relatively healthy person can change masks from one context to the next. For example, one woman may play business executive, mother, and student on different occasions, experiencing little stress as she shifts among the roles. The rigidly "good mother" mentioned earlier may be "stuck" behind her mask, finding it impossible to move easily into the role of student; perhaps she is so preoccupied with her child that she can't concentrate in class.

HERO. The Hero or Heroine is an archetype that often serves as a Persona. Heracles (Hercules to the Romans) is a typical embodiment of the Hero archetype. He performed practical tasks in the world, doing his Twelve Labors at the bidding of the Goddess Hera (Juno). Heracles began his career in the cradle by strangling two serpents and never deviated from his Hero role (Hamilton, 1942/1969). He was not a notable thinker or a good husband or father; he was the first workaholic.

Ulysses (the Greeks called him "the wily Ulysses") was a more flexible and ambiguous hero, since he sometimes lied or cheated to get what he wanted. He played the roles of lover and husband as well as adventurer. Rather than connecting the dots of a prescribed solution, like Heracles, Ulysses shrewdly figured out solutions to the puzzles put to him.

Ulysses is often cited by Jungian writers as the "Wounded Hero"—a hero who carries a reminder that he is not perfect. Ulysses had been wounded in the thigh, and his old nurse recognized him by this scar when he finally returned from his wanderings. In the contemporary period, the person who carries a well-healed psychic wound is considered likely to be a better therapist than someone who has never consciously confronted his or her fallibility (Hillman, 1979, pp. 100–128).

Heracles and Ulysses were mortal heroes. Mortal heroines are harder to find in mythology. Perhaps Psyche will do; although not quasi-historical like Ulysses, she is well known. After casting a forbidden light on her husband Eros, she was forced to undertake a series of impossible tasks by Aphrodite, his jealous mother. Psyche secured help from the forces of nature, and eventually reunited with Eros, after which Zeus made her a goddess. Her actions fell between those of Heracles and Ulysses in that she did not always follow directions from the gods, but created trouble from her personal attachment to her husband, and from curiosity—like Eve, she suffered as a result of disobedience. In contrast to Ulysses, though, she was not a liar or a cheat.

SHADOW. The Shadow is the antithesis of the Persona. If your Persona is made up of all the qualities you and others most admire, then the Shadow includes all the qualities you most loathe. Thus in Jungian theory, the Persona is *ego-syntonic* (an acceptable part of your picture of yourself) and the Shadow is *ego-dystonic* (an aspect of yourself that makes you uncomfortable and that you may even repudiate). In classical Jungian analysis, after an analysand (person undergoing analysis) recognizes the limits of the conscious Persona, the Shadow is the next archetype he or she encounters in the course of psychological development.

Shadow characteristics have an *emotional* nature, a kind of autonomy, a possessive quality. The Shadow is mostly unconscious, and you *project* it onto others. It includes all the qualities that you hate most about your enemies and that you refuse to believe could describe yourself. However, if you or I look closely at the characteristics of someone we cannot stand, we may be surprised later to realize that our antagonist detects and complains about many of the same qualities in us (Beebe, 1993c). You could say that it takes one to know one—especially to *hate* one.

Projections are the hardest aspects to assimilate into the conscious personality. As Jung put it, "One meets with projections, one does not make them" (CW 9ii, para. 17). They are not voluntary; the reasons for our emotion really appear to lie in the *other person*. Moving beyond projection to accept this negative side can be a bitter task.

Even when the activated shadow side is not projected you may still disown it by saying "I'm not myself right now," or "I was swept away by a sudden impulse." It is also possible to identify with and actively embrace your negative-Shadow side, both personally and culturally (Harding, 1952, pp. 25–43). Perhaps this is what happens to some criminals or to societies that go down destructive paths. In this connection, an intriguing aspect of Jung's concept of the Shadow is that it resembles the Christian notion of original sin.

Henderson (1990c, p. 83) points out that the Shadow may not be a person at all; it may just be

> a state of mind or of being or a way people react to life or to their own psychic disposition. When we talk of the shadow it is not always easy to determine where it is; instead, it is part of an atmosphere and manifests itself in a general way.

Henderson also helps us to distinguish the personal shadow from the archetypal Shadow when he says that the personal shadow manifests itself as self-doubt: "We think we are doing fine and suddenly we doubt ourselves" (p. 70).

Our personal shadow is relatively easy to deal with, because it is human in size and meaning and is directly related to the rest of our personality. The archetypal Shadow, however, because it stands for the negative side of the Self, partakes of the impersonal nature of the collective unconscious. Its evil goes infinitely deep and is by definition the incarnation of all that is alien to us.

Jung felt that it is relatively easy to see through the personal shadow but that the archetypal Shadow is as hard to assimilate as the Anima/Animus: "It is quite within the bounds of possibility for a man to recognize the relative evil of his nature, but it is a rare and shattering experience for him to gaze into the face of absolute evil" (CW 9ii, para. 19).

If an archetypal Shadow exists within the Self, it represents the negative pole of the Self. This reminds us that the Self must be bipolar like every other archetype. When Jung posited the archetypal Shadow as a negative aspect of the Self, he brings us up against the fundamental religious problem of good and evil.

Toward the end of his life Jung was haunted by the problem of archetypal evil as acted out in World War II and as reflected in the threat of nuclear extinction. His *Answer to Job* (CW 11, para. 553–758) was written at this time. The film *Matter of Heart* also shows Jung's concern with these issues.

POSITIVE PROJECTIONS OF THE SHADOW. Not all Shadow qualities are negative (Jung, CW 9ii, para. 423). This creates the paradoxical possibility that a vicious criminal will have as part of his Shadow a tender heart, since the Shadow contains any quality alien to a person's ego, no matter whether it would be considered positive or negative by the world at large.

Not all projections are Shadow projections. When we fall in love, the other person seems to embody all the world's virtues. Such a romantic (classically "contrasexual") projection belongs to the Anima/Animus archetype, not to the Shadow, since the Shadow archetype, when it appears as a person, is (by the classic definition) always of one's own gender (Jung, CW 9ii, para. 19). Some problems with these classic contrasexual definitions are discussed in the sections on feminine development and same-sex love in Chapter 6.

OPPOSING PERSONALITY. This archetypal influence may cause the individual to behave in a way opposed to his or her own best interests as well as against the well-adapted, Hero identification. Beebe (1993c) tells us that this personality can be adversarial, passive-aggressive, suspicious, or avoidant. Beebe

(1993a) also says that the Opposing Personality arises as a way to defend oneself and often impersonates the other gender.

There is no familiar archetypal figure to personify this concept, but I think of it as the state of mind familiar to all of us from our "terrible twos," when we shouted, "I don't care if it's 'my own way,' I still want it!" This fierce and desperate ego state, a special aspect of temper tantrums, is mostly neglected in psychology literature.

In an adult, perhaps the archetype of Lucifer, the angel who rebelled against God, is not too stark. Recovering from a relatively benign or witty attack, we sometimes say, "The devil made me do it." The Devil here needs to be distinguished from the Demon/Daemon, discussed below, which is more unconscious and is occasionally apt to produce positive results.

RELATIONSHIP BETWEEN THE PERSONA AND THE SHADOW. The Persona and the Shadow are more-or-less reciprocal. The Persona is your conscious adaptation to the world, and the Shadow is your unconscious compensation for the Persona. The "higher" the Persona, the "deeper" the Shadow and the more unlikely it is that you will be able to see yourself realistically.

Even if you become more conscious of the Shadow, the two personality aspects still depend on each other:

> There is a very peculiar paradox where persona and shadow are mixed up together. . . . The origin of the persona can be found in the shadow—in the recognition of the shadow and the attempt to dress it up so that it looks better to those around us. (Henderson, 1990c, pp. 71–72)

So by tinkering with the Shadow to dress it up, you can trap yourself in further attempts at social adaptation. A more effective move would be to accept your negative side, giving up any attempt to appear faultless. As Joe E. Brown said to Jack Lemmon in *Some Like It Hot,* "Nobody's perfect."

Wise Old Man or Woman Versus Witch or Senex

This archetypal cluster forms a double syzygy with the next one—the Puer/Puella versus the Trickster. We will first consider the parental figures in their positive and negative incarnations, looking at the Good Mother or Father as the opposite of the evil Witch or Devouring Mother and the punitive, rigid (masculine) Senex.

WISE OLD MAN OR WOMAN: THE GOOD MOTHER OR FATHER. The Good Mother appears as Gaia, the spirit of the earth, and as Demeter, Kwan-Yin, the Virgin

Mary, or other familiar incarnations of nurturance and forgiveness. In the male version, he is Zeus, Jesus, the Divine Lover of the Sufi tradition, or the Buddha. This parent takes good care of his or her children by fostering, enabling, and giving permission to do things (Beebe, 1993c). The parental style may range from total acceptance to acceptance with a tinge of moral sternness, but one may rely on the Good Parent's support under all conditions.

This parental style is not always in tune with the prevailing culture. Some people have quite individual, even eccentric inner parental archetypes that support them when the world does not. We can think of religious martyrs, artists, or political reformers who proceeded undaunted by opposition. Sociologist David Riesman (1961) called such people "inner-directed"; they carry their Good Parent inside them.

You could think of the Self as a Good Parent. Often without your knowledge, even against your conscious wishes, some insistent internal influence may nudge your actions toward what is best for you rather than what you want. This influence often shows up in dreams, guided imagery, sandplay, or other symbolic modes of expression.

Sometimes this parental aspect of the Self becomes apparent in retrospect—for example, when you see that unbeknownst to your ego, the events of your life have created a recognizable pattern. It is as if a magnetic pole had guided the voyage, in spite of the vagaries of wind and weather. One reward of being old can be the gradual appearance, like a developing photographic print, of such a pattern in your life.

WITCH OR SENEX.   We are familiar with witches from Halloween and from folktales (Figure 4.1). In Jungian theory, the Senex (old man) stands for a correspondingly frightening male principle.

The most active, violent aspect of this archetype is vividly expressed as the Terrible Mother. Consider the Hindu goddess Kali, who both creates and destroys life. She stands for the morally neutral, inexorable birth/death cycle of existence. Many matriarchal religions emphasize this bloody and repetitive nature of being, expressed through planting and harvest rituals.

Kronos, the Titan of Greek myth who ate his children, was unusual in being a male example: He attempted to arrest the cycles by destroying all new life as it emerged, foreshadowing Herod's slaughter of the innocents when Jesus was born.

Rather than always being hot and active, the Witch or Senex can be icy cold, freezing all action. Think of Medusa, whose gaze turns men to stone, or Saturn (the more familiar Latin name for Kronos), whose leaden influence suppresses hope. The Witch creates terror, so that it becomes impossible to

FIGURE 4.1
The Witch

think, while the Senex is likely to engage in more active forms of destruction such as chopping something down or cutting it off (Beebe, 1993c).

The Witch is the source of the little imp that sits on your shoulder and whispers in your ear, "You're no good. You never were any good, and you never will be any good." Depressive illness occupies this realm, where the smallest action seems like an impossible demand. When projected, this imp finds fault with everyone around you, making them all seem pompous fakes or malicious and devious people you can never trust. We can speculate that paranoid issues arise here.

Sometimes the Witch is confused with the Animus in women. The Animus is positively or negatively active in a woman's Opposing Personality, not in the Witch (Beebe, 1993a, 1993c). The Witch or Senex can, however, take over and horribly misuse the Anima/Animus. When the Witch seductively takes over the Animus (the thinking aspect for women), nobody can think at all. Beebe says that correspondingly, the Senex can seize control of the Anima by bringing up emotions or values in a dogmatic way, creating an oppressive, poisoned atmosphere in which everybody feels bad.

Both the Witch and the Senex are antilife, since they cripple soul and spirit. The Anima and Animus (soul and spirit, respectively) involve us in life. All Shadow functions serve power, aggression, and excitement, and of these functions the most powerful are the Witch and Senex (Beebe, 1993c).

Besides being different from Anima/Animus, the Witch or Senex is also different from the Trickster, which provides access to the Anima; once you discover your Trickster you are on the road to discovering your Anima. Situated on the opposite end of the horizontal personality axis from the Trickster, the Witch or Senex has an uncanny capacity to find and touch weak spots (Beebe, 1993c).

Beebe says that the Witch's job is to stop you in your tracks. Occasionally this can be a good thing. Also, if you habitually fly too near the sun and are in danger of crashing, the Senex may cruelly clip your wings. The unwelcome opposition of the Witch or Senex forces you to be creative, to outwit some challenge by finding a way around it. To succeed, you must have enough vitality to keep going in the face of powerful opposition.

Puer/Puella Versus Trickster

These archetypes express eternal, creative youth. In addition, they evade the settled expectations and laws of the Senex. Their sometimes sneaky refusals tend to annoy people in authority. They can get the person who relies on them into various kinds of internal or external hot water or even lead to tragedy.

PUER/PUELLA. The Puer/Puella archetype has been discussed in detail by Marie-Louise von Franz (1970) and James Hillman (1979), who approach the archetype differently. It is gendered, like the Witch and Senex. The Puer is the masculine aspect and the Puella is the feminine; less has been written about the Puella, but her characteristics can be derived from descriptions of the Puer.

The Puer is a symbol of the Eternal Divine Child and represents creativity, spirituality, youthful enthusiasm, and new beginnings. Many religions are founded on a description of the miraculous birth of such a child who brings enlightenment to the world.

On the negative side, the Puer never grows up, doesn't have his feet on the ground, can't hang on to a job or a relationship, and repeatedly crashes as a result of flying too high. Icarus and Phaëthon are mythological Puer figures. Icarus flew out of a dungeon on wings his father had assembled with wax; he approached the sun too closely, the wax melted, and he dropped to his death. Phaëthon tricked his own father, the sun god Apollo, into letting him drive the sun chariot; the sun horses were too much for him to control, and he also fell out of the sky.

Von Franz emphasizes the perils of being a Puer, while Hillman's view is more positive. Hillman sees the Puer/Senex opposition as more significant than the opposition of positive-negative poles in the youthful archetype. He feels that the positive Senex (stability) and positive Puer (innovation) balance well. Both authors remind us, as did Jung, that to retain the youthful, creative aspects of our personality we need to keep the Puer alive.

Nathan Schwartz-Salant (1982) connects the Puer with Narcissus, the god associated with self-love or, as his name suggests, narcissism. Schwartz-Salant says that the Puer's path is unique in clinical practice:

> Negative emotions, called shadow problems, are the last thing the puer assimilates. His process . . . is the inverse of the classical view of individuation: it goes from the top down, so to speak, from being concerned first with spirit and then with instinctual and shadow issues (p. 21).

When you try to assimilate the Puer/Puella archetype you confront the individuation puzzle: How can you work with the hand you've been dealt and the people you have made promises to, and still keep room for new things in your life? Eventually you may learn to be content, realize that you can't have it all, and face the limits of human existence. This archetype is one of the most troubling in our own culture—not surprisingly, since as a nation we have run out of new frontiers to explore.

Some growth processes require continuity. For instance, Donald Sandner (1994) has said that a long, relatively successful marriage is the sine qua non for developing your contrasexual attributes. This process can start over only a few times; otherwise you will never experience the full development of a relationship, or the difficult but rewarding experience of exploring and loving the true Self of your partner (or friends).

Too close adherence to either the Senex or Puer aspects of this syzygy will lead to trouble. Overreliance on the Senex would result in a stultifying dullness; too much of the Puer would mean unreliability. Our task is to walk a fluctuating path between them, without sacrificing flexibility to dependability or vice versa.

TRICKSTER. The Trickster is ambiguous. It can represent the seamy side of youthful enthusiasm and the dangers of foolish enterprise or selfish pursuit of a goal. However, in Beebe's (1993c) personality schema, the Trickster provides the only means of working with the Anima/Animus archetype, by bringing the Anima/Animus closer to consciousness and changing its habitual (and therefore previously unnoticed) expression in our lives.

Mythology offers many examples of Trickster figures. In Norse myth, the shape-shifting, mischievous god Loki tricked Balder's blind brother Hoder into shooting at Balder with an arrow made of mistletoe, thereby killing the good god (Hamilton, 1942/1969, pp. 310–311).

Similarly, Hermes, the immortal Greek guide, often treacherously leads you astray, into the blinding fog of *liminality*, the shadowy border zone between places or states of being (Stein, 1983). Hermes also helps you laugh at yourself when you do go astray (Schwartz-Salant, 1982, p. 153). Or, to take another example, the court jester was typically a Trickster who used sly wit to get away with telling the king some painful truths.

Goats often symbolize Trickster phenomena. They suffer for it in their role of scapegoat, in which they divert the wrath of the gods by carrying the tribe's sins into the desert. Native American myth gives us the greedy coyote who plays tricks on the other gods and is killed over and over, only to pop up again somewhere else.

Anima/Animus Versus Demon/Daemon

These pairings represent some of the least-conscious, hardest-to-assimilate parts of our personality.

ANIMA/ANIMUS. The Anima and Animus are a much-disputed pair of archetypes. As Gareth Hill (1992, pp. xiii–xiv) reported, "As recently as . . . 1990, they were the subject of a major Jungian conference . . . reportedly producing one of the most acrimonious debates some participants had ever experienced at a Jungian gathering."

This is partly because Jung originally called the Anima and Animus *contrasexual* qualities of the psyche, giving a mother/son example (CW 9ii, para. 20). Jung conceptualized the Anima as the soul or feeling function of a man. He had experienced a female presence in visions and had worked out its attributes over several years. The *Animus* (women's thinking function) was somewhat of an afterthought, created for the sake of symmetry: If Jung had an Anima, then women must have something corresponding to it. Contemporary women tend to take offense at Jung's descriptions of the Animus because these descriptions often reflect gender stereotypes. The "genderized" Anima and Animus seem to be based on perceptions of the strangeness of the other gender and its representation within our psyches. Some Jungians get around the controversial aspects of Jung's theory by speaking of the Anima/Animus as the "other" within us, without referring specifically to gender.

Hermes and Psyche (the Trickster and the Anima) are well acquainted, as illustrated in Rilke's (1907/1984) poem "Orpheus, Eurydice, Hermes." In the myth of Orpheus and Eurydice, Orpheus tries to rescue his wife Eurydice (who has just died) from Hades, the Greek underworld. He is told that she may follow him out of Hades, but he must not look back at her. They are escorted by Hermes, messenger of the gods. Just as they approach the exit, Orpheus can't resist looking over his shoulder, and Eurydice is lost to him.

Rilke's poetic version describes Eurydice as having already given up the world and her connections to Orpheus; she has retreated into her own person and is no longer interested in him. She glides back into Hades totally indifferent to Orpheus's pain. Eurydice stands for Orpheus's Anima, and in the poem Hermes understands her, while Orpheus, intent on "saving" her, doesn't have a clue. In Hades, she is no longer his Anima; she is only herself.

The Anima/Animus is often connected with the concept of longing or desire for the other, originating in the child's (incestuous) desire for the opposite-sex parent. Sandner's (1994) description of the Anima is less forbidding: He calls it "the force that holds families together" and says it is the source of all transference relationships. Transference is the process by which we see qualities in other people that are not necessarily theirs. We "transfer" these qualities from our early experience with our own families. For example, we may think all men like steak or all women like to hike because our own father, mother, or siblings liked those things.

If we don't learn to contain the desire inherent in the love for and from our parents, we may sexualize desire in all contexts. Hillman (1972) argues that the failure to contain desire results in a *fear* of desire, smothering emotional and sexual development. The Jungian concept of containing desire and suffering frustration as a result resembles Freud's concept of sublimation; however, containment keeps desire accessible, while sublimation represses it or arbitrarily substitutes other objects.

Anima/Animus attraction creates high energy in the personal field for both genders and can be attributed to the relationships between contrasexual principles in the participants. In other words, we are attracted to elements in another person that we perceive ourselves to lack. Often these elements are contrasexual, as when a man is attracted to a woman's nurturing qualities. Since both heterosexuals and homosexuals have attributes of both genders, sexual orientation does not matter.

DEMON/DAEMON. The two spellings of this word differentiate a totally ego-alien aspect (the Demon) from an aspect (the Daemon) that goes so deep that it may create an enantiodromia and turn into something positively valued by the ego.

This archetype is a bit like the Terrible Mother but adds a malicious twist to her impartial creation and expenditure of life. It seems to delight in destroying the old, only occasionally going on to create the new. The most deeply unconscious part of our personal unconscious, it has to do with a destructive

FIGURE 4.2
Mandala

creativity and in rare cases with genius. We can speculate that it provides a connection from the personal to the collective unconscious and can be our access route to the negative pole of the *Self* archetype.

Archetypal Symbols Not on the Personality Diagram

The following archetypal images do not appear on Beebe's personality diagram (discussed in Chapter 5) but are widely used in myth and legend. They include some of my personal favorites.

CHILD. The Child archetype can be younger than the Puer/Puella. When a baby or child appears in dreams or fantasy, it can signify elements of any level of the unconscious. At the personal level, it might stand for the ego, or a relative, or some of their attributes. At the collective level, the appearance of a child can suggest a change or new start in life. A divine or magical child can stand for creativity and growth or may carry religious overtones as a redeemer or Christlike figure.

MANDALA. A mandala is a compact, symmetrical design, most often a circle surrounded by or enclosing a square (Figure 4.2). Mandalas occur in the religion and art of widely diverse cultures and were a central symbol in alchemy. Jung described the archetype underlying the mandala in several ways. In a radio broadcast during World War II he said:

There was often terrible suffering and destruction; but when the individual was able to cling to a shred of reason, or to preserve the bonds of a human relationship, a new compensation was brought about in the unconscious by the very chaos of the conscious mind, and this compensation could be integrated into consciousness. New symbols then appeared, of a collective nature, but this time reflecting the forces of *order.* There was measure, proportion, and symmetrical arrangement in these symbols, expressed in their peculiar mathematical and geometrical structure. They represent a kind of axial system and are known as *mandalas.* (CW 10, para. 450)

Thus the symmetrical, orderly mandala sometimes emerges as an effort to compensate for chaos. During his crisis after the break from Freud, Jung himself produced many beautiful mandala paintings. In another paper, he wrote:

In so far as the mandala encompasses, protects, and defends the psychic totality against outside influences and seeks to maintain the inner opposites, it is at the same time a distinct *individuation symbol* and was known as such even to medieval alchemy. The soul was supposed to have the form of a sphere. (CW 10, para. 621; Jung's italics)

Like all archetypal symbols, the mandala has two implications. The negative aspect is its revelation of a struggle against chaos, and the positive aspect is its indication of the possibility for containing the tension of the opposites. The enclosure of the parts of the mandala by its circumference can stand for individuation—like the development and assimilation of all our multiple contradictions within a larger whole.

SUN. In alchemy, the sun stands for the masculine principle (see Chapter 7). It also connotes the element of fire, the metal gold, the spirit (versus the soul), heroic effort, the light of reason, dryness, and power. Its god is Jupiter (Jove) and its animal is the lion, the king of beasts and a denizen of hot, dry countries. Its color in alchemy is red-gold.

MOON. The moon in alchemy is feminine, cool, moist, and mysterious. It stands for the element of water, the metal silver, and the soul; since it changes shape, it signifies recurrent, cyclic time. Pictures often show it as sickle-shaped or as the horns of a cow, and the Virgin Mary is sometimes depicted as standing on a crescent moon. The moon is associated with the goddess Hecate when below the horizon and with Artemis (Diana) when up in the sky. Its animals are nocturnal and include the cat, hare, and frog.

DRAGON. In myth and symbol, the dragon and serpent are often equivalent; the winged dragon or serpent stands for matter and spirit conjoined. Ancient matriarchal religions venerated the serpent, since it sheds its skin every year, signifying renewal (Meador, 1992).

The dragon guards "the pearl of great price," and a hero must defeat it to attain the treasure he seeks. If the Hero is in touch with his Anima, defeating the dragon need not involve slaying the dragon but can mean confronting and subduing forces in the hero's own psyche. Christian tradition emphasizes the dark side of the dragon/serpent; St. George slays his dragons, and the serpent in Eden represents the Devil. Gnostic tradition praised the serpent for bringing knowledge to humanity against the wishes of the Demiurge, whom the Gnostics considered to be a secondary, flawed deity, not the God we know from the Old Testament.

UROBOROS. This circular serpent or dragon biting its tail signifies the eternal round; Neumann (1954b) used it to mean the infant's undifferentiated unity with nature. It also stands for other unities—for example, between male and female, birth and death, end and beginning, or chaos and creation. In alchemy it stands for the undifferentiated material to be transformed through the alchemical process.

COSMIC EGG. The Cosmic Egg is related to the serpent as uroboros, since the serpent is sometimes shown wrapped around the egg. The Cosmic Egg is the germ of all creation and can stand for hope and new beginnings. In alchemy, it is the vessel in which the process of transformation takes place. According to many traditions, at the time of creation the egg split, and the two halves formed heaven and earth.

COSMIC TREE. Sometimes the Cosmic Tree is shown as growing from the Cosmic Egg floating in a sea of Chaos. The tree stands for active life (perhaps the Psyche, as contrasted to the Self, as in Chapter 3), and joins the three worlds of heaven, earth, and water. The Trees of Life and Knowledge in Eden derive from this tradition. Many cultures consider the tree to be the axis of the world and embody it in the central pole of their temples.

The "Christmas" tree predated Christianity and has always reminded us of the light and growth absent in winter, promising their return after the winter equinox. The Cabbala, a book of esoteric Jewish lore, describes the Tree of Life or Sephirotic Tree as having its root in the air, symbolizing the transmission of faith from above to the crown on earth below (Scholem, 1974, p. 106).

The tree has both masculine and feminine connotations, since it nourishes and shelters and also has phallic aspects. In alchemy it often appears with seven branches, which stand for the seven ancient planets and their associated metals.

This concludes our overview of some major Jungian archetypes. These are selected, partial, and personal interpretations, which the conscientious student of archetypal symbols should supplement with wide exposure to myth, folklore, religion, and popular culture. You may want to consult books on symbolism, such as Cooper (1978), Jobes (1962), or Walker (1983), for richer descriptions of these and many other archetypal symbols. Entire books have also been written that amplify the meaning of particular archetypes (see Mullett, 1991; Monick, 1987; Perera, 1986).

What Is a Symbol?

In the previous section, archetypes were not distinguished from their *symbols*. Archetypes, themselves free of content, are unknowable; they are expressed in theory, dream, and fantasy by symbols.

The Oxford English Dictionary indicates that the word *symbol* comes from *symbolon*, a Greek word meaning to "throw together." It gives the following as a definition of *symbol:*

> "Something that stands for, represents, or denotes something else (not by exact resemblance, but by vague suggestion, or by some accidental or conventional relation); *esp.* a material object representing or taken to represent something immaterial or abstract, as a being, idea, quality, or condition; a representative or typical figure, sign, or token; a type (of some quality)."

Jung was careful to discriminate between symbols and mere *signs:*

> Those conscious contents which give us a clue to the unconscious background are incorrectly called *symbols* by Freud. They are not true symbols, however, since according to his theory they have merely the roles of *signs* or *symptoms* of the subliminal processes. The true symbol differs essentially from this, and should be understood as an intuitive idea that cannot yet be formulated in any other or better way. (CW 15, para. 105; Jung's italics)

A symbol is also "the expression of a spontaneous experience that points beyond itself to a meaning [that is] only partly conceivable" (Whitmont, 1969, p. 18). Signs, on the other hand, express themselves in allegories and are "products of *conscious* mental activity" (p. 18; Whitmont's italics).

Symbols interpret ordinary experiences in terms of our predisposition to see meaning in them, so that events come to stand for much more than their face value. The memory of previous situations contributes to this process. The whole conglomerate of archetypal predisposition, symbol, and the idiosyncratic perception of experience operates as a complex—a topic we take up in the next section.

Transcendence as the "Telos" of the Symbol

Symbols provide the way out of a dilemma, a transcendent coming together of the opposites. Jung wrote:

> The will can no longer operate when every motive has an equally strong countermotive. . . . This would lead to an insupportable condition did not the tension of opposites produce a new, uniting function that transcends them.
>
> From the activity of the unconscious there now emerges a new content, constellated by thesis and antithesis in equal measure and standing in a *compensatory* relation to both. It thus forms the middle ground on which the opposites can be united. (CW 6, para. 824, 825; Jung's italics)

The term *constellated*, common in Jungian writing, means "activated" or "highlighted." Here Jung explicitly equates his term *transcendent function* with Hegel's philosophical *synthesis*, mentioned in Chapter 3. This paradoxical unification is sometimes called the *telos* of symbolic images, since *telos* is the Greek word for "goal." Symbols emerge into consciousness *to* connect logically disparate elements.

The connection can be compared to achieving a bird's-eye view of a previously confusing warren of passages, as when you look down at an old-fashioned garden maze from the top of a tree. What formerly seemed complicated and contradictory appears from the new perspective to have order and direction. By occupying a "new" dimension, your viewpoint has transcended the old limits of the problem. A well-known example of such symbolic insight is the chemist F. A. Kekulé von Stradonitz's vision, when riding on a bus, of the benzene ring as a snake biting its tail (CW 16, para. 353).

A symbol, then, throws together disparate elements to arrive at a new concept. There are many symbols for each archetype; they express the underlying archetype in ways determined by their setting. Thus, the archetype of the Terrible Mother is depicted in each culture through symbols derived from her context; she appears as Kali, Ranga, Hecate, or any of a myriad of other guises.

Complexes

People in different cultures evolve personal symbols influenced by their own experiences, by the conventional cultural form of the symbol, and by the underlying archetype. Taken together, with the addition of our emotional reactions to them, these factors compose our *complexes*. My "mother complex" may be "good" or "bad" or mixed, for example; it is unique to me but defined by my culture and organized by the Great Mother archetype.

> A complex is a collection of images and ideas, clustered round a core derived from one or more archetypes, and characterised by a common emotional tone. When they come into play (become "constellated"), complexes contribute to behavior and are marked by affect whether a person is conscious of them or not. They are particularly useful in the analysis of neurotic symptoms. (Samuels et al., 1986, p. 34)

Complexes provide the link between archetypes, symbols, and behavior. An archetype lies at the core of every complex and can be expressed in fantasy and dream images or in emotional attitudes and actions (Whitmont, 1969, p. 68). Complexes, along with symbols, organize all three realms of being (personal, cultural, and collective), and so may create confusion among personal, cultural, or archetypal events.

For example, a father complex affects, and may seriously distort, memories of interactions with a personal father. The action of complexes may help to explain faulty memories of childhood abuse. Such memories can stem from distressing experience, but they can be overamplified by the rising concern with abuse in our culture and further conditioned by archetypal images like the one of the Greek god Kronos eating his children.

The existence of complexes was first demonstrated by Jung's innovative use of the Word Association Test (see Jung, CW 2). Jung's resulting description of a "complex of injury" described a pattern of narcissistic impairment and vulnerability close to what we today would call a paranoid syndrome. Freud adopted the term *complex* from Jung to describe the Oedipus struggle, but after their rupture, he dropped it in favor of *conflict*.

Like archetypes, complexes are multiply bipolar: First, each has both a negative and a positive valence; then, when activated, one complex always relates structurally to another complex, as mother to child, power to love, and so on (Perry, 1970). They connect to both conscious and unconscious aspects of our minds. Furthermore, complexes are "psychoid" (a concept Jung used to mean "including aspects of both body and psyche") since they include a psychic pole of thought and intuition plus a somatic pole of emotion and sensation.

Complexes Are "Feeling-Toned"

Complexes organize more than simple experiences; they color concurrent emotions and pattern both with archetypal connotations. The emotions may be at odds with perceived or ideal circumstances and can create internal conflict. For instance, if I have a negative complex about cats, I may hate or fear a kitten that most people see as harmless and adorable. Although I may be embarrassed by my irrational reaction, I am unable to feel or act differently.

Some aspects of complexes are projected onto others. When mutual projection occurs, it becomes hard for those involved to sort out fact from fancy. Beebe's schema of personality types (covered in Chapter 5) provides one way to visualize the process by which these tangles may be generated.

Complexes, archetypes, and symbols often seem overly reified in Jungian writing. Samuels (1985b, p. 48), for instance, writes as if the psyche were made up of separable parts capable of acting on each other:

> Structurally, the complex can be studied in relation to the ego. There may be conflict ("two truths") or the ego may repress the complex or, conversely, be overwhelmed by it. The complex can become completely dissociated from the personality, as in psychotic breakdown.

Samuels may not intend to imply that the ego or the complex is an object. Here the metaphor of a vortex or field of energy may serve better than our earlier one of a whirlpool of water: Like other aspects of "structure" in Jungian theory, a complex (and an archetype) can be visualized as a *vortex or field* of energy, rather than as a *structure* like a skeleton. In these terms, a neurotic complex can spin off from the collective archetypes when a symbol encounters cultural or personal energy fields. Further, in psychosis, minivortices might become established within the larger ego complex, like permanent eddies or subfields of energy within the vortex.

Neutral and Multiple Nature of Complexes

Popular use of the term *complex*, as in "You'll give him a complex if you do that!" distorts the meaning of *complex* by suggesting that it is exclusively negative. The function of complexes is to organize our experiences. Their positive or negative value derives from their individual content. Samuels (1985b, p. 47) gives the example of the mother complex, which includes and organizes actions and emotions "from numerous archetypal configurations: the individual, the mother, the individual and mother, mother and father, . . . individual and sibling and mother, . . . etc., etc." To sum up, complexes are normal, essential components of every psyche. They may be more or less accurately attuned to others' perceptions of what is happening, and they may carry positive or negative emotion.

Negative Aspects of Complexes

Given that complexes are normal and necessary, when do they become drawbacks? Basically, unconscious complexes can cause trouble. Whitmont (1969, p. 58) lists four possible negative relationships to an unconscious complex:

1. *Identity* with the complex (it takes over and devours your consciousness to a greater or lesser degree)
2. *Compulsivity* (the complex drives you until it has expended enough of its energy for you to get a grip again)
3. *Primitivity* (the activated complex regresses you to a less adaptive level of behavior and expression)
4. *Projection* ("It's the other guy's fault")

Growth and individuation can occur when you consciously anatomize and assimilate your complexes. This means that you must separate the archetypal from the personal elements in a complex, recognizing and consciously accepting the differences. Once you can own and take responsibility for the existence of your complex, its power to drive you is reduced. Much of this work, a central feature of Jungian therapy, corresponds to the work outlined by object relations theory. Object relations theory considers our perception of real objects (usually people) to be distorted by early experience and encourages us to separate the symbolic object inside us from the actual person facing us.

Now that we have reviewed some basic archetypes and briefly discussed symbols and complexes, we are ready to consider personality types in detail. This is the task of the next chapter.

READINGS

Hamilton, E. (1969). *Mythology: Timeless tales of gods and heroes.* New York: Mentor Books. (Original work published 1942)

Jung, C. G. (1970). Flying saucers: A modern myth. In CW 10: *Civilization in transition* (2nd ed, para. 589–824, pp. 309–433). Bollingen Series XX. Princeton, NJ: Princeton University Press.

Meador, B. DeS. (1992). *Uncursing the dark: Treasures from the underworld.* Wilmette, IL: Chiron.

Samuels, A. (1985). *Jung and the post-Jungians.* London: Routledge & Kegan Paul.

von Franz, M.-L. (1970). *Puer Aeternus* (2nd ed.). Santa Monica, CA: Sigo Press.

CHAPTER 5

Personality Types

Jung's (1961, p. 206) work focused on the mysteries of personality:

> My life has been permeated and held together by one idea and one goal: namely, to penetrate into the secret of the personality. Everything can be explained from this one point, and all my works relate to this one theme.

Many later analysts share this interest. One of them—John Beebe (1992, p. 136)—has written vivid thumbnail sketches of personality type. Here is a sample:

> The introverted feeling function concerns itself with the values expressed in the archetypal aspects of situations, often relating to the actual situation by measuring it against an ideal. When the actual is found wanting, introverted feeling can become intensely disappointed. Although it often finds it hard to articulate its judgments, or simply prefers to keep them to itself, introverted feeling also tends to ignore social limits regarding the communication of critical responses, to the point of appearing to depreciate others. It may withhold positive feelings as insincere and fail to offer healing gestures to smooth over difficult situations. In its shadow aspect, introverted feeling becomes rageful, anxious, and sullen. It may withdraw all support for attitudes it has decided are simply wrong, even at the risk of rupturing relationship and agreed-upon standards of fellow-feeling.

Many people will instantly recognize this as a description of one aspect of their own personality. How does Jungian psychology develop the basis for such a vignette? In this chapter, we will try to answer this question by first looking at Jung's thinking, then focusing on Beebe's system, and finally exploring a novel approach to life development—based on Jungian theory—that I myself have proposed.

Jung's Theory of Personality

We introduce some fundamental concepts in this section.

The Attitudes: Introversion and Extraversion

Jung's reflections led him to conclude that everyone falls into two basic personality types that he called *attitudes*. He termed one attitude *introversion*; members of this group are called *introverts*. Introverts need to establish autonomy and independence from external objects. They derive energy from and direct their attention toward inner events, subjective meanings, and reactions. The other attitude is *extraversion*; group members—called *extraverts*—habitually seek, move toward, and react to external objects. Beebe (1993a, 1991, 1986) suggests that in general extraversion is broad, while introversion is deep.

Jung worked out his theory of personality partly because he suspected that theoretical disagreements between his colleagues Freud and Adler stemmed from basic differences between their characters. Austrian psychiatrist Alfred Adler was one of the original three prominent psychoanalysts, along with Jung and Freud. He is not as well known now as he used to be, but he developed the idea of the inferiority complex, which compensates for our inferiorities by developing them into strengths.

Jung categorized Freud as extraverted and Adler as introverted. An extraverted theorist will emphasize object relationships and the influences of early childhood, while the introverted theorist "sees the subject as having to protect himself against the undue significance of external objects" (Storr, 1988, p. 86). Jung's own approach to theory was largely introverted.

Introversion and extraversion are *attitudes of consciousness* that don't exist by themselves but that *modify* the *functions* (see below) of our personalities. The attitudes are evenly distributed among the four functions, but the *attitude of the dominant function* is the one with which you meet the world and that determines whether others are likely to think of you as extraverted or introverted. Beebe thinks the attitude of the dominant function (as well as which function is dominant) is innate, part of the person's "hard-wiring" at birth. The genetics of type has never been studied. However, environmental influence may cause someone to adapt through a different function that dominates the culture and family into which he or she is born.

The terms *introversion* and *extraversion* are possibly the best known of Jung's innovations and have entered common usage. A psychologists' joke runs that you can identify someone's attitude by his or her reaction when the telephone rings: Introverts say "Oh, damn!" and dread answering, while extraverts say "Oh, boy!" and can't wait to find out who's calling.

Recent Jungian theory emphasizes the mixture in each person of introverted and extraverted elements, as discussed in detail below.

INTROVERSION. Introverts react to internal events and are forever comparing worldly happenings with internal, archetypal standards. They are often concerned with ideals. Anthony Storr (1988, p. 146) says that some introverts relinquish their need for personal intimacy in favor of creating relationships with their activities or interests: "For them, the meaning of life is less bound up with intimate relationships than it is in the case of most people." Storr gives Kant as an example of someone who was well adjusted and happy, but introverted and absorbed in work rather than in personal relationships (pp. 155–159).

Healthily introverted people don't mind being alone and may distinctly need solitude from time to time. Introversion has often been confused with "maladjustment" in our mostly extraverted North American culture. Sometimes it does accompany psychological dis-ease, but depressive and schizoid people need to be alone for their own, different reasons (Storr, 1988, pp. 93–105). The tendency to withdraw can be ego-syntonic or ego-dystonic, healthy or neurotic, depending on how it develops in the individual personality organization.

EXTRAVERSION. Extraversion leads people to make a sympathetic merger with the reality of another person or object. If your dominant function is extraverted, you are likely to be sociable and will argue rather than withdraw if events run against you. Extraverts make good team players and are often successful in business.

Storr says that naturally extraverted children who are isolated and must rely on their imagination for entertainment may develop an active fantasy life. He gives as examples the writers Anthony Trollope, Beatrix Potter, Rudyard Kipling, and P. G. Wodehouse, all of whom suffered lonely childhoods (pp. 106–122). He speculates that depression resulting from the loss or absence of attachments drove them in on themselves, and in compensation, they produced richly imaginative stories about people (or animals) whose lives they entered vicariously.

The Four Personality Functions

Within and expressing the two attitudes of introversion and extraversion, Jung named four *functions* of personality. Both introverts and extraverts operate out of some combination of the same four functions: *thinking, feeling, intuition,* and *sensation.* These capacities are paired; thinking and feeling are called the *rational* functions, while sensation and intuition are known as the *irrational* functions. Jung defined these terms quite specifically, and the technical meanings of *rational* and *irrational* do not correspond to their everyday meanings. Each pair of functions is usually considered to create two ends of a continuum, so that the two rational functions are opposites, as are the two irrational functions.

The following descriptions of the four personality functions are skeletal. For further detail and case examples, you should read further in the relevant literature, starting with Beebe (1992), Sandner and Beebe (1995), von Franz (1971), and Clarke (1992).

THE RATIONAL FUNCTIONS: THINKING AND FEELING. By Jung's definition, the "rational" functions make a discrimination about something, in a quick two-step process; you perceive a stimulus, then perform a sorting or classifying operation on it. The rational functions involve an element of choice. The use of a rational extraverted function to adapt oneself to environmental demands is equivalent to Judgment (J) in the Myers-Briggs Type Indicator (MBTI) (Beebe, 1993c).

When you are in the *thinking* mode you discriminate among events or ideas; you name things, you separate them into logical groups, arrange them in a particular order, or link them logically to other things or events. This definition is close to our everyday use of the word *thinking.*

Feeling, the other rational function, is the most difficult one for most people to understand in the Jungian way. Jung himself provided several different definitions, but we can simplify by saying that the feeling function is an evaluative ability. When you are in the feeling mode you are categorizing stimuli as good or bad, pleasant or unpleasant, comfortable or uncomfortable. You are expressing your perspective and determining whether something has a positive or negative value for you.

Emotions often are confused with the feeling function. Affects do tend to be associated with the feeling judgment; if you experience negative emotions like fear or anger about an event, you may be more likely to decide that the situation is "bad." Nevertheless, the immediate emotional states are not in themselves *rational;* the feeling judgment, a rational sorting decision, is not made until you distinguish the nature of your excitement from the context in which it occurs. The feeling function, therefore, is relatively conscious and is the tool used to sort feelings emerging from the unconscious.

This process is related to the question discussed in Chapter 3: When we see a bear, do we run because we are afraid, or are we afraid because we run? First the adrenaline pumps, and we react, instinctively, often with some bodily reflex (James, 1890/1950, pp. 449–450). It is later, even if only by a split second, that we categorize the event as "fear" or "anger." The first reaction is *sensation* (see below); the second is *feeling*.

In everyday speech we may use the word *feel* when we mean we are *affected*. We say, for instance, "I feel anxious," which makes it easy to confuse the feeling *function* with the verb *to feel*. They are not the same. Familiarity and practice with the concept of the feeling function make it easier to understand.

THE IRRATIONAL FUNCTIONS: SENSATION AND INTUITION. The irrational functions are immediate reactions to stimuli and involve only one-step processing. When you perceive a stimulus in the irrational mode, you register it directly, without labeling it; you straightforwardly recognize its existence.

The Jungian definition of *irrational* does not connote being illogical or unreasonable, as the word *irrational* would in daily conversation. It refers to the absence of the step of categorizing an event; categorizing is done only in the rational mode. You may find it useful to mentally substitute *nonrational* for the more loaded term *irrational* when considering personality type.

"In the irrational mode we are taking on the riot of sensations from outside," Beebe (1993c) notes. When we approach a situation with an extraverted function that accepts the riot of perceptions as an irrational given, that orients us to what is out there. This corresponds to Perception (P) in the MBTI (Beebe, 1993c).

The *sensation* function tells you the color of someone's eyes, the placement of furniture in a room, how wet leaves smell after a summer shower, that your belly aches. Those are "just-so stories," representing how things are according to any of your senses; no logic or judgment is involved. You are mapping your interior or exterior sensory world.

Intuition deals more with the invisible world; it enables you instantly to guess the outcome of a situation when there is little information available. Intuition tells you the minute you enter the room if the party will go well, or more generally, whether you'll ever be a topnotch child therapist. It's rooted in data but immediately flies far beyond data to the big picture; intuition includes implications for other times and other places, not just the immediate situation.

Beebe's Personality Schema

Beebe (1988) has developed a clear system to approach the complexities of personality organization from a Jungian viewpoint. Jung originally proposed a system of only four personality functions, ranging from most to least conscious. Beebe found that arrangement too limiting, because clinical experience had taught him that each function has an acceptable and an unacceptable side. We are happy to own some aspects of our personalities but refuse to acknowledge others.

Beebe has doubled Jung's personality functions, adding a second set of the Shadow (unacceptable) aspects of each. Every one of this second quaternity of functions is less conscious than any of the first four, but the second four also are arrayed in a descending order, from relatively ego-accessible to deeply unconscious. I find Beebe's schema to provide an enriched rationale for many complex interpersonal problems and so have decided to use it here, in place of Jung's more widely known set of four.

The First Four Personality Functions: Beebe's First Quadrant

To understand Beebe's system, we first need to become familiar with his use of personality diagrams.

SPINES AND ARMS: UNDERSTANDING THE GRID DIAGRAMS. In the grid diagrams below, as in those of classical Jungian personality theory, the rational properties of consciousness are not considered to be "opposite" to the irrational properties. We can call them *orthogonal*; they exist as independent variables, not correlated qualities or polar opposites. Beebe calls the vertical axis in each grid the *spine* of the personality.

BEEBE'S FOUR PERSONALITY "SPINES"

	Irrational			*Rational*	
EN		ES		ET	EF
IS		IN		IF	IT

There are two rational and two irrational spines. Either one when arranged upside down is considered to be the "same" in many respects. In each diagram, as in the MBTI, the first letter (E or I) stands for Extraversion or

Introversion, and the second letter (N, S, T, or F) stands for (I)Ntuition, Sensation, Thinking, or Feeling. The function at the top of the spine is the *dominant function,* which can be introverted or extraverted in attitude. The first spine shows extraverted intuition at the top and introverted sensation at the bottom, and so on across the series.

You become acquainted with your personality spine only through the interactions of friendship, therapy, family, or other long, intimate relationships; it must be identified over time. Your natural spine can be shifted by various experiences, making it hard to figure out.

Besides a spine (vertical axis), Beebe's personality grid has two *arms,* forming a horizontal axis. The four functions of consciousness are distributed on the four ends of these axes. Traditional Jungian theory calls the functions at the four positions the *superior* (or *dominant*), *auxiliary, tertiary,* and *inferior* functions. They are illustrated in the accompanying diagram.

TRADITIONAL JUNGIAN PERSONALITY GRID

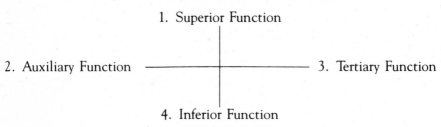

1. Superior Function

2. Auxiliary Function   3. Tertiary Function

4. Inferior Function

The superior function is called that because it is pictured at the top; the inferior function is situated at the bottom. The superior is also the most conscious and the inferior the least conscious of the (first) four functions. (Beebe's second set of four functions, mapping the portion of personality adaptation that is unconscious, is developed later.)

Having considered the function positions, we turn now to the nature of the functions.

PERSONALITY CONFIGURATIONS. Although it is usually easy to know when you are acting primarily out of an attitude of extraversion or introversion, the rest of the picture is less simple than it first appears. The various aspects of your personality serve to balance out your introverted and extraverted approaches to events.

Jungian theory limits the number of possible personality configurations. Thus, most writers consider the two rational functions to be "opposites," arranging them at the two ends of an axis. This approach implies that one function excludes the perspective of the other: If you are primarily a thinker, you tend not to be a great "feeler."

In the sample personality diagram that follows, the thinking function appears at the top and the feeling function at the bottom. A line—the spine or vertical axis—connects these two rational functions.

SAMPLE PERSONALITY DIAGRAM

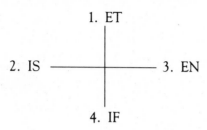

Similarly, in this diagram the two irrational functions occupy the ends of the arms or horizontal axis at right angles to the spine. Like thinking and feeling, sensation and intuition are usually considered poles apart. (It is possible to use these poles as complements along a single axis, but often the axis is split by the exclusive use of only one of the poles, producing one-sided adaptation.)

The vertically arranged pair of functions represents the most conscious (first, or top) and least conscious (fourth, or bottom) attributes of the ego-syntonic aspects of personality. Classical Jungian theorists call the bottom position the position of the Shadow, which is ego-dystonic. Beebe, however, regards the bottom position as the place of the Anima/Animus, which carries an ideal for the functioning of the "inferior" function and therefore regards this position, too, as ego-syntonic. Traditionally, in addition to being a bridge to the unconscious, the fourth function has been considered to represent the individual Shadow, the ego-dystonic and projected aspects of one's personality. In this role the Anima or Animus carries the projections of one's contrasexual aspects. The contrasexual is considered "strange" enough to make it ego-alien.

Although this is indeed the least conscious of the first four functions and is not under control of the will, Beebe considers it *more* conscious (in the sense of being part of what the person is aware of) than are any of the second four function positions. In addition, he does not consider it a Shadow function, since it may carry personality aspects that are highly valued, even if in relatively unconscious ways. In other words, Anima/Animus values are still ego-syntonic; that is why they can "inspire."

SEQUENCE OF ATTITUDES ON THE PERSONALITY DIAGRAM. According to Beebe and Isabel Briggs Myers (Myers & McCaulley, 1985), if a person's most used, best developed function is extraverted, then the next most developed function must operate in the introverted mode. Beebe feels that the third function will be extraverted again, and the fourth introverted. The sequence is completely reversed if the first function is introverted; based on clinical observation, this theory asserts that the attitudes of the four functions always follow an alternating sequence.

In the example we are using, the first function is extraverted thinking (ET), so the second function must be expressed in the introverted (I) mode. Here it could be either of the two irrational functions; in this case it is sensation, giving us introverted sensation (IS).

Now the other two functions are known. The third must be extraverted and must be the other irrational function: It is extraverted intuition (EN). The fourth must be introverted and must be the other rational function; it is introverted feeling (IF).

Diagnostically, then, once we have identified a person's first two functions accurately, we know all dimensions of that person's typology. Many people are familiar with the MBTI, a popular personality test based on Jungian theory (Myers & McCaulley, 1985). We do not have room here to discuss the MBTI in detail, but its use is compatible with the information given in this chapter. No paper-and-pencil test is likely to accurately reflect a person's way of relating to the world, though. Some reasons for this should become evident as we proceed.

MISLABELING. In clinical contexts, according to Beebe, *mislabeling* of a person's typology is a common problem. He points out, for example, that it is easy for a therapist or other observer to "collapse" the attitude of the first function with the function in the second position, as illustrated in the accompanying diagram. The arrow in the diagram indicates that the attitude of extraversion at the Hero position is collapsed with the function of sensation

MISLABELING PERSONALITY FUNCTIONS

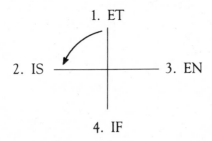

at the Parent location. Thus, instead of being identified as an extraverted thinker with a helping function of introverted sensation, the person will be labeled an extraverted sensation type. As you can imagine, this leads to misunderstandings. Often even a skilled Jungian analyst needs months of meetings with a client to accurately figure out the individual's natural personality type.

The Second Four Personality Functions: Beebe's Second Quadrant

Beebe bases his theory on Jung's but adds a second quaternity of function positions to the four discussed above. He calls the functions in the first four positions the "ego-syntonic" functions; these are the ones we are more-or-less happy to acknowledge. The fourth function is the least conscious, but it is not regarded especially unfavorably.

Beebe's second group of four function positions differentiates among the elements of our "ego-alien" or Shadow personality. This second quaternity is shown below. The diagram includes both the first four functions as diagrammed on page 67, and the fifth through eighth functions for the same person.

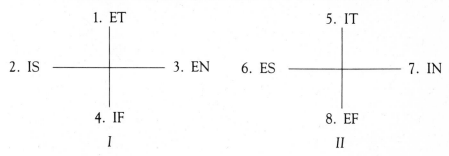

ATTITUDE CHANGES IN THE SECOND FOUR FUNCTIONS

At the top of the second grid, in the fifth position, the function is still "thinking," but it is introverted, not extraverted. The other three functions are similarly modified. Each function occupies the same relative location but has switched from its original attitude to the opposite attitude. You can readily imagine that people with the same functions but opposite attitudes are likely to clash; each represents the Shadow of the other.

Archetypal Correlates of the Personality Positions

We will next consider the influence of archetypes at each grid position. The archetypes are discussed only briefly; Chapter 4 gave them a fuller treatment.

In addition to describing new functions 5 through 8, Beebe has inferred from clinical observation that a major Jungian archetype "rules" each of the eight positions. By addressing the influence of these archetypes on the operation of the functions, he hopes to increase our understanding of personality dynamics.

Beebe's first four archetypal labels are shown below.

BEEBE'S POSITION LABELS FOR THE FIRST FOUR FUNCTIONS

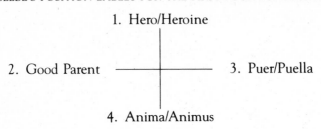

1. Hero/Heroine

2. Good Parent   3. Puer/Puella

4. Anima/Animus

The first two labels are in English because they are the two most conscious of the four functions; the third and fourth are Latinized to show that they are relatively less conscious.

As Beebe has pointed out, a simple approach to these position labels is to think in terms of transactional analysis, originated by Eric Berne (1964). Berne's *Adult* is the Hero, representing the superior or dominant function; the *Parent* is equated with the auxiliary function; and the *Child* equals the tertiary function. (Berne does not deal directly with the inferior, Anima/Animus function.)

All but the inferior function are "trainable." This fourth function, being less conscious, resists conscious control and must be approached indirectly, through the Trickster archetype at the seventh (usually ego-alien) position if it is to change.

FIRST OR DOMINANT POSITION: HERO/HEROINE. The first function has for its archetype the *Hero*, or the Ego Achiever. This is the protagonist in the Hero's journey through life. This function is associated with the Persona in an extraverted person and represents adaptation to life's demands. For an introvert, it still represents one's ego or primary conscious identity, but in closer relation to the Self.

This function is often mislabeled when people take a type test such as the MBTI, or when we try to assign types to our friends, because of the observer's tendency, mentioned earlier, to "collapse" attributes of the first and second functions.

The heroic superior function can be grossly entangled with the Persona if it is overdeveloped at the expense of the others. Another function, more favored by the culture or family, may also be used as a Persona in a falsely heroic way. Thus, if I am naturally an intuitive person but my parents favor a thinking approach to life, I may be forced to favor my thinking function in my adaptation to life's demands, even though it is really my secondary, or even tertiary personality function. The Persona is the mask with which we face the world. James Yandell (1993), a Jungian analyst, claims that "we all sold out to satisfy our parents" and so must all cope with our Persona problem.

In therapy, the clinician's first task often is to identify and help the client develop his or her dominant, Hero or Heroine function. Beebe feels that this is less often done well for women than for men in our culture. Male therapists especially tend to evoke the Child or Parent archetype from their women patients. They may be threatened by, and may even actively discourage, the Heroine function. The most perilous case is when the therapist is attracted to the patient as Anima; this can lead to damaging emotional and sexual entanglements.

SECOND OR AUXILIARY POSITION: GOOD MOTHER/FATHER. This is the position ruled by the Good Mother or Father archetype. Beebe says that you use your auxiliary parent function to take care of others. To identify the auxiliary function, he suggests that you ask yourself how you (or another person) would care for a person in deep distress. He has found that these modes of caring are often the helpful voices of wisdom and experience.

THIRD OR TERTIARY POSITION: PUER/PUELLA. The third position is occupied by the *Puer/Puella* archetype. This is the eternal child, a source of creativity and new beginnings, but also the enemy of a settled life.

FOURTH OR INFERIOR POSITION: ANIMA/ANIMUS. This position marks another departure of Beebe's theory from classical Jungian descriptions of the personality functions. Beebe sees the fourth function as less unconscious than, and its Anima qualities as different from, traditional formulations.

In much Jungian writing, the fourth, "inferior" position is associated with the Shadow and with the Anima/Animus, the "other" or "alien" aspect of either gender. Being the least conscious of the four primary functions, it resists being drawn into consciousness; approaching it is considered instead to draw the other functions closer to the unconscious. Rather than being able to draw the fourth function up from the unconscious, one must approach it by allowing or encouraging less consciousness to rule in the other three functions.

For Beebe as well, the fourth position is that of the Anima/Animus, which provides a bridge between the conscious and unconscious. In his view, the Anima/Animus is not necessarily projected onto a person of the opposite gender, even though it may be represented contrasexually in dreams. Rather, it gets lived as the individual's *purpose* in life, an inspiration, ideal, or "cause" that represents the person's highest value in life. When operating out of this position, the individual is inspired by the Anima/Animus, as by a mythological muse.

For instance, the person whose dominant function is introverted intuition will have extraverted sensation in the fourth position. The normal goal of introverted intuition is to sense gestalts. In Jung's own case, this process involved hunting down primordial images. When his extraverted sensation came up in midlife, however, his "cause" became to establish the *reality* of the psyche he had discovered. During his near-breakdown, Jung conducted dialogues with visionary figures (see Chapter 1) in developing his concept of archetypes. In later life, he also did much stone carving of archetypal subjects by the lake at Bollingen. The primordial images became living archetypes of the collective unconscious for him, to be carved in stone and dramatized and talked to like real people.

When Beebe says that in this fourth position the Anima/Animus provides a transition between conscious and unconscious parts of the psyche, his approach is consistent with classical Jungian theory. Beyond this, Beebe's theory of personality type begins to diverge from standard Jungian descriptions.

MALADAPTIVE DEVELOPMENT. Some people don't use their second or auxiliary Parent function, or use it only in a restricted way; as small children they were prevented from competing with a powerful parent or other environmental pressure. They learned to use their third function, the Puer/Puella or child, instead. Beebe believes, for example, that many American women have been forced to behave in a childlike way because they couldn't compete with a strong mother (he gives the television character of Lucy in *I Love Lucy* as an example of a childlike woman). In addition, subordinate groups in society are often encouraged to be "childlike."

When forced into using the third function and neglecting the second, a person becomes unbalanced; in this situation the two most commonly used functions are both extraverted or both introverted, rather than one being of each attitude, as is normal. Individuals can be forbidden the third, child position also. These people are overly sober, because they use only the Hero and Parent positions. A popular name for them these days is *parentified children*.

Beebe calls being forced into the second or third position *rotating the personality*. Instead of operating out of the true vertical spine, a person with this condition is meeting the world with one of the functions on his or her true horizontal axis.

The Second Quaternity of Archetypes

This is Beebe's original contribution to personality theory. He classifies the Shadow processes into the same four functions as exist in the ego-syntonic personality, and spells out the ways the two quadrants compensate each other.

BEEBE'S POSITION LABELS FOR THE SECOND FOUR FUNCTIONS

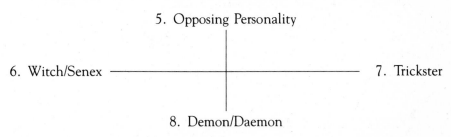

5. Opposing Personality

6. Witch/Senex

7. Trickster

8. Demon/Daemon

FIFTH POSITION: OPPOSING PERSONALITY. The fifth position is held by the *Opposing Personality*. This is Beebe's discovery through typological analysis. Not as well known as other archetypes, it is the shadow of the Hero, the origin of obscure stubborn refusals of life's challenges. It opposes the heroic approach to life and refuses to play the game. When the Greek hero Achilles sulked in his tent, refusing to come out and fight, he could have been in the grip of his Opposing Personality. The Opposing Personality can be oppositional, passive-aggressive, suspicious, or avoidant. On the positive side, for the extravert, it can represent the inner striving not derived from response to collective demands; for the introvert, it can involve externally stimulated response tendencies. Often the opposing personality is contrasexual: the "domineering" woman, the "bitchy" man.

SIXTH POSITION: WITCH/SENEX. Next comes the *Witch/Senex*—the bad or "negative" mother/father that criticizes, condemns, immobilizes, or demoralizes you, or relentlessly attacks others in a shadowy way. In some configurations, Freudians might call this function the *negative superego;* it is similar to the ego appraisals one has introjected (taken as an internal standard) from the censure of others (most often one's parental images, or symbolic representations of one's parents) and can be the basis of the severe self-attack seen in depression.

SEVENTH POSITION: TRICKSTER. The next-to-last position is that of the *Trickster*, an androgynous shadow of the Puer/Puella. The Trickster fools and confuses you or people who encounter you, depending on whether this function is introverted or extraverted. Beebe says its hallmark is to put other people into double binds. In a double bind, you are forced to make a choice that is wrong either way. An anecdote about a simple double bind goes as follows: A man received two neckties from his mother. He wore one for their next visit. She greeted him by asking, "What's the matter, don't you like the other tie?"

EIGHTH POSITION: DEMON/DAEMON. Finally we see the *Demon/Daemon*. This is the most rejected aspect of personality, the source of evil in many people, and (more rarely) the deepest source of creative inspiration. As with all Jungian polar dimensions, if you go far enough out in one direction you experience enantiodromia—the quality turns into its polar opposite.

Dyadic Personality Interaction

As mentioned before, Beebe says that it is most difficult for people of the same primary function but opposite attitude to get along. This becomes a problem in various contexts such as business, friendship, marriage, or therapy. It is helpful to be aware of one's type, the type of one's partner, and the difficulties in mutual understanding that will probably result.

The greatest personal conflicts arise between persons of opposite genders who have the same dominant function but paired with opposite attitudes. Sometimes the conflict is less intense between same-sex dyads. Members of such dyads often fall madly in love with each other; if they understand each other and the relationship survives, they can form an intense connection. Together, their personality distributions make up one completely balanced personality.

Problems arise because we speak from one of the eight archetypal positions at all times. When we address someone, says Beebe, the other person not only switches modalities (attitude and function) to match the ones from which we spoke, but also switches into the archetypal position those modalities occupy for him or her. This complicates the way one person "comes across" to someone else. A brief example will illustrate this complexity.

If my functions are distributed as in the diagrams above, then we see that my second function will be introverted sensation, in the position of the Good Parent. Suppose I am chatting while giving a check to George, who cuts my hair. I make a little ritual of getting out my checkbook, entering the figures, and so on, and since George once lost a check of mine, I always remind him to put it in his wallet right away.

Beebe's system predicts that George will respond to me in the same modality in which I am addressing him—in this case, introverted sensation. But let's say that *George's introverted sensation resides at his eighth position and is Demonic, tending to twist things.* Matching the modalities I used, but from this radically different position, George starts to feel sick to his stomach over my benevolent, if perhaps slightly patronizing, remarks. Our relationship is in trouble. After a few months of this, my friends begin to wonder why I have so many bad hair days. On a good hair day, however, the creative Daemonic side of George comes through with a final flourish of the comb after my caretaking ritual, which sometimes hooks his (Daemonic) gratitude and veneration for a caring mother figure. Making up other hypothetical misunderstandings—or looking at quarrels with one's intimates—with the aid of Beebe's schema can be an amusing exercise.

Personality Assessment

Several measures of personality based on Jungian theory have been developed. Jung's Word Association Test was the first projective test to appear. It inferred the presence of a personality complex from the delay between a stimulus word and the individual's response. If the associated word doesn't pop out readily, it has been intercepted. The person is searching for a substitute. The immediate response feels too scary to say, usually because it taps into a complex, with all its extra meanings and associations. Later Hermann Rorschach, a Swiss psychiatrist, used Jungian concepts such as introversion and extraversion to develop his projective Rorschach inkblot test (Exner, 1986). A projective test is a test where a purposely vague stimulus (a word or picture) is presented and the subject is asked to give a response or tell a story. The subject is presumed to "see" in the picture whatever theme is currently on his or her mind, and so the response reveals the subject's own story, not that of the stimulus.

Psychologist Henry Murray was familiar with Jung's work and used it in his projective Thematic Apperception Test or TAT (Bellak, 1993), in which subjects are invited to tell stories about a standard series of pictures. From the themes of the stories told, the TAT scoring system infers the presence in the subject of "needs" (somewhat like Jung's "complexes").

How can we accurately determine someone's personality type? In an effort to be objective and to provide statistical data, several investigators have constructed self-report, paper-and-pencil tests aimed at reflecting the respondent's personality configuration at a given moment, insofar as this can be reported consciously.

The MBTI (Myers & McCaulley, 1985) is the best-known of the personality assessment tests, followed by the Gray-Wheelwrights (Wheelwright, Wheelwright, & Buehler, 1964) and Singer-Loomis tests (Singer & Loomis, 1984). The Singer-Loomis differs from the other two by assuming that the personality functions are not opposing pairs but can be expressed as separate percentages.

These latter three tests share drawbacks. Any person's score can change over time and under varying conditions. People are too likely to label themselves forever as a particular type after taking one of the tests. Self-reports are also full of pitfalls when one is operating from a "rotated" personality grid. As Beebe points out, early family pressures force many of us to operate out of a substitute dominant function, but this problem is one that the tests are unlikely to detect. For further discussion of the use of typology in Jungian therapy, see Quenk and Quenk (1982).

The most reliable way to assess someone's personality configuration is to interact over long periods and gradually figure out his or her reactions to different stimuli. Many therapists believe that this kind of extended, intimate personal contact is the only way to arrive at a correct and useful assessment of personality type.

Therapy Implications of Personality Distribution

Good therapists should be able to voluntarily "rotate" their own type enough to speak the client's language and avoid the worst position/modality conflicts. In some cases therapists can expect to diagnose, and tailor their responses to, a client's specific type in just a few sessions; identifying others may take years, if the client has undergone distorting experiences early in life. If someone's shadow aspects are deeply repressed, you often can infer what they must be from observing the first four functions; even so, actually approaching and dealing with the Shadow will take a long time. More implications of personality type for therapists and clients are discussed in Chapters 7 and 8.

Life Development Theories and Individuation

This section represents my own attempt to visualize the course of life development in Jungian terms. The more usual approach describes life as having a morning, noon and evening, followed by the dark night of death. Jung's

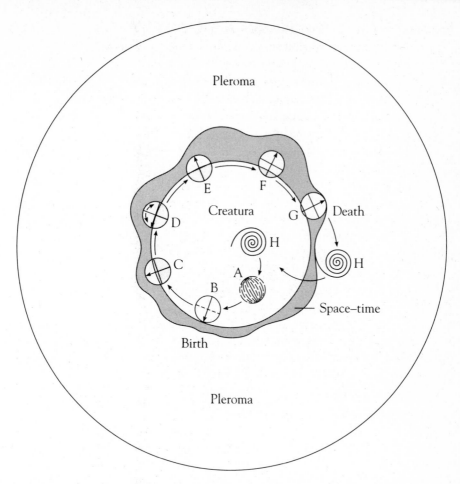

FIGURE 5.1
A Possible View of Jungian Life Development

theory of the collective unconscious, and his emphasis on the absence of time and space in the cosmic order, seem to imply a less limited trajectory for the individual than the usual approach just mentioned. Beebe's personality theory, described above, provides diagrams for the individual; I have risked envisioning a diagram of human development in a larger context.

The Diagram

We can approach Jungian concepts of life development through several levels of abstraction. Of these the most general is the progression experienced by a "generic" human being of either gender. The diagram in Figure 5.1 depicts one vision of that general development of personality. It is built on concepts presented earlier but speculates about the relationship between Jung's view of personality and his wider worldview.

The following comments on the diagram give one of my interpretations of development in some detail and touch on a few other interpretations. The central circle of the diagram represents one aspect of the *objective psyche*—the part that includes everything in the "lower world" of the created universe (see Chapter 3). Jung's (1916/1967c) term for this created world, which includes our own "creatureliness" as human beings, was *Creatura*.

The periphery of the diagram is, paradoxically, also the objective psyche, but its boundary is wider and its total contents more diffuse than the dense center. The broad area bounded by the large circle represents the chaos before creation, which Jung (1916/1967c) called the *Pleroma*. Physicist David Bohm (1980) refers to this region of potential being as the *implicate order*, and he calls the Creatura the *explicate order*. (Some other ties between Jung's thought and contemporary models of physics and mathematics are discussed in Chapter 10.)

The Pleroma contains one kind of consciousness—the consciousness inherent in all things. This pleromatic consciousness is faint and weak, at least as far as we can make out. Consciousness is stronger in the Creatura, where even inanimate objects manifest their being. This conception of the consciousness of things is perhaps best grasped through poetry, although it has been recently stressed in psychology by Hillman.

To repeat, the center and periphery of the diagram are *both* the objective psyche, but the consciousness in the center is dense while that of the outside is diffuse. We can extend the metaphor by saying that from the objective psyche, the diffuse consciousness of the archetypal periphery *precipitates* or condenses into the denser consciousness of the central self. One way to describe the human being is as a *precipitate of consciousness* (J. Beebe, personal communication, October 22, 1993).

Now we are ready to consider the labeled circles in Figure 5.1. It will help if we think of the whole diagram as more than two dimensional, so that the circles are "really" spheres in three (or more) dimensions. Each sphere is intended to be a diagrammatic snapshot of a stage in the sequence of the development of an abstract, generic human being's consciousness. This development is pictured as moving through time in the direction of the arrows connecting the spheres. The movement, suggested by the letters accompanying the spheres, is shown as outward and *clockwise*, because in the conventional iconography of symbol perception, clockwise movement leads us out of the unconscious.

EARLIEST DEVELOPMENT. Taking the spheres in alphabetical order, sphere A represents the gradual but considerable organization of an individual psyche around the time of birth. In an analogy to cellular meiosis, we could say that the personality becomes aligned along a major polar axis, as disparate but corresponding elements are incorporated into larger structures.

This first personality axis is what Beebe (1984, 1986, 1988a, 1993a) has called the spine of the personality, as discussed earlier in this chapter. Erich Neumann (1954) and Edward Edinger (1972) call this personality spine the ego-Self axis, and it represents the orientation of individual consciousness to wider consciousness of both the creatura and the pleroma.

INFANT DEVELOPMENT. Sphere B depicts the emerging consciousness of the newborn baby. After birth, during the cycles of coming apart to relate to others and coming together to relate to the self that Fordham has called the integration-deintegration process (see Chapter 6), the baby's personality structure gradually develops, with its wealth of self and object relations. In this way, the consciousness and unconsciousness of the individual, and the individual's areas of health and pathology, gradually emerge from the objective psyche.

During this process of accommodating to the outside world, most babies are compelled by pressure from their caretakers to "rotate" their personality axes so that the innate primary function of consciousness—the natural psychological type—is demoted in favor of a personality attribute more pleasing to the parents. (Such rotation can turn either way, as indicated by the arrows in sphere D.) We assume that relatively few parents are either the same, typologically, as their children, or well enough developed themselves to be able to tolerate a baby's innately different personality tendencies. Some of the painful vicissitudes of this process of adaptation have been described by Alice Miller (1981) and by Stella Chess and her associates (Chess, Thomas, & Birch, 1965; Thomas, Chess, & Birch, 1968).

ADOLESCENT DEVELOPMENT. Sphere C depicts the person's consciousness in youth. At this stage the apparent superior function becomes inflated. This may be the "true" superior function or the "false" superior function produced by rotation of the grid of individual consciousness in childhood. In either case, the function that has been providing the greatest measure of adaptation is the one that gets inflated in adolescence. Inflation is a normal event; the adolescent's job is to develop and even exaggerate an identity as a way to separate from the parents and deal with the rest of the world. Erikson (1963) calls this exaggerated sense of identity *ego identity*, and in Beebe's view, its strong assertion does not depend on knowledge of one's true Jungian type. This dominant function represents the adolescent's Persona. However, if the ego identity does not, finally, correspond to the true psychological type, there will be something overdrawn about it and it will eventually break down, as a belatedly recognized false self. Beebe has given the example of Jung, whose adaptation broke down after his periods of strong self-assertion in the (for him) false position of trying to be Freud's leading disciple (Beebe, 1984a, 1984b).

STAGNATED DEVELOPMENT. Sphere D is a diagram of an adult whose personality is rotated (adapted to external demands) and who is not very individuated. Much of the personality is still embedded in the unconscious. The person still may be mostly identified with the Persona, with success defined by the family and culture, rather than responding to any internal standards.

MIDLIFE RECTIFICATION OF PERSONALITY. Sphere E shows rectification of the personality; this can happen at midlife, if all goes well. *Rectification* means that the personality axes are re-rotated so that the true spine aligns with the ego-Self axis, rather than being at right angles to it.

Rectification of one's personality is for most people a vital part of the individuation process; somewhere between the ages of 25 and 45 to 50, we can wake up to who we really are. Rectification includes two simultaneous tasks. First, aligning the personality axes in the "true" direction requires that the person recognize and liberate the true superior function. At the same time, the individual must also recognize and accept the true inferior function, which serves as a permanent compensation for the tendency of the superior function to become inflated.

Rectification is an arduous process. It usually means the breakup of an adaptation that has seemed to serve well, a resulting state of confusion and depression, and a laborious process of reorienting to and assimilating the "true" personality type that has been neglected since childhood. The process is eased considerably if the person is fortunate enough to obtain effective psychotherapy relatively early.

The acceptance of the inferior function means that the individual begins to assimilate contrasexual aspects of the psyche (see the discussion of the Anima/Animus archetype in Chapter 4). This process helps us to withdraw projections (Chapter 7) from objects around us and is part of one's acceptance of the Shadow (Chapter 4). When we come to terms with the Shadow we are taking a first step on the road to individuation, in which our personality components are more equally balanced. Thus the Anima/Animus development associated with the inferior function (described in the last two paragraphs) makes the fourth function an important route of access to the unconscious at this stage, rather than just a place of faulty ego adaptation.

At this stage the compensation of the unconscious for inflation of the superior function really starts to count; no longer can one say about a failed marriage or lost job, "Oh well, I don't care; that wasn't really me." It was "me," and the personal roots of the loss must be dealt with. This development often corresponds to the grounding of the Puer archetype (Chapter 4), which so often participates in the inflation of the area of apparently greatest adaptation in youth.

We may speculate that a re-rotation of the personality in the "wrong" direction may lead some people to live out the inflated shadow, rather than the true superior function. Perhaps they become psychopaths, criminals, and so on.

FURTHER DEVELOPMENT. If the developmental tasks at sphere E go well, the person may next be pictured by sphere F. This is an individuating individual, operating out of a rectified superior function compensated by a healthy inferior function and open to the wider consciousness. The area of unconsciousness recedes somewhat as the inferior function and shadow aspects of the rest of the personality are assimilated, or at least acknowledged. Interestingly enough, as the least-developed function becomes conscious, the most-developed function begins to decrease in importance and to lose its sharpness (J. Beebe, personal communication, October 22, 1993).

DEVELOPMENT IN OLD AGE. Sphere G shows a person in old age, perhaps in his or her 80s. Here what amounts to a burst of Self often occurs; consciousness is beautifully concentrated and can be said to radiate outward, so that some aged persons become for others symbols of the Good Parent. Herbert Maslow (1973) is possibly the only psychologist besides Jung to speak of the unity achieved by a developed personality. This state leads to an immersion in the present and an exit from "time."

HYPOTHESIZED PRE- AND POSTEXISTENCE STATES. Spheres labeled H appear twice, in the center and on the periphery of the diagram. In the center, sphere H represents archetypal elements of the Creatura available to be selected and organized in the process of personality formation. On the periphery, sphere H stands for the redispersal into the Pleroma of the personal elements of the psyche.

These dissolving elements include personal consciousness. Under this hypothesis, the objective psyche is changed by the addition of these elements at the death of each individual. People differ in the degree of consciousness they are able to attain, and as more people travel farther along the individuation process, they can be said to create more consciousness. This is a purposive act; we earn our way to luminous clarity through human effort. We create "more" diffuse consciousness in the Pleroma, which is then available for precipitation into the Creatura of the next generation. (See Chapter 10 for Sheldrake's related concept of "morphogenetic fields.")

This, obviously, is a metaphorical description of an unknown and perhaps finally unknowable process, but it provides one way to assign meaning to life. It implies that each life makes a difference to the objective psyche. In this way, Jungian esoteric thought is different from Buddhist spiritual theory; the Buddhist notion that this life is Maya, illusion, implies that we never should have left the Mother archetype. It tells us, like a mother to a youth who has left home, that all human psychic development outside the sphere of the original Home is illusion.

THE ARENA OF OUR LIVES. Now look at the wavy band between the center and periphery of the diagram. This represents the universe as we experience it. It includes both consciousness and unconsciousness, whether collective, cultural, or personal. This is the playing field on which we pursue the game of life as we know it.

The main difference between this area and the other two is that it is anchored in a space-time continuum. While we can only speculate about the universe before we were born and after we die, we actually know something, or think we do, about this area, which is a place of conscious imagination. Conscious imagination can be seen as actually creating the dimension of time.

The boundary between the center band and the Pleroma is shown as ameboid, which is meant to indicate that it expands with the sum or volume of all forms of consciousness, wherever they appear. We can imagine consciousness as spreading out over unconsciousness like an oil slick. Consciousness here is less concentrated than in the center of our diagram, but more extensive.

The ameboid shape of the boundary expresses a belief that there is continual change in the topography of the objective psyche; this may correspond to Bohm's notion of the unfolding of the implicate into the explicate order (see Chapter 10) and follows Jung's assertion that the psyche is an open system—a place of continuous creation. However, there are limits. The Pleroma is altogether outside of the space-time dimension. The Creatura contains the possibilities of space and time, but only our conscious world embodies them.

This concludes our first view of Figure 5.1, which helps us organize the basic Jungian concepts taken up in the following paragraphs. By visualizing through a meandering pattern the concepts of the objective psyche and human development we have set the stage for the drama to follow. This is the individuation process, in which consciousness precipitates, develops, and renews itself. It is a wonderful thing to participate in this drama, as therapists will confirm who have been privileged to trace the progress of individual lives.

OTHER INTERPRETATIONS. The explanation just given is not the only way we can look at the diagram. Like all symbols, it hints at many possible meanings. Here are a few:

1. It is probable that the developmental stages, depicted here as separate spheres, do not necessarily succeed each other, as in time-lapse photography, but actually coexist throughout a lifetime. For better or for worse, we may never lose some aspects of our original character no matter how effective our therapy or how complete our process of individuation (Beebe, 1993b). This would help explain how our earliest defenses of *splitting* (categorizing persons or events as all-good or all-bad) or *denial* (refusing to recognize that something exists) stick with us and can be pressed into service during a crisis.

Thus sphere A in the diagram could represent an observing standpoint that coalesces during our birth, and only dissolves with our death.

2. Simultaneous with or alternative to the view that the diagram represents the objective psyche, we could think of it as something alive, like an organic cell; the center is then the nucleus, and the periphery is the cytoplasm.

In a physiological cell, the nucleus contains the potential for growth such as the genes and the mitochondria, and it is here that the cell initiates the mysterious biological processes of mitosis or meiosis (cell division). Individuaton is a lot like these biological processes in that both are natural procedures apparently working against nature, or at least against the structures created by nature. The most natural thing to do would be to stay undifferentiated and undeveloped, but something inherent in living things impels them to break up this primal unity.

3. We could think of the Pleroma as being a primal, archetypal hologram (see Chapter 10), which precipitates pieces of itself into the Creatura, each piece being an individual who contains all the elements of the original. However, we know that as one enlarges a tiny piece of a mundane hologram it loses detail. Similarly, in our analogy, since the elements making up the individual are embodied—realized in matter—they inevitably must be more coarse-grained than the original archetype and lose something as a result.

Furthermore, unlike bits of holograms, the arrangement of elements is unique in each fragmented piece of the objective psyche. As Clyde Kluckhohn and Henry Murray (1951, p. 35) said, we are each like everybody else, like somebody else, and like nobody else.

4. We might use the language of physics and mathematics and call the archetypes in the Pleroma *strange attractors* (Chapter 10). These mathematical

functions generate what seems to be a chaotic process, but through infinite repetitions create a recognizable set of patterns, identical in form up and down the scale of their expression. That is, each large pattern comprises identical smaller patterns, right down to the submicroscopic level. This concept is like that shown in the mathematical patterns known as *fractals*, in which each tiny part of a pattern replicates the whole.

In looking at the "paths" around the attractor, it is evident that each repetition is similar to but separate from every other cycle. This is a vivid illustration of the uniqueness of each individual process within a recognizable archetypal pattern.

I offer these additional ways to look at this diagram of human development because different people may respond better to one metaphor than to another. The multiplication of ideas also illustrates a principle that applies to all symbols—that they are subject to more than one interpretation, each of which may contain some truth even if they seem to contradict another facet of the total "meaning" of the symbol.

INDIVIDUATION. No matter which metaphor we choose to visualize the developmental process, the underlying premise is the same: Individuation of the personality is a major goal in life. Samuels et al. (1986, p. 76) define individuation in part as follows:

> A person's becoming himself, whole, indivisible and distinct from other people or collective psychology (though also in relation to these). . . . The person becomes conscious in what respects he or she is both a unique human being and, at the same time, no more than a common man or woman.
> Because of this inherent paradox, definitions abound.

Here we find a central paradox in Jungian thought. We are unique but "common," distinct but related. It's as if we must find the hole in a jigsaw puzzle into which we are the only piece that fits.

Individuation is a search that never ends, but the process of searching may produce what Jung called one's "true personality." He said:

> Personality is the supreme realization of the innate idiosyncrasy of a living being. It is an act of high courage flung in the face of life, the absolute affirmation of all that constitutes the individual, the most successful adaptation to the universal conditions of existence coupled with the greatest possible freedom for self-determination. (CW 17, para. 289)

Jung believed that not everyone achieved a true personality; although you needn't be an exceptional figure to achieve your true personality, it does take inner guidance: "Only the chosen few have embarked upon this strange adventure. . . . For the ordinary man the outstanding personality is something *supernatural*" (CW 17, para. 298, Jung's italics). "True personality is always a vocation," he added, noting further that "anyone with a vocation hears the voice of the inner man: he is *called*. That is why the legends say that he possesses a private daemon who counseled him and whose mandates he must obey" (CW 17, para. 300, Jung's italics).

This is another area where Jung's belief in the individual rather than society is strongly expressed. He acknowledged that the conventions are necessary but reserved his admiration for people who were not unthinkingly governed by collective standards. This is the arena of the daemon, as he indicated; it takes great courage to act on your convictions when most people think you are wrong. There is no guarantee that the call comes from the Self and not from the Shadow—or even from the Shadow side of the Self!

READINGS

Edinger, E. (1972). *Ego and archetype: Individuation and the religious function of the psyche.* New York: Putnam.

Hillman, J. (with von Franz, M.-L.). (1971). *Lectures on Jung's typology.* Dallas, TX: Spring Publications.

Myers, J. B., & McCaulley, M. H. (1985). *Manual: A guide to the development and use of the Myers-Briggs Type Indicator.* Palo Alto, CA: Consulting Psychologists Press.

Samuels, A. (1989). *The plural psyche: Personality, morality, and the father.* London: Routledge.

Sandner, D., & Beebe, J. (in press). Psychopathology and analysis. In M. Stein (ed.), *Jungian analysis* (2nd ed.). LaSalle, IL: Open Court.

Storr, A. (1988). *Solitude: A return to the self.* New York: Free Press.

Theoretical Components

Developmental Theory

This chapter is divided into two main sections. In the first section, we sketch Jungian developmental theory, looking both at Jung's own view of the developmental process and at some competing theories offered by his colleagues and successors. The second section focuses on gender in Jungian developmental theory.

Jungian Developmental Theory: An Overview

Jungian developmental theory encompasses many points of view; we can only touch on some of the highlights here.

Child Development

Jung had little to say about early development, apparently choosing to leave that period to Freud. Volume 17 of his *Collected Works* includes about 100 pages written between 1910 and 1932 on the subject of children, partly taking issue with Freud's view of sexuality and the Oedipus complex. Children turn up only here and there in his other books. Like others at that time, he directed what he did write about children mostly to educators, since he felt that they exerted great influence on child development.

Jung (1933) concentrated on the adult psyche and considered work with children to mean work with the parents. He viewed children as more closely identified with their parents than most people would today. Children now grow up faster than they did in a more sheltered age, or among the families Jung knew.

Jung's developmental interests were centered on changes in adults, usually around the ages of 30 to 50. Jung sometimes sought out the child in the adult; he focused on the unconscious residues of childhood experience when treating severely disordered patients, since he saw that such disorder is likely to stem from early trauma (see Jung, CW 5).

Although he did not write much about childhood himself, Jung knew the child-focused work of a number of Jungian contemporaries. He wrote an introduction to *The Inner World of Childhood* (1927) by Frances Wickes, a Jungian child analyst. Her book is a rich collection of case examples, rather than a theoretical work, but it is firmly grounded in Jungian principles. Wickes was much less widely recognized than Erich Neumann, although her book first appeared over 40 years before Neumann's (1973) book on the child. Neumann, building on both Jung and the field of anthropology, was the first theorist to present a Jungian interpretation of child development. Dora Kalff (1981) used Neumann's theories to explain some of the phenomena of sand-play therapy.

NEUMANN'S THREE-STAGE THEORY. Neumann (1973) believed that after birth the baby gradually emerges from a state of undifferentiated unity with the world, as symbolized by the mother. He called that state *uroboric*, after the *uroboros*, the symbol of a snake biting its tail, signifying the eternal round of nature. As this primary unity with the mother gives way to emerging ego consciousness, the baby seeks active relationship with the world (Sullwold, 1982).

Neumann (1973) described three stages of development in the child as it emerges from the uroboric unity with nature: the animal-vegetative stage, in which the child actively explores the physical world; the battle or defense stage, in which the child becomes aware of dangers and ways to protect itself from them; and entry into the collective by adaptation to the demands of the parents and other caretakers.

If all goes well, the child retains a reliable connection between its ego and the self. This maintains the support of the self at each stage. As we saw in Chapter 5, a less fortunate child may be forced to adapt to parental demands in a way that cuts off the connection to the self. In severe cases, this experience may encourage the development of a flight from reality or even major dissociation.

Children are connected to, and influenced by, archetypes besides the self. Parental archetypes seem at first identical to the actual parents, who are experienced as human personalities only as the child progresses developmentally.

The child can sense the archetypes as spiritual, nonpersonal forces that help compensate for negative experience with the actual parents. On the other hand, a child who has not developed a strong enough ego can get lost among the archetypes and remain identified with them (Sullwold, 1982, p. 243).

FORDHAM'S THEORY OF THE DEINTEGRATION-REINTEGRATION CYCLE. Michael Fordham's (1961, 1963) group is closely associated with the British object relations school, and he has combined object relations and Jungian theory in his principles of child development. The theory is a valuable addition to Jungian knowledge.

No writer mentioned so far has told us exactly how a child progresses along the developmental path. Fordham's (1957, 1961) descriptions of infant development provide a detailed account of this process. Jung believed that developing consciousness was composed of fragments that emerged from unconsciousness and gradually came together (CW 17, para. 103). Fordham and his associates modified this aspect of Jungian developmental theory as a result of detailed observations of infants at home with their families. Observers, who are analysts or trained by analysts, spend several hours a week in the home of the family, from the day a child comes home from the hospital until it is about two years old. The experience has a tremendous impact on the observers. They are asked to watch without intervening, but as they become acquainted with the family they often find it hard to resist being drawn into other roles. They are required to participate in discussion groups and therapy to help contain these excursions.

The core of Fordham's theory describes a cyclical *deintegration-reintegration* (*DI-RI*) sequence in the infant. In the birth process the baby is assumed to deintegrate as it emerges from a preconscious (uroboric, in Neumann's terms) identity with the primal *Self* (see Chapter 3).

In deintegration the baby's preconscious unity with the world shatters, activating archetypal drives and constellating opposites in the psyche. Sphere B in Figure 5.1 gives one possible schematic representation of this process.

Before birth, the baby possessed little or no consciousness, all its needs were instantly gratified, and it was merged with the primal Self. The incomprehensibly painful birth process initiates a complete change of circumstances. You can't explain any of this to a newborn; it is alone with the unmediated experience. There is no personality to filter or interpret events and no means to anticipate future change. The repercussions of the newborn's experience of fragmentation are archetypally extreme, absolute, and nonhuman. It is likely that the wound of the initial rupture from the prebirth primal Self never disappears. Our subsequent developmental course essentially depends on how well our primary caretaker, most often the mother, handles the recurrent DI-RI cycle (Matthews, 1985).

If the caretaker manages the DI-RI cycle well, the baby's distressing deintegration due to hunger, cold, heat, or other factors is caught early enough to enable the infant to quickly reestablish equilibrium. This constitutes *reintegration*.

For the sake of convenience we will call the primary caretaker the "mother" here, although it could be any person most closely involved with the baby's care. Both members of the caretaking dyad act to *humanize the archetypes*. This means that the infant depends on the mothering one as a mediator between its interior, archetypal environment and the human experience. Otherwise it finds itself abandoned to the power of the archetypes.

The baby's earliest task is to evoke instinctive response patterns in the caretaker. In the traditional family, women and girls were the ones most exposed to this activity, while fathers' and sons' nurturant and affective needs and abilities were left undeveloped (Chodorow, 1978). This differential training has begun to wane, as old assumptions about the nature of men and women are given up.

If the caretaker acts as a "good-enough mother" (Winnicott, 1969), the baby is unlikely to pass beyond deintegration into a state of disintegration. For example, imagine a hungry baby squirming, wrinkling up its face, whimpering, and starting to wail. In a secure household, at about this time the good-enough mother picks up the baby and soothes it while she prepares to feed it. When she gives it the breast or bottle, the baby latches on to the nipple, gulps greedily, and soon regains its equilibrium.

In a disorganized or hostile household, the baby's cries may go unheeded for a longer time. When the baby's needs are frustrated beyond its tolerance level, the DI-RI sequence deteriorates into an experience of *disintegration*, and the infant is engulfed in a storm of rage or sorrow that resists ordinarily effective interventions of comfort. If still ignored, the baby may eventually "give up" and fall asleep. Severely neglected babies become apathetic and may even die. Pediatricians call this condition *failure to thrive*, or in the worst cases, *marasmus*.

Once a baby is in a disintegrated state, it cannot easily be soothed, even when picked up. Its continued thrashing may knock away the nipple it so desperately craves. Jungian theory assumes that it is now in the grip of archetypal rage and despair. (If you remember the archetype of the Opposing Personality, you might consider whether such occasions as these could enable this archetype to emerge and strike root in the baby's world.)

Every infant suffers some failures of mothering, since no family can avoid an occasional lapse, but in healthier households the positive experiences far outnumber the negative, so that gradually a baby can begin to anticipate that its needs will dependably be met. The tempering of almost-out-of-control reactions is both physiological and psychological. By their successful interactions, the mother and baby cooperatively organize the neurological and emotional integration of the infant and ease its adjustment to the environment.

The DI-RI cycle is a natural flow of events, by which the baby's ego gradually develops. As the infant introjects and assimilates the sequence, it can "keep" the experience of the mother's care for longer periods. During cycles of DI-RI, a separation of the baby's and mother's ego and self is going on. In these interchanges, the baby acquires the experience of a personal self different from the archetypal self, which begins to recede. This is another aspect of "humanizing the archetype." Mother and baby learn to perceive and love each other as separate individuals, and as a result the infant's ego gradually begins to substitute for that of the mother, so it can increasingly bear anxiety, frustration, and waiting.

As we have seen, for healthy development to be possible, the times of loving care must exceed the times of frustration and deprivation if reintegration is to occur. If negative experiences overshadow the positive, then the archetypal Self continues to be predominant, archetypal imagery intrudes, and the deintegrated state falls into disintegration.

When all goes relatively well, the child eventually develops the ability and courage to stand the experience of deintegration and to reintegrate on its own. How soon and how well this happens depends on the child's experiences, ego strength, and budding faith in the caretakers. A certain amount of anger builds up in the process, and at adolescence, in a final readjustment, all hell may break loose.

This second rupture will be especially severe in families where the parents have been intolerant of a child's innate personality tendencies. The developing adolescents must either break away to become their own person, or remain trapped in a false Persona adaptation to parental demands.

Stella Chess and her associates (1965) have described the consequences of poor fit between the personalities of a child and its parents. If a baby is born with a set of responses to a world that the parents consider burdensome, a barrier to understanding and love often springs up, so that by the time the baby is two years old, the parent/child relationship has badly deteriorated, with dire results.

When caretakers have severe problems of their own, they may see any normal baby as "difficult" and refuse or feel unable to give adequate responses to the baby's ordinary needs. The caretaking adult's problems may be situational or characterological; the results are similar.

Problems in the baby, in the caretaker, or between them can foster the development of a narcissistic or borderline personality. A person whose personality qualifies as borderline needs immediate gratification, or will "split" into an archetypal state of rage. Borderline people are fragmented people.

The borderline person has both ego and boundary difficulties; Jungian theory attributes these problems to an early deficiency in humanizing the archetypal experiences and to the resulting interference with maintaining the ego-Self axis. These events occur earlier than the Oedipal events proposed by Freud, and so paradoxically Jungian theory now extends both earlier and later into the life cycle than did early psychoanalysis.

Some aspects of Fordham's theory are closely comparable to Kohut's (1971) object relations explanations of early development: The infant needs others to promote development of an identity, and if this fails to happen, problems show up later, in part as fears of disintegration. We relate to the objects (others) we have introjected, rather than to contemporary events involving actual persons. Our introjected objects often are based on outmoded early relationships with parents. If they did not meet our early need for recognition as a separate person, our ego remains weak. The Fordham school also draws heavily on the work of Winnicott (1951, 1969) and Klein (1953, 1975). All these theorists believe that narcissistic and borderline conditions involve deficits in ego strength.

Because of this broadly accepted assumption of the importance of relationship in identity development, Jungian therapy, especially as used to help a fragmented patient attain greater inner coherence, often focuses on interpersonal *feelings*, especially in the transference relationship (see Chapter 7).

This emotional/relational approach contrasts with the Freudian approach, which is based more on cognitive interpretation. It is also different from the theory of individual development advanced by Erik Erikson, another major theorist.

Development at Midlife

Jung's description of individuation starts with the changes of midlife. Recognition of the need to develop all sides of personality, not just the "adapted" aspects, is one of his main contributions to psychological theory. In this section we look at Jungian developmental theory, modified to fit current cultural conditions.

Midlife in mainstream Western culture seems to bring crisis. The conditions are somewhat different for men than for women. At midlife, many a typical middle-income man will look around and say "Is this all there is?" He has devoted his energies to achieving status and money, with varying degrees of success. He has been in a number of close relationships, perhaps married one or more times, and his sexual powers are beginning to dwindle. His children may or may not have "turned out well." He may feel that his whole life has been spent running in place.

Many women at midlife have two divergent tracks to deal with. Like her male counterpart, the woman who is a breadwinner has poured energy into achieving recognition and success. In addition, she has probably been the primary person responsible for running her household. With the departure of adult children, she may for the first time have leisure to consider who she is, and what she might like to do, apart from multiple caretaking responsibilities. It is fashionable lately to frighten us with the apparition of menopause; this biological "change of life" is indeed a crisis for some, but many women sail through it with hardly any symptoms and few regrets.

The midlife woman may have lost intimate contact with her husband or partner, or a culture-bound man may have dropped her during his own midlife crisis and turned to a younger woman.

The woman, educated or not, who has followed a domestic path exclusively may be faced with even harsher questions of personal identity in her middle years. She may pick up a former interest or avocation, intending to move out into the larger world just as her "outside" partner is getting ready to spend more time at home. More than for most men, a woman may be dismayed by the loss of her youthful appearance. She too has reason to ask, "Is this all there is to life?"

This is the traditional time for someone to enter Jungian therapy. Jungian theory emphasizes that midlife will bring a reevaluation of goals. Energy turns away from outer achievement toward inner development, as neglected areas of personality cry out for attention in dreams or through symptoms, whether cognitive, emotional, or psychosomatic.

The more one-sided you have been, the more you have narrowly focused your goals, and the more you have subordinated your natural personality to collective pressures, the greater you can expect your midlife crisis to be.

If a person can hang on to (or recover) equilibrium through these stormy waters, he or she will emerge with a renewed sense of enjoyment and purpose. Severe crises are not inevitable. Some people manage to distribute their energies relatively evenly in the first half of life and negotiate midlife with only minor upheavals. Others who became unbalanced early, may by their middle years have worked some matters out, with or without help.

In many ways, a midlife crisis provides a chance to come to terms with one's life before it is too late—to square away difficulties at work or with a life companion; to sign up for a course in some creative activity; to quit voting the way your parents told you to; in short, to make time for whatever or whomever you had neglected up to now.

JUNGIAN FORMULATION OF THE MIDLIFE TASK. According to Fordham and others, the repetitive childhood DI-RI cycles, separating the ego from the primal self, led to the establishment of the complex of the ego. At midlife, to allow a newly introverted relationship to the Self, the person must experience a new deintegration of that complex. This often creates feelings of a chaotic diffusion of ego boundaries.

The renewal of the ego-Self axis occurs at a more nearly conscious level at midlife, as contrasted with the unity of the baby-nature relationship. Neumann saw the baby as merged with the mother, representing the unconscious archetypal Great Mother. During Fordham's DI-RI cycles the increasingly conscious individual separates from the archetype and by midlife is ready to forge a new, more conscious bond with nature and the unconscious. Persons who are naturally introverted must take an effectively "extraverted" view of their previous inclinations, while the natural extravert will be required to turn attention inward, perhaps for the first time.

The tasks of women in later life have been addressed by analyst Jane Wheelwright (1984, p. 7), who maintains that "it is important for us as modern women to develop, to make conscious, and finally to integrate the animus." She feels that for women such a process is the only source of real autonomy.

Development in Later Years

The main point Jung made about aging is that development is a lifelong process, not a prerogative of youth. In the years of active older age from about 55 on, people can find Jungian therapy extremely valuable.

Many older people continue the inward-turning process initiated at midlife, gradually developing a personal philosophy that establishes a satisfying meaning for their life story. Simply retelling life events to family or others may reveal and develop unsuspected patterns that emerged too gradually to be noticed amid the rush of other concerns.

As we retire, move to a smaller home, lose some of our physical abilities, and experience all the other shifts that result from the aging process, therapy may help us sort out life events and carry out the necessary changes with purpose and zest. Betty Friedan (1993, p. 328) says:

> After, finally, coming to terms with the parameters of my own age, I became more and more convinced that it *was* possible—though it will not necessarily happen unless we make it happen—to "go beyond" one's previous limitations and pitfalls, the self-defeating, paralyzing traps and plateaus, in both work and love, responding to and using serendipity as it might emerge, or even painful tragedy, in the most surprising ways . . . to that new place that can expand, rather than restrict, the parameters of our age.

The Last Stage: Death and Dying

Much good work can be done with dying patients, to enable them to let go of mundane concerns, work through unfinished problems, and achieve a sense of completion. As an example, Wheelwright (1981) has written about the death of a 37-year-old woman who, with the help of therapy, successfully faced the task of dying before her time.

The task here for therapists and families is to stay in emotional contact with the dying, instead of isolating them in hospitals behind barricades of white coats, tubes, and machines. A person who is able to attend a loved person through a dignified death is fortunate indeed. People often say that such an experience changed their life for the better.

Gender in Jungian Theories of Development

Jungian developmental theory is being modified under the influence of the feminist and gay rights movements; new thinking (involving issues related to both gender and age) has also had an impact on the concept of a life trajectory. We touch on each of these three areas of controversy in turn.

Why Do Women Criticize Traditional Developmental Theories?

Like Freud, Jung defined elements of his theory in a male-centered way. Modern Jungians, especially women, are reexamining these concepts in an attempt to create a gender-neutral set of definitions. These efforts are, in my opinion, doomed to partial failure because the essential nature of archetypes such as the Anima/Animus includes intrinsic gender implications. Even so, it should be possible to make conscious, if not to eliminate, many conceptual biases originating in our culture.

The unquestioned assumptions of psychology have, understandably, corresponded to those of the rest of Western culture. Freud, who built his developmental theory around the experiences of the male child, valued logic over feeling, and saw a woman's personality as the result of a developmental failure. "Women show less sense of justice than men, . . . they are less ready to submit to the great exigencies of life, . . . they are more often influenced in their judgements by feelings of affection or hostility," he insisted (Freud, 1925, pp. 257–258).

Jung was in many ways ahead of his time, as when he postulated the existence of opposite-sex characteristics (Anima/Animus) in every person.

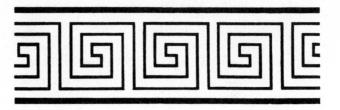

FIGURE 6.1
Greek Key Design, Illustrating a Repetitive Path
from Periphery to Center and Back Again

However, his views were definitely conditioned by his culture. Jung's views are being revised by women theorists, both Jungian and non-Jungian.

Although gender roles are to a great degree culturally established, and can be expected to vary from one society to the next, in the last few hundred years the majority of cultures holding world power and resources have been androcentric (male-oriented). In these cultures, people have generally worshipped a male supreme deity. Consequently many women perceive that laws, customs, and even psychological precepts are one-sidedly developed from a masculine viewpoint.

In Jungian theory, the masculine principle is seen as encouraging the use of exclusive categories; it employs logical thought to split issues into yes/no or good/bad. In her book *Psychotherapy Grounded in the Feminine Principle* (1989), Barbara Stevens Sullivan uses what she describes as a more feminine, inclusive approach. This approach deemphasizes the systematic diagnosis and even the pathology of mental disorder, maintaining that we exist on all levels of our psyche and need to preserve access to even the deepest of them for optimal mental health.

Access to early developmental levels often requires a sequence of progression and regression between more and less conscious psychic elements. Henderson (1990c, p. 50), an early advocate of this view, has provided a diagram of the repetitive involution/evolution process in the form of a Greek key design, shown in Figure 6.1. If we imagine our attention as following the thin black line, we see a diagram of how an individual may gradually change from an extraverted to an introverted attitude and back again. We can shift our attention as needed between exterior and interior events—but it takes time.

As we oscillate between progression and regression, our position on the associated spectrum of sanity/insanity appears to depend on our ego strength and on the strength of the Ego-Self axis. These create stability in regressed states and contain turbulent energies strong enough to prevent diffusion of our sense of identity. To work effectively, this strong ego must be flexible, not rigid, and it must be tolerant of ambiguity.

Henderson's idea shows the limits of Sullivan's argument: If the ego is not strong enough to preserve a sense of identity in regression, the person will no longer be in a normal but in a pathological state.

THE FEMINIST THEORY OF DEVELOPMENT IN RELATIONSHIP. Before we turn to feminist theory, we should note by way of background that Erikson (1963) gave us one of the best-known explanations of the course of human development. He outlined eight major stages:

1. Basic trust versus mistrust
2. Autonomy versus shame and doubt
3. Initiative versus guilt
4. Industry versus inferiority
5. Identity versus role confusion
6. Intimacy versus isolation
7. Generativity versus stagnation
8. Ego integrity versus despair

Erikson's last two stages are roughly where Jungian theories of midlife development begin. Other theorists such as Jean Piaget (1954) speak of "ages" as well as "stages" of development. Most stage theorists assume that the steps are coordinated with age, though some writers are more rigid than others in their descriptions of the timing and sequence of stages. The point here is that these stages describe *individual* development, and (except in Erikson's stage 6) deal very little with the person in relationship to others. Students interested in further exploring the relationships between Jungian theory and Erikson's stages or Freud's psychosexual stages of development are encouraged to consult the references. Other well-known, nonanalytically oriented developmental theories can also be found in the psychological literature.

Recent developments in feminist developmental theory concentrate on the person in relationship but say less than they might about Jungian theory.

Women writers go along with Erikson and Piaget's age-stage concepts, but argue that models of self-development advanced by those male psychologists do not reflect the female experience (Chodorow, 1978; Gilligan, 1982; Mercer, Nichols, & Doyle, 1989). For example, Jean Miller (1976, p. 12) criticizes Erikson as follows:

> In Erikson's scheme, after the first stage, in which the aim is development of basic trust, the aim of every other stage, until young adulthood, is some form of increased separation or self-development. . . . When the individual arrives at the stage called "intimacy," he is supposed to be able to be intimate with another person—having spent all of his prior development striving for something very different.

This exaggerates Erikson's position; relationship has some place in his early stages. As Miller points out, however, it is not emphasized.

Many feminist writers believe that women's development, more than men's, occurs in a context of relating to others, but Jungian analyst Anthony Storr believes that relationship is important to both genders. As early as 1960 he said that

> one cannot even begin to be conscious of oneself as a separate individual without another person with whom to compare oneself. A man in isolation is a collective man, a man without individuality. People often express the idea that they are most themselves when they are alone; and creative artists especially may believe that it is in the ivory tower of the solitary expression of their art that their innermost being finds its completion. They forget that art is communication, and that, implicitly or explicitly, the work which they produce in solitude is aimed at somebody. (p. 24)

By relating to someone or something else, you get a different slant on your experience. Comparison, by recognizing different views, creates the possibility of change.

In his later book on solitude, Storr (1988) departed somewhat from this position. He allowed for the possibility that introverts have a different set of priorities: "the great introverted creators are able to define identity and achieve *self-realization* by *self-reference*; that is, by interacting with their own past work rather than by interacting with other people" (p. 147; Storr's italics).

The notion of development through relationship has grown over the years. Jane Loevinger (1976) said that in the autonomous stage of moral development, recognition of one's own emotional interdependence with others develops alongside a growing sense of individuality. Loevinger's view was echoed by Carol Gilligan (1982, p. 22) who wrote of a "more contextual mode of judgment and a [consequently] different moral understanding." This is the kind of feminine moral understanding deplored by Freud, as you saw in the earlier quotations from him.

The feminist approach to development suggests that previous investigations have been one-sidedly concentrated on the male experience, and that women's experiences have been largely ignored or denigrated. It proposes that cooperation, cyclic growth, life stories, and the individual experience are just as valuable to human development as competition, achievement, and statistical averages.

Many of these points have been recognized by Jungian theorists. For instance, Schwartz-Salant (1982) speaks of the unifying goal of the Eleusinian mysteries, in which the women of ancient Greece took part. These ceremonies celebrated a return to wholeness through a nonheroic form of initiation, sacrificing the heroic, solar "greater light" and reuniting two aspects of the Great Goddess (pp. 133, 149). Polly Young-Eisendrath and Florence Wiedeman (1987) have written about a feminist approach to Jungian therapy.

Readers interested in the details of theories developed at women's studies centers such as the Stone Center and at Harvard are referred to the works by Belenky, Clinchy, Goldberger, and Tarule (1986), Chodorow (1978), Gilligan (1982), Mercer et al. (1989), and Miller (1976) listed in the reference section.

Same-Sex Love and Development

Gay, lesbian, and bisexual development is complexly different from heterosexual development, in part because the interactions of *Anima/Animus* attraction to parents and others does not fall into the better-known heterosexual gender patterns. Its nuances are just being explored now and are beyond the scope of this introductory Jungian text.

Jung himself had little to say on the subject (Hopcke, 1988), but Jungian writers such as Hopcke (Hopcke, 1992; Hopcke, Carrington, & Wirth, 1993) have recently begun to fill this gap. The Ghost Ranch conference reported in Schwartz-Salant and Stein (1992), and a conference held in Chicago titled "Who Do We Think We Are? The Mystery and Muddle of Gender" (1993) have addressed issues of gender and homosexuality. Tapes of the latter conference are available for purchase (see the reference section under the title of the conference).

Generally speaking, these contemporary theorists develop the implications that result from dropping the simple equation of sex with gender and emphasize the fact that, since members of both sexes contain aspects of both the masculine and feminine principles, personal relationships transcend cultural gender-role stereotypes.

Sandner's (1993, p. 229) sensitive discussion of Animus/Anima development among gays and lesbians provides a last word on the subject:

> It matters little whether the other person is man or woman, for the face of the soul is androgynous and can be loved in marriage or in any sexual union experienced as a sacred event, and in same-sex relationship as of bonding and initiation. Through this love the most difficult spiritual realization can be made—the need to sacrifice the ego to something beyond itself, which alone allows the blossoming of the soul.

New Perspectives on the Life Trajectory

The classic view of the life trajectory sees life as "up like a rocket, down like the stick"—at least as far as life in the world goes. We have been told

FIGURE 6.2
Tombstone Rubbing: A New Cycle Begins

that the second half of life is primarily a time to prepare for death through
a growing awareness of the transpersonal (Jung, 1961, p. 320; Satinover &
Bentz, 1992, p. 56).

We do indeed proceed from birth through life to death; who could argue
about that? Nevertheless, the trajectory, as visualized in Figure 5.1, could be
considered more of a recursive or repeated pattern of ascent than a linear fall.

Women have been more aware than men of the complexity of the life
cycle. Friedan (1993) cautions us not to assume that decline is inevitable. She
says that

> The process of *individuation*, becoming more oneself . . . which I found so
> striking in my own interviews of women and men at sixty-five, seventy, and
> eighty, shapes our third age uniquely, *unless we succumb in stagnation or
> denial to the self-fulfilling prophecy of age as decline and despair.* (p. 115;
> Friedan's italics)

After each developmental achievement, we confront the next, right up to
death, and optimists see even death as the start of a new cycle, as the tombstone rubbing in Figure 6.2 hints.

Many feminist writers, both Jungian and non-Jungian, emphasize our experiences of constant rebirth, multiple initiations, and continual deepening
of psychological awareness. The transitional stages of later life echo the process described by Fordham's DI-RI sequence in infants. As we move from one
age or stage to the next, we must break up old identifications, pass through
a time of chaos and depression, and, if all goes well, finish by composing
a new version of our identify.

Among male Jungian writers, Hillman (1979, p. 10) states most clearly that life cannot simply be divided into first and second halves. It seems likely that if we can consciously experience multiple, overlapping, sequential transitions, we may not need to undergo a traditional, major midlife crisis in order to rebalance a one-sided adaptation to the world.

We have reviewed Jungian approaches to the development of personality. Next we will see how Jungian therapists conceptualize psychotherapy.

READINGS

Fordham, M. (1957). *New developments in analytical psychology.* London: Routledge & Kegan Paul.

Friedan, B. (1993). *The fountain of age.* New York: Simon & Schuster.

Henderson, J. L. (1990). *Shadow and self: Selected papers in analytical psychology.* Wilmette, IL: Chiron.

Hopcke, R. H., Carrington, K. L., & Wirth, S. (Eds). (1993). *Same-sex love and the path to wholeness.* Boston: Shambhala.

Neumann, E. (1973). *The child: Structure and dynamics of the nascent psyche.* New York: Pantheon Books.

Sullivan, B. S. (1989). *Psychotherapy grounded in the feminine principle.* Wilmette, IL: Chiron.

Wheelwright, J. H. (1981). *The death of a woman.* New York: St. Martin's Press.

CHAPTER 7

Alchemy

In this chapter we look at a difficult but rewarding topic: the role of alchemical symbolism in Jungian psychology. Three main parallels between alchemy and the therapeutic process will concern us. The first involves the symbolism of the *temenos* or alchemical container, which can serve as a metaphor for the therapeutic "frame." The second concerns resemblances between the stages of the alchemical and therapeutic processes. The third has to do with transference/countertransference (the feelings or energy field between therapist and client) and analogous ideas in alchemy.

We will start with a dictionary definition of alchemy, as done for previous terms, and amend it to fit Jungian usage. According to the *Chambers Concise 20th Century Dictionary*, alchemy is the "infant stage of chemistry, its chief pursuits the transmutation of other elements into gold, and the elixir of life: transmuting potency." Lynne Ehlers's (1992, p. 14) comprehensive review of the history of alchemy underscores the fact that "from the beginning, alchemy had a twofold nature: the practical laboratory work . . . and the more philosophical speculations or 'mystical' visions which accompanied the process." Alchemy appears always to have incorporated spiritual (psychological) properties. Also, aside from its history as the precursor of chemistry, alchemy provides a metaphor for what the psyche goes through in deep, long-term analysis.

Jung was fascinated by the relevance of alchemy to psychology. He studied alchemy from 1926 until the end of his life, concluding that what the alchemists "really discovered, and what was an endless source of fascination for them, was the symbolism of the individuation process" (CW 13, para. 393). "The entire alchemical procedure," he explained, "could just as well represent the individuation process of a single individual, though with the not unimportant difference that no single individual ever attains to the richness and scope of the alchemical symbolism" (CW 14, para. 792).

The alchemical process involved several steps and entailed complex symbolism. Writers such as Edinger (1985) and Hillman (1980, 1981, 1982, 1991) have explored the process in detail. In a 1977 lecture, Edinger offered a useful introduction:

> In spite of the confusion generated by the alchemical literature, the basic scheme of alchemy is quite simple: the alchemist or *adept* was committed to a sacred work, called the *opus* or *grand arcanum*. The goal of the work was to create a transcendent miraculous substance, a supreme or ultimate value, symbolized by the *Philosopher's Stone*, the *Elixir of Life*, or the *Universal Medicine*. The first step was to find a suitable material on which to work (the *prima materia*) and submit it to a series of *operations*. The vessel, *vas*, *curcurbit*, or *alembic*, in which the operations took place was to be kept well sealed, the equivalent of containment in the analytic process. The attitude to be taken toward the work was one of patience, courage, and perseverance. It was considered a sacred work, requiring a prayerful, religious attitude. . . . The work was highly individual and often lonely; the adept might have one helper [often female], but no more. It was a process started by Nature but completed by the conscious work of man. The knowledge gained was a result of direct experience, something each seeker had to discover for himself, and the result was equated with the creation of the world [the Self, in Jungian terminology]. (quoted in Ehlers, 1992, pp. 25–26)

Three main factors are relevant to our topic. First, the symbol of the *temenos*, the cooker or container in which the process occurs, implies a need for privacy, safety, and concentration in treatment. Second, the *process* described by the alchemy metaphor has a surprising number of parallels with the latest developments in physics. Third, the mutual effects of therapy on client and therapist, implicit in the alchemy metaphor, were first emphasized by Jung and are now gaining recognition among other schools of thought. These effects constitute the system of *transference/countertransference*.

The alchemical analogy is most likely to appeal to therapists who follow the *symbolic* approach to Jungian thought (Chapter 8), although the three factors above are present to some degree in all Jungian therapy. Obviously they are most salient in long-term, intensive work. Shorter-term therapy provides less opportunity for rising pressure within the therapeutic container to affect the participants.

FIGURE 7.1
Temenos or Alchemical Container

In the remainder of the chapter, we explore each of the three major areas of overlap between alchemy and Jungian psychology in greater detail.

The Frame or *Temenos*

The word *temenos* originally meant "square citadel" or "temple precinct." It was borrowed by the medieval alchemists to describe the alchemical container or early chemical beaker, which had a rounded, womblike shape (Figure 7.1). When the enclosed container was placed over a fire, the resulting heat and pressure enabled the adept to "cook up" new chemical substances.

In psychotherapy the "frame" or rules of therapy are the container. A safely limited setting provides the equivalents of heat and pressure: It keeps the client's examination of current distress on the fire and prevents an escape to other subjects. The goal of the process, rather than to create gold from dross, is to create a new way of experiencing the world.

Privacy, confidentiality, and responsibility are essential to maintenance of an effective therapeutic container. This is one reason many Jungians are reluctant to give in to requests from insurers for details of diagnosis or symptomology. Many are also reluctant to use drugs to alleviate symptoms; by reducing the pressure to change one's circumstances, drugs can sabotage the effects of the container. Even the processes of diagnosis and prescription, as practiced in the traditional "objective" medical model of therapy, to some degree compromise the boundaries of the frame.

Every therapeutic interview, Jungian or not, is conducted according to certain conventions or rules. Among Jungians, the choice and strictness of these parameters vary with theoretical preference and with environmental constraints. But the creation of the *temenos* is made possible by the extensive and thorough training required to become a competent Jungian therapist, especially an analyst. No person who has not experienced the meaning of the *temenos* can provide such a container for another.

Independent Practice and the Strict Frame

Jungian therapy is mostly, though not entirely, done as individual, private practice. In this modality, as contrasted to work in clinics, you set the rules yourself. Some therapists feel that a tight, reliable set of rules helps the client contain troublesome issues, while others like to preserve more flexibility.

PRIVACY. Practitioners differ on the amount of privacy they require for appointments. Advocates of a strict frame will not share even a waiting room or secretary with other therapists. They will arrange for patients to come in one door and go out another without returning to the waiting room, fostering the transferential illusion that each client enjoys the therapist's sole attention.

CONFIDENTIALITY. Such frame-conscious persons will not provide treatment reports to third-party insurers or other outside agencies. To protect clients' confidentiality, some keep minimal notes, or none at all, to guard against their being seized and exposed in legal proceedings. This ethical choice can conflict with legal regulations and is also a problem for therapists whose professional organizations require a defined standard of record keeping.

APPOINTMENTS AND FEES. Strict-frame practitioners are meticulous about never changing appointment times, and usually require that clients pay for every missed appointment, no matter how "good" the reason for missing it. In turn, these therapists try never to break appointments, drop a patient, surprise a client with sudden news of a vacation, or move to a different town. They feel obligated to observe the rules as faithfully as they ask their patients to do. These measures are all aimed at preserving the frame by keeping the therapist/client relationship totally reliable.

A strict frame minimizes extrinsic variables in therapy, enabling the client to concentrate on personal events and focus on the transference/countertransference.

Independent Practice and the Flexible Frame

Other practitioners in private settings advocate more flexibility. Given sufficient notice, they will not charge for canceled appointments, and they will themselves cancel an occasional appointment, or change the meeting time, if they have a schedule conflict. They may share a waiting room with other therapists, where patients sit together and see each other's arrivals and departures.

Flexible-frame therapists feel less constrained to observe the strictest rules of confidentiality and so may accept the paperwork of third-party insurers, testify in court cases, and so on. These specific decisions depend on the focus of practice (whether they take forensic cases, for example) and on the personal preference or theoretical background of the therapist.

A flexible frame admits discussion of transference issues arising from random occurrences; it's all grist for the mill.

CLINIC SETTINGS. Many therapists (but hardly any analysts) work in clinic settings where the frame is strictly open, rather than being flexible. A business office sets fees and cancellation policies, and client charts are kept in a master file, accessible to certain administrators, to clinic inspection or accreditation teams, and to the file clerks.

Clinic patients must usually wait together in one room for any of several therapists and have to set up their appointments with harried secretaries at a crowded desk. Encountering other clients in the waiting room, they may become jealous about who is seen more promptly or is allowed to run overtime. These issues, although bothersome to some clients, can be used for therapeutic discussion, as in the flexible frame of private practice described above.

The Alchemical Stages
and the Therapeutic Process

We now turn to some comparisons between alchemy and the therapeutic process.

Alchemical Stages

Within the medieval alchemist's container, base matter underwent a series of transformations. Each stage of the alchemical process was associated with a color: black, white, yellow, and red. The "red" was not ordinary red but the red of gold and represented the philosopher's stone—the goal of the work. Some writers name other, intermediary colors.

FIRST ALCHEMICAL STAGE: THE NIGREDO: LEAD-BLACK: EARTH. In alchemical literature, the start of the alchemical process is called the *nigredo*, or black stage. The black color is associated with chaos and is also called the *massa confusa*. This is a formless mass of soul, spirit, and body together, connoting dirt, earth, darkness, and weakness of spirit, often shown as an old man shut up in a cave or vessel.

The symbolic colors were derived from archetypes that, like all archetypes, have both positive and negative attributes. All colors are concealed in black, and at this stage their negative qualities are considered most influential.

In a substage of the *nigredo*, soul and spirit separate from the body and form the *unio mentalis*, or mental identity. This stage is experienced as a symbolic death; the body has lost its animating principle.

SECOND ALCHEMICAL STAGE: THE ALBEDO: SILVER-WHITE: WATER. In the second stage, following the symbolic death, soul and spirit recombine with the body. This stage is associated with the color white and with symbols such as mercury (quicksilver), the moon, cooking, ashes, and salt. At the beginning this is still a deathlike state, as if the soul were waiting, imprisoned in the body. Neumann (1954a) associates this stage with *matriarchal consciousness*, a state of pregnant, receptive, creative waiting. It is a timeless point, free of habitual effort and striving and associated with the feminine principle.

THIRD ALCHEMICAL STAGE: THE CITRINITAS: SULPHUR-YELLOW: AIR. In the third stage, transitional between white and golden-red, soul and spirit join the *unus mundus*, or oneness of the universe. The yellow color represents change (Ehlers, 1992, p. 95). Its animal is the eagle, who enters the air, soars above the earth, and provides a new perspective. Hillman (1991, pp. 84–85, 94) says that in this stage the yellow taints the white (relating spirit to the earth) and represents a more "jaundiced," critical view of the world.

The yellow stage of the alchemical process is sometimes equated with the red and is omitted from some descriptions of alchemy. This is congruent with its ambiguous nature, representing a stage somewhere between feminine and masculine, night and day, expectation and achievement, and so on.

FOURTH ALCHEMICAL STAGE: THE RUBEDO: GOLDEN-RED: FIRE. This stage is associated with the sun—Western culture's active masculine principle—and with the metal gold, into which the earlier base metals have been transformed. Another, compound image calls the metal of this stage "red sulphur," as

FIGURE 7.2
The Alchemical Process

compared to the yellow sulphur of the third stage and the white or feminine sulphur of the second. (In a typical Jungian-style enantiodromia, sulphur changes from being part of the corrosive *prima materia* of the first stage to a constituent of the final *philosopher's stone* of the fourth.)

SACRED MARRIAGE OF RED AND WHITE: THE CONIUNCTIO. Red and white together form a pair of opposites, which become united in a symbolic "sacred marriage" during the alchemical process. Since all colors and elements are present in the blackness of the first stage, the colors or metals must first be separated and refined before being reunited in the final end stage of the *rubedo*. This marriage is called a *coniunctio*. Jung (CW 14, para. 1) used this concept to describe the transformation of the archetypal opposites into a transcendent whole.

Before they have been separated, the masculine and feminine principles are pictured as a two-headed hermaphrodite. A "premature" uniting of opposites (a union occurring before the elements have been adequately refined) may also be seen as a hermaphroditic union, too merged and unconscious to be effective.

Alchemy and Therapy

The alchemical process cannot always be fully developed in our current therapeutic milieu, although in every therapeutic modality a Jungian therapist will provide a shelter within which the innate healing tendencies of the psyche may emerge.

Directed, short-term, problem-solving therapy is essential for many situations, but in a crowded clinic it takes a cool head, faith, skill, and patience to create a bit of secure space for a client before jumping in with suggestions and interpretations.

In the long quotation given earlier, Edinger said that the healing process is started by nature and completed by human beings. The *temenos* provides a place for the natural processes to occur. In a safe environment, and given sufficient time, order will often spontaneously appear out of chaos. In Jungian psychotherapy, the *temenos* comprises the consulting room, the rules of conduct, and the ability of the therapist to contain difficult material in an attitude of calm acceptance. The alchemical analogy is also used to describe the sequence of events.

FIRST AND SECOND STAGES. The stages of the alchemical process can be interpreted to correspond with stages of long-term therapy. The client arrives in a state of dark, leaden chaos (the first alchemical stage) and proceeds to the second, silvery stage, protected by the therapeutic container from daily cares. Healing images may emerge in this tranquillity, as attention turns inward, creating a state of lunar consciousness. Attaining the second stage is a considerable achievement in itself. This stage is not reached by everyone, but it is not the goal of therapy.

THIRD STAGE. The third stage, associated with the color yellow, begins as the "light" of the sun, or consciousness, tries to break through the white, lunar fog (Ehlers, 1992, p. 91). Hillman (1991) says that the yellowing is like milk turning into cheese and involves a process of useful corruption. In therapy, at this point the client may become conscious of negative aspects of transference; this stage signals that the first, nebulous part of therapy is over. Insightful, clarifying work is needed to attain the next stage.

FOURTH STAGE. This stage corresponds to the symbolic fire and to the sun. In therapy, it is the stage of illumination—of active understanding or insight (Ehlers, 1992, p. 101). At this stage, attention returns to outer life, as old problems are re-viewed in new, transcendent ways.

Alchemy and the Chaotic Process

Jung's intuitive use of the alchemical analogy anticipated a number of current developments in science. In *Psychology and Alchemy*, he wrote:

The way to the goal seems chaotic and interminable at first and only gradually do the signs increase that it is leading anywhere. The way is not straight but appears to go around in circles. More accurate knowledge has proved it to go in spirals. . . . The whole process revolves about a central point or some arrangement round a centre. . . . Dreams . . . circumambulate around the centre . . . drawing closer to it as the amplifications increase in distinctness and scope. (CW 12, para. 34)

Jung's observations parallel the description given in Chapter 10 of the spontaneous generation of order out of chaos in such phenomena as the human heartbeat. For Jung, the center, analogous to the mathematicians' "attractor," is the Self. The "field" of the Self is considered to influence the personality, much as an attractor influences other natural events. Joining the new language of science to the old language of alchemy, we can say that events are drawn toward the "attractor"—formerly called the philosopher's stone.

Transference/Countertransference

Within the therapeutic container, indeed in any close relationship, *transference* processes develop. The psychic mechanism mediating the transference is called *projection*. When transference emerges in a therapist, it is called *counter-transference*.

Projection

Projection is a defense against anxiety, in which one person attributes to another (*projects*) emotions or qualities that are difficult to own, or that belong to a third person, and that are not necessarily characteristic of the person to whom they are attributed. Often the projected qualities properly belong to a parent of the person doing the projecting, since it is in early life that we create our internal pictures of how other people are likely to behave.

Projection is most familiar as a major feature of "falling in love." We see our beloved as possessing all the properties we lack; together we can conquer the world. This enchantment is usually followed by a troublesome period of disillusionment when the beloved comes to be seen as his or her natural, ordinary self. Besides projecting our Anima or Animus, as when falling in love, we may also project our Shadow or any other archetypal trait. Examples include the archetypal father/son projections of the Freud/Jung letters.

There must be some correspondence, whether obvious, subtle, or even unconscious, between the nature of a projection and the nature of its human target in order for the person targeted to "hook" that projection. For instance, you are more likely to perceive a small, soft-spoken woman therapist as your domineering father if she is having personal difficulties with your hypersensitivity to being bossed around. If your strong need for autonomy mobilizes some complex of hers, she will feel disturbed, and you may detect that response even in the absence of an overt reaction.

Many, if not most, analysts consider it a central analytical task to encourage the emergence of projections, which are then "worked through" (discussed, amplified, dissected, and unraveled from early associations). This process goes on whether the therapy focuses primarily on the *relationship process* in the treatment or on the *symbolic material* that emerges. If all goes well, as projections are gradually contextualized, they are withdrawn, the transference disappears, and the client reclaims the previously projected qualities as aspects of his or her own psychic history.

Transference

A relationship involving projection is called a *transference* relationship when it happens in a therapeutic context. The transference relationship is a powerful, experiential connection. It largely involves the feeling function but includes intuition and thought and in some circumstances—such as body therapy, dance therapy, art therapy, and so on—may include sensation (Sandner, 1994). We normally develop transference relationships with many people, but they are not usually recognized or labeled as such. In these ordinary social interactions, any person can project traits onto any other, and the resulting transference relationships can develop further over time.

The transference relationship, originating in the psychic mechanism of projection, takes a year or more to develop fully and is reflected in dream material. In classical analysis, following Freud's lead, the patient was considered to be doing the projecting, while the therapist maintained "professional objectivity." We now know that a mutual process of projection occurs between each therapist/patient pair.

Sandner (1994) describes transference/countertransference as the same force that holds the human family together and says it is evoked by sitting face to face. The transference molds itself to what's there. It is always framed in terms of family relationships, but since a therapist is *not* the patient's father, daughter, sibling, and so on, the participants may also incur feelings of erotic (not parental or sibling) love.

Transference can be *positive* or *negative*. A client may feel great love or great hate for the therapist, neither of which may be founded on anything the therapist has done, said, or even thought. There are nevertheless some *valid aspects* of transference, and also of any projective reactions between people in ordinary life. We react to nonverbal, subliminal, or unconscious stimuli by building on our memories of similar situations, accurately or not. This reaction to the other is variously called *empathy, intuition,* or "reading between the lines."

There are always *two active forces* in transference—attraction and repulsion. Practically speaking, their balance determines the physical distance at which one person sits or stands relative to another. In addition, each culture has strong rules regulating this distance, which must be respected (Sandner, 1994).

FREUD'S VIEWS. Freud, reviewing one of Josef Breuer's analytical cases, discovered what he called the *transference neurosis.* In 1880, "Anna O.," one of Breuer's patients, had become excessively enamored of Breuer, who eventually dropped her treatment as being too much for him to deal with (Fordham, 1978; Tansey, 1994).

In those early days, all projection was attributed to the patient. Freud used the word *transference* specifically to describe the result of the projective process by which every patient transfers to the therapist feelings about significant people in the patient's life. Thus when Anna O. "fell in love with" Breuer, she was said to transfer to Breuer feelings about her own father.

Freud was not able to see Breuer's subsequent reaction to Anna O. as *countertransference,* and only later coined that term in a letter to Jung about the latter's erotic attraction to his patient Sabina Spielrein (Tansey, 1994, p. 143). Freud's letter made it clear that he had experienced similar feelings, although he denied ever translating them into action.

JUNG'S VIEWS AND EARLY PITFALLS OF TRANSFERENCE/COUNTERTRANSFERENCE. Jung and his first students gave most of their attention to symbolism in therapy and understood little about transference. Sandner (1994) reports that as late as 1959, although by then Jung himself was too ill to teach, analysts like von Franz were still passing on Jung's thought in pure form, and it was almost all about symbolism. Attention to the issue of transference was missing.

In analytical therapy, if you don't know about transference you won't attend to relevant patient/therapist boundaries. For the early analysts, the dream provided the boundary. The patient talked at will about his or her dreams in a "living-room" setting, often in the analyst's home. *Within* the dream the transference was acknowledged, so in that sense it was there, but its presence in the consulting room was not recognized.

Often the analyst and patient knew each other socially, presented papers at the same professional meetings, and too often conducted romantic affairs.

The first two circumstances still freely occur; at an analytical meeting there are not only hundreds of analysts present but also hundreds of patients, and the categories overlap markedly.

CURRENT PITFALLS OF TRANSFERENCE/COUNTERTRANSFERENCE. Although nowadays everyone is aware of the dangers of unrestrained interaction between patient and therapist, there is "appalling, documented evidence of sexual abuse of female patients by roughly 7–10% of male therapists of every stripe and level of experience" (Tansey, 1994, p. 140).

Besides being immoral, illegal, and destructive to therapy, any sexual contact between therapist and client is grounds for expulsion from most professional organizations. Nevertheless,

> Virtually every institute and society [of psychotherapy] harbors "family secrets" involving analysts who have married former patients and others who have referred patients on to other colleagues after engaging in sexual relationships and ending the treatment. The closets of our institutional houses are full of skeletons. (Gabbard, 1994, p. 203)

Only recently, as in the articles cited above, has this issue been substantially addressed in professional journals.

It is no wonder that early analysts were confused and often personally entangled by transference/countertransference phenomena. Jung was only one among many in the same predicament. Ignorance of these issues contributed to Jung's problems with Freud, and then to his entanglement with Sabina Spielrein and at least two other women patients, as detailed by Carotenuto (1982) and Kerr (1993). Jung's problematic relationships with these three women are discussed in Chapter 11.

PREVENTIVE MEASURES. Few therapists can comfortably discuss their sexual attraction to a patient with their peers (although doing so can prove extremely helpful with the right consultant), and seldom should a therapist venture to discuss any kind of countertransference issues with a client. How can we employ these troublesome impulses therapeutically?

Gabbard (1994) suggests that useful symbolic "enactments" of countertransference issues often occur. He says that these moderately sanitized analogies of forbidden impulses "must be drawn out and shepherded into a transitional area where they can be subjected to the 'play' of containment and interpretation" (p. 206).

When incestuous impulses are expressed only symbolically, the cultural taboo against incest may seem diluted, but the therapist must still be careful to keep the process verbal and confined to the office. The transference must be placed under control.

LEVELS OF TRANSFERENCE. Just as unconscious processes occur on more than one level, so do transference phenomena. The latter are anchored in the former—although Sandner (1994) is the only person I know to discuss *cultural* transference/countertransference. Jung described these phenomena as being either *personal* or *archetypal*, while Freud confined them to the *sexual*.

Traditional Freudian analysts thought that transference only reflected affects from the client's early years and used it to reveal the origins of the client's neurotic problems. Jung built on this part of the transference to describe what he called *personal transference*. He expanded it to include other elements and connected it to a deeper kind of transference he called the *archetypal transference*.

Jung included in the personal transference not only affects concerning past relationships, but also those concerning undeveloped (potential) or denied (Shadow) aspects of the client's own personality. For example, a woman who sees her therapist as a hated authority figure may have failed to develop her own capacity for assertion. The reasons for this lack of development may or may not be related to childhood experiences.

Jung's major innovation in this area was his expansion of the concept of transference to include the archetypal. This kind of transference has two parts. The first includes the transference of projections based on *unconscious fantasy*, not on the patient's ordinary history. Thus, without being in the least psychotic, you may become convinced that your therapist is a divinely appointed guide to the meaning of your life, in a way quite beyond rational explanation. The second meaning derives from the web of relationships in the analytical encounter. Complex *unconscious communication* occurs between patient and therapist, who both make archetypal projections. That is, you may connect to the Good Parent archetype through your therapist's deep concern for your welfare. Similarly, as a therapist, you may sense a childlike trust in your client that is anchored in the Puer/Puella archetype.

CULTURAL VARIATIONS IN TRANSFERENCE PHENOMENA. *Shamans* in northern Russia portray the most vivid transference (Sandner, 1994). In shamanic healing rites, the patient is very passive, while the shaman powerfully enacts the symbols, the ceremony, and the transference. The symbols enacted come from the culture, not from the individual patient.

The *Navaho* have the largest, most complete healing system of all Native American cultures (Sandner, 1994). Here the element of transference is interpersonal but not psychological. The Navaho *use* symbols; they don't enact them like the shamans, but in both cases the transference always goes and comes through one person—the leader of the ceremony.

In each of these cultures, the experience is carefully structured and contained in its own kind of alchemical *temenos*. The strength of the container allows safe expression of powerful emotions.

In *Jungian analysis* patients bring out their own experience of transference in their dreams and visions: They provide the symbols used in healing. Such healing symbols usually only surface during a series of hundreds of dreams. Extended attention paid to dreams activates the underlying matrix from which arise the "Big Dreams" or "Archetypal Dreams" that express symbolism. Sandner (1994) says that if he loses track of what's happening in an analysis, he will read over the last six months of the patient's dreams, because they always tell what's going on.

Countertransference

Projections from the therapist onto the patient were originally named *countertransference* because they were considered reactions to stimuli from the patient, but this turns out to be only part of the story.

A TWO-WAY RELATIONSHIP. Therapists still call the therapist's projections *countertransference*, but they define it in differing ways. Freud first saw it as the analyst's unconscious reaction to the patient's transference. Later he wrote that the analyst must "turn his own unconscious like a receptive organ towards the transmitting unconscious of the patient . . . so that the doctor's unconscious is able to reconstruct the patient's unconscious" (Freud, 1958, pp. 115–116). Here Freud recognized an accurate and helpful aspect of countertransference, based on the therapist's attunement to the patient. In traditional Freudian analysis, however, countertransference continued to be attributed to unresolved conflicts within the therapist, including overidentification with the patient, and was a fault to be eliminated through personal analysis or consultation.

Jung (CW 16, para. 422) disagreed with this view and developed the accompanying diagram to depict the pattern of cotransference between patient and analyst. This complicated diagram maps all possible interactions among the conscious and unconscious processes of a therapist and patient, showing that Jung believed the members of the analytical dyad to affect each other in all the ways indicated.

Jung explicitly saw the therapeutic relationship as complex and reciprocal, making his definition of countertransference broader than Freud's. (Arrow 6 in the diagram indicates the communications between unconscious aspects

JUNG'S RELATIONSHIP DIAGRAM

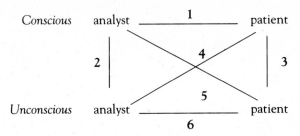

Source: Adapted from A *Critical Dictionary of Jungian Analysis,* by A. Samuels, B. Shorter, & F. Plaut, 1986, p. 20. Routledge, Chapman & Hall Publishers. Adapted by permission.

of both therapist and patient that underlie some countertransference phenomena.) Jung believed that both participants *must* be affected for therapeutic change to occur:

> You can exert no influence if you are not susceptible to influence. It is futile for the doctor to shield himself from the influence of the patient and to surround himself with a smoke screen of fatherly and professional authority. By doing so he only denies himself the use of a highly important organ of information. (CW 16, para. 163)

This is an alarming aspect of therapeutic work; if you hope to help the client change, you must be willing to let the client change you.

EMOTION IN COUNTERTRANSFERENCE. Jung, like Freud, urged the therapist to attune his or her own unconscious to the unconscious of the patient. Jung took Freud's idea one vital step further by advocating the use not only of one's "objective" perceptions, but also of one's personal, emotional reactions. Consistent with this approach, Machtiger (1982, p. 89) has said that countertransference utilizes "the analyst's capacity for empathy, antipathy, sympathy, and other affects."

CONSTRUCTIVE COUNTERTRANSFERENCE: REFLECTIVE AND EMBODIED. When therapists are conscious of countertransference phenomena, they can use them in constructive ways. More and more writers have become interested in the usefulness of bodily countertransference, by which therapists can consciously attend to their physical sensations during therapy with their patients (see Rutter, 1989).

Andrew Samuels (1985a) defines two main categories of constructive countertransference response, calling them reflective *and* embodied. In *reflective countertransference,* the analyst accurately picks up a thought or intuition still unconscious in the client. A therapist might have sudden insight into the sources of a client's difficulty, based on his or her own words, before the client comprehends the significance of what was said.

Samuels's emphasis on embodiment in *embodied transference* is innovative. He includes under this heading bodily and behavioral, feeling, and phantasy responses. Rutter (1989, p. 69) summarizes Samuels's views as follows:

> "Bodily and behavioral" responses range from the analyst forgetting to mention something important (i.e., vacation plans) to wearing clothes similar to the patient's clothes to actual somatic reactions, such as chest pain, feeling drowsy, or experiencing "a strange sensation in the solar plexus."

As these comments suggest, it is useful to pay attention to bodily reactions during a therapy session. Various aches, restlessness, boredom, and genital agitations are expressions of countertransference phenomena and are often clues from the therapist's psyche to subtle information about the psyche of the client.

"Feeling responses," according to Rutter, "include such reactions as anger, annoyance, envy, boredom, depression, feeling flooded, and so on" (p. 57). He explains that

> "phantasy responses include imagery and thoughts ("countertransference thoughts"); for example, the analyst may have the sudden thought, "If I leave the room the patient will look at my appointment book," or "The patient is considering another therapist." An example of an image is "The patient is receding into the chair and wall and is disappearing." (p. 57)

THE MUNDUS IMAGINALIS (SHARED IMAGINARY WORLD). Embodied sensations, felt by a therapist in response to projections of a patient and mediated by empathy, are discussed by a number of Jungian authors, notably Samuels, as we saw above, and Schwartz-Salant (1989). These sensations often relate to the concept of the *mundus imaginalis* or *subtle body*, which are too arcane to be discussed in this introductory text.

SANDNER'S CLASSIFICATION OF COUNTERTRANSFERENCE. Sandner (1994) divides countertransference into four elements. The first is *countertransference proper*, where feelings arise in the therapist because of feelings in the client. This represents your reaction to the client's actions, or the effects on you of his or her complex.

The second element, *psychological transference* to the client, is conditioned by the therapist's own early childhood experience. This arises from the therapist's personal complex; you react to this client as if she or he were your mother, father, or another member of your childhood family.

The third is the therapist's Shadowy *love for power, sex, money, and so on*; this element is more fixed and less malleable than a complex. This may include *identification* with a positive or negative projection from the client. Such Shadow influences inflate a therapist's personality and explain why Sandner thinks each full-time practitioner should have one or two regular hours of supervision a month for his or her entire professional life. He says that standing consultation appointments and a routine with a familiar person make it easier to bring out your Shadow transference, as compared to making a special appointment to discuss each incipient problem. Such routine preventive consultation might stave off therapeutic catastrophes.

Finally, a *genuine liking for or dislike of* the client contributes to countertransference issues. As Sandner puts it, "liking a client helps you to be more willing to go through *all that* with *them*." He recommends referring out clients to whom you have a real aversion; no therapist can handle all possible tasks, and a negative process may be disastrous for both therapist and client.

PITFALLS OF COUNTERTRANSFERENCE. While appreciating the positive aspects of countertransference, a therapist still needs to look out for neurotic reactions originating in his or her personal complexes. By later life, Jung had learned something about this problem. He came to consider countertransference to be an inevitable component of psychotherapy, writing in 1937 that it

> is one of the chief occupational hazards of psychotherapy. It causes psychic infections in both analyst and patient and brings the therapeutic process to a standstill. This state of unconscious identity is also the reason why an analyst can help his patient just so far as he himself has gone and not a step further. (CW 16, para. 545)

Jung had good reasons for saying this, as we have seen.

Other, more specific pitfalls should be mentioned. *Projective identification* is a neurotic aspect of countertransference in which two distinctly unhelpful processes occur, one in the client and one in the therapist. First, the client projects an internal object on you, as the therapist, and treats you as if you were the projected object. In turn, you develop a corresponding countertransference, and feel like, may think or act like, and in short, identify with the object projected on you, whether or not it fits your actual personality.

For instance, if you are a juicy, easy-going woman of 60 whose client experiences all women over 50 as dried-up, unattractive nags, after a few months of sessions you may find yourself grieving over the loss of your looks and often reminding the patient that the time is up. You realize that you are identifying with the client's projections only when you notice that you never feel or do these things around anyone else.

On the other hand, projections from clients will sometimes represent your unrecognized shadow (or some other archetypal) aspect. In these cases, also shown by some client dreams, clients have "hooked on" to one of your own unconscious complexes. This is a signal to address the issue in personal therapy or consultation.

An additional pitfall of countertransference concerns empathy. Although realistic empathy can be useful, empathy is dangerous when it is markedly countertransferential: Both you and the client may be so focused on your mutual acceptance of a positive projection that the client's problems in which it originated are neglected, or may even remain unconscious for both of you.

This chapter began by explaining the analogous features of alchemy and Jungian therapy. It continued with descriptions of various ways a protective container, like the alchemist's *temenos*, is constructed to hold the strong emotions aroused in therapy. The mutual immersion of therapist and client in the process was illustrated by the transference/countertransference discussion.

READINGS

Edinger, E. (1985). *Anatomy of the psyche.* La Salle, IL: Open Court.

Schwartz-Salant, N. (1989). *The borderline personality: Vision and healing.* Wilmette, IL: Chiron.

CHAPTER 8

Varieties of Jungian Therapy

Since the dynamics of the psyche underlie everyone's behavior, understanding them is always useful. Jungian therapists may approach the *treatment* of psychic problems differently, according to their own training, work setting, and personality, but some generalities apply to all Jungian modalities. We discuss these general points first, then turn to variations.

Clinical Assumptions of Jungian Therapy

Jungian psychology takes a relatively benign view of the less extreme symptoms of emotional disturbance. Jung wrote:

> The symptoms of a neurosis are not simply the effects of long-past causes, whether "infantile sexuality" or the infantile urge to power; they are also attempts at a new synthesis of life—unsuccessful attempts, let it be added in the same breath, yet attempts nevertheless, with a core of value and meaning. They are seeds that fail to sprout owing to the inclement conditions of inner and outer nature. (CW 7, para. 67)

This passage appeared in the essay that initiated Jung's split from Freud, who saw symptoms solely as evidence of pathology. Freud attempted to reduce all mental symptoms to their primary causes, ultimately rooted in sexual, Oedipal traumas. Jung did see a reductive approach as necessary and useful in treating young children or persons with severe mental disorders, though he did not conceptualize this approach in exclusively sexual terms. He felt that under some conditions growth was possible only through regression to the deepest, earliest levels of the unconscious psyche, from before the Oedipal period (see Jung, CW 5). With his usual adult patients, Jung took a more forward-looking stance.

The Goal of a Balanced Personality

The most comprehensive goal of Jungian psychotherapy is to work with the individual toward a relatively harmonious relationship among conscious and unconscious processes of the psyche. Other terms for this are *relativizing the ego* and *strengthening the ego-Self axis*. The person who achieves this is considered to be more *developed* and well launched on the process of *individuation*. These terms simply mean that if your life unfolds satisfactorily, your energy will become more evenly distributed among the functions of your personality, and you are likely to be operating consistently from the true spine of your character.

"Development" does not imply perfection, or achievement of a concrete goal, after which you may relax and bask in bliss. To the contrary, Hillman (1972, p. 78) says that true involvement in life means to experience yearning and suffering. Development occurs only as a result of involvement. It is an endless process, since new possibilities open up as previous ones are realized.

TELEOLOGY. Jung's assumption that behavior is directed toward a goal mediated by the Self is called *teleological*, after the philosophical doctrine of final causes in nature. To serve the nonspecific goal of facilitating individuation, therapy can be centered on intermediate or individual subgoals. Over the life span, these subordinate aims of therapy tend to shift. Jung emphasized the impossibility of setting any goals of therapy by rote:

> The great decisions in human life usually have far more to do with the instincts and other mysterious unconscious factors than with conscious will and well-meaning reasonableness. . . . There is no universal recipe for living. . . .
>
> What the doctor then does is less a question of treatment than of developing the creative possibilities latent in the patient himself. (CW 16, para. 81–82)

Many people come for Jungian therapy at midlife, seeking creative alternatives, even though they have had earlier competent, more focused treatment and have no pressing emergency to address. This was the case with Jung's patients:

> Thus my contribution to psychotherapy confines itself to those cases where rational treatment does not yield satisfactory results. . . . About a third of my cases are not suffering from any clinically definable neurosis, but from the senselessness and aimlessness of their lives. Fully two-thirds of my patients are in the second half of life. (CW 16, para. 83)

The Jungian therapist seldom actively pushes a patient toward any goal, but will instead trace emergent themes with the client and help him or her "circumambulate" and untangle issues as they arise in the course of life's everyday interactions. Everything is subject to interpretation, since all issues are connected through the substrata of our personal life story, active complexes, relationships, and the collective unconscious.

As mentioned elsewhere, many Jungians are averse to the use of medication. Schwartz-Salant (1982, p. 15) says that you can inhibit an archetypal process in several ways: with medication, by ignoring its existence, or by subjecting it to reductive interpretations.

What are some of the variations in Jungian therapy?

Some Therapy Modalities

This section looks at Samuels's classification of Jungian "schools" of psychology, reviews Sandner's sorting of preferred styles of therapy according to personality type of the therapist, adds a few notes on the overlap between analytical psychology and object relations theory, and touches on Kohut's self psychology in relation to Jungian psychology.

You may not be interested in becoming a Jungian analyst; you might want to be a Jungian psychotherapist, to stay eclectic, or to reject Jungian psychology altogether. After learning about Jungian therapy styles, and about differences in the training of Jungian therapists and analysts, you may be more prepared to decide. The variations in analytical psychology discussed here are intended to be useful for anyone who is at all curious about Jungian psychotherapy. They provide a background for the even more concrete details of Jungian practice that follow.

Samuels's Classification of Jungian Therapies

Samuels (1985b) identifies three major schools within analytical psychology: *classical, developmental,* and *archetypal.* He considers three aspects of theory and three aspects of practice when classifying a school (or a practitioner). The three theoretical areas are as follows:

1. the definition of archetypal;
2. the concept of self;
3. the development of personality.

The three clinical aspects include:

1. the analysis of transference-countertransference;
2. emphasis upon symbolic experiences of the self;
3. examination of highly differentiated imagery.
   (p. 15)

Samuels weights each factor for each school: "I think the Classical School would weight the [theoretical] possibilities in the order 2, 1, 3," and so on (p. 15).

A simplified matrix of Samuels's classification appears in the accompanying table. Although the details are not central to this discussion, the major variables are relevant. The table locates each analytical school at the intersection of its major theoretical and practical emphases. For example, the classical school emphasizes the Self concept and its symbolic expression, the developmental school uses personality development and transference/countertransference, and the archetypal school attends mainly to archetypal imagery.

The classical school corresponds to Jung's own approach and is closest to what is taught at the Jung Institute in Zurich. The developmental school is like Fordham's London school. The archetypal school was defined by Hillman and emphasizes symbolic imagery. Samuels reminds us that analysts may move among or combine approaches and that his categories are only approximate.

SAMUELS'S CLASSIFICATION SYSTEM AS APPLIED TO THIS BOOK. Most of the discussions in this book have fused the classical and archetypal approaches, since Hillman's offshoot of Jungian therapy is rather specialized. The developmental school is addressed as part of the larger subject of life-span development (Chapter 6), and this book, more than Samuels's, considers recent aspects of feminine relationship psychology in the context of Anima/Animus theory (Chapters 5 and 11).

Sandner's Classification of Jungian Therapies

Sandner (1994) takes a different approach to therapy style, dividing it according to the personality type of the therapist. He identifies three kinds of therapy in our culture: *dream-centered, regressive,* and *interpersonal.* A fourth approach, mostly absent from the mainstream, would be *body-centered.* Certain kinds of massage, Gestalt work, "family modeling," psychodrama, and other modalities occupy the body-centered fringes of our therapy practice.

SAMUELS'S TABLE

	Transference/ countertransference	Symbolic experiences of the self	Examination of highly differentiated imagery
The definition of archetypal			Archetypal
The concept of self		Classical	
The development of personality	Developmental		

Source: Adapted from *Jung and the Post-Jungians*, by A. Samuels, 1985, p. 17. Copyright © 1985 by Routledge & Kegan-Paul. Adapted by permission.

In one way or another, all Jungian therapies allow patients to drop the Persona and regress, (that is, drop back to an earlier, more authentic state of being than the one with which they face everyday life). A therapist's preference for one modality over another depends on his or her personality type.

DREAM-CENTERED OR INTUITIVE THERAPY. Jung himself was highly intuitive, so the Zurich school attracts therapists whose dominant personality function is intuition. In this style of therapy, the *dream is the center of attention;* it carries the regression and the relationship. At a certain point one can see the transference enter the dream. The dream does not necessarily reveal the appearance of the therapist undisguised, but his or her presence is often shown symbolically.

Dreams are valuable in any depth therapy. Some people can awaken after each rapid eye movement (REM) sequence and record a series of dreams each night. A typical nightly dream series first presents a dramatic dilemma, then moves toward a solution, often achieved in the last dream before waking.

Sandner says that under some conditions of heavy regression, within a strong therapeutic relationship, it is hard to dream. People need some psychological space to relate to the dream itself. Perhaps dreams allow you to get *more* from therapy by carrying their own opportunity for self-expression.

REGRESSIVE OR THINKING THERAPY. This modality encourages more regression than does the dream-centered style. It is preferred by therapists who operate best in the thinking mode. Here the *regression is the main fact* of the therapy, which is usually done on the couch. This framework allows the patient to regress to early-childhood states, in the care of the therapist's thinking, ideas, and concepts, which "hold" the patient safely. Having the patient lie down, with the therapist out of sight (rather than sitting face to face), both fosters regression and reduces some kinds of transference. The early, regressive family issues are what highlight the transference.

INTERPERSONAL OR FEELING THERAPY. This is a highly interpersonal style of therapy, favored by therapists with a dominant feeling function. Sandner believes that here the *relationship itself is the center*, and thus sessions are conducted sitting face to face. As the relationship develops, the therapist becomes more and more like the parent, and the patient becomes more and more like the child, creating a present-anchored regression.

BODY-CENTERED OR SENSATION THERAPY. Here the *body is central*; this style would appeal to therapists of the sensation type. They usually have little opportunity to practice it. Sandner (1994) vividly describes the experience of a Sioux sweat lodge ceremony, which definitely includes the body as the main thing, though other elements come in. In that ceremony, the intense heat makes you regress; you are often naked like a baby, sitting on the ground in mud created by your own sweat. These factors create an instant transference, done by the body. Paradoxically, this agony brings out what you long to feel—anger, tears, or whatever else is needed (Sandner, 1994).

Jungian Psychology and Object Relations Theory

Object relations theory originated in Freud's experience of transference phenomena, when he realized that not every memory of childhood abuse is factual. To this he added the concept of a "lost love object, which cannot be properly mourned and let go of, but rather remains inside the person's own psyche and goes on relating to it there" (Solomon, 1991, pp. 316–317). This entity is an *introjected object*. (Objects are, of course, more often people than things.) Melanie Klein took the next step, saying that internal objects are representations of instincts, modified by experience of the real object.

Klein's additions were applied by Michael Fordham to Jung's theory, in his own view of child development that succeeds, says Solomon (1991, pp. 317–324), in healing the split between Freudian and Jungian theory caused by the rupture of the personal relationship in 1913. Solomon's statement may be optimistic: Jungians are still divided over the relative merit of Kleinian and archetypal theory. The reader can consult Fred Plaut's *Analysis Analyzed* (1993) for further discussion of what Plaut calls the "Klein-Jung Hybrid."

Object relations theorists tell us that from birth onward, we seek *relationships*, not merely instinctual satisfaction. Storr (1988, p. 7) also views neurosis as resulting from a failure to make relationships, rather than being a result of inhibited or undeveloped sex drives. Storr reminds us that "even very young infants show interest in objects which provide novel visual and auditory stimuli, and such stimuli cannot be regarded as anything to do with satisfying basic drives like hunger, thirst, or the need for contact and comfort" (p. 152). We remain attached to others throughout our lives, even while becoming increasingly independent. Earlier writers confused the meanings of *attachment* and *dependence*. Storr (1988, p. 11) explains that "attachment is not evident until the infant is about six months old. Dependence gradually diminishes until maturity is reached: attachment behavior persists throughout life."

Winnicott (1969), in a related theory, says that our ability to be alone depends on a secure experience of being alone as a baby in the presence of the good-enough mother (read "primary caretaker"). Such experience enables a child to become aware of its true self, consisting of its own inner feelings, needs, and impulses (Storr, 1988, pp. 19–20).

Winnicott, unlike Jung, depicts the Self as evolving and differentiating from relationships, rather than existing a priori, as an archetype. This is one of the differences between object relations theory and classical Jungian psychology, as well as a departure from Fordham's concept of the DI-RI cycle (Chapter 6).

Winnicott paves the way for the development of symbolic thought when he says that imagination and play lead to the development of *transitional objects* such as a favorite blanket that *stands for* the mother in her absence (Storr, 1988, pp. 69–72). This fits well with the Jungian theory that the purpose of symbols is to enable us to transcend conflict.

H. M. Solomon (1991) has also updated some correspondences between object relations theory and Jungian psychology. Both theories are grounded in Hegel's philosophy of dialectical change (see Chapter 2), and both rely on a concept of "deep structures" in the dialectical relationship. Solomon summarizes his conclusions as follows:

> The connection between the concept of the archetypes of the collective unconscious and concepts from object relations theory . . . can be . . . conceived thus: *in all of us there are certain fundamental psychic structures through which the primal self mediates its inner experiences and its earliest relationships;* the interactions between the primal self and inner and outer experiences with their multitudinous imageries build up over time to make the person who we are: a kind of inner and outer family. (p. 309; Solomon's italics)

This formulation places individual development in an integral relationship with other people and events. Earlier, Jung had recognized the personal and archetypal importance of family images. He saw the mother and father complexes as

The sum of the individual's personal experience, positive or negative, of their real mother and their real father *and* the collective experience, the "mother" and "father" imagoes [idealized images], which we have all inherited by virtue of being human. In ethological terms, an individual's personal experiences of their own mother and father are functions of an innate inherited predisposition to experience them in particular ways. (Solomon, 1991, p. 313)

Solomon emphasizes that Kleinians see aggression as an aspect of the death instinct, whereas the Jungian view "encompasses conflict, anger, and aggression within a potentially positive, albeit contentious, framework, without necessitating viewing them as ultimately destructive" (pp. 325–326).

Solomon also relates our experience of our parents to theirs of their own parents, and so on back through the generations. This relativizes an archetypal encounter, and avoids the bitterness intrinsic to the Kleinian premise of inherent destructive impulses directed by an infant toward its mother.

Jungian Psychology and Kohut's Self Psychology

Kohut's psychology, like Jung's, departs from the pessimistic stance of classical Freudian theory. Kohut has in fact been criticized for paying too little attention to the psychic conflicts posited by drive-based psychologies. In another "correction" to Freud's negative attitude, he was one of the first theorists to say a good word for narcissism. Kohut also anticipated recent developments that blur distinctions between occurrences "inside" and "outside" the individual (see the discussion of transference/countertransference in Chapter 7).

Choice of Therapeutic Modality

One's practice of psychotherapy is colored by individual style. We have seen that therapies can be classified in several meaningful ways, but doing that is basically a pedagogical exercise. All kinds of therapy overlap in practice, and the transference takes multiple forms in each.

On the other hand, Sandner (1994) says that in his experience, although some analysts may be good at two of the modalities he describes, he doesn't know anyone who can do three kinds very well. After their initial training, most therapists ease into the mode they find most compatible, whether it is a Jungian style or something more objectively codified, like behavior modification. (In behavior modification one may, for example, create a schedule of observed frequency of a problem behavior and attempt to change the frequency to a more desired level.)

In this context, Jungians point out that even the most "objective" approach to treatment inevitably includes the subjectivity of the therapist. A therapist whose own psyche is unfamiliar territory risks getting into deep trouble.

Specific Therapy Goals

Within the general framework of the developmental goal, designated subgoals can help orient therapy. Some typical objectives for each stage of life development are given next.

SUBGOALS OF THERAPY WITH INFANTS AND CHILDREN. Jungian therapists have not been especially known for their work with children. As noted earlier, Jung himself most often worked with people at or past midlife, in many cases after previous therapy had failed. However, you can find Jungian therapists for clients of all ages.

Sandplay, as developed by Dora Kalff (1981) is widely used with children as well as with adults, as we will see in Chapter 9. Other approaches to child therapy include play therapy, art therapy, and some work with dreams. Recent years have brought more interest and discussion to Jungian child therapy.

A great deal of work with infant and child development has been done in England by Michael Fordham and his associates (1957). Mara Sidoli (1989) has described her process of child analysis. These Jungian authors have been influenced by the work of the (Freudian) British object relations school, and because Sidoli relies heavily on verbal interpretation, the reports of her child therapy read much like reports of Freudian child analysis.

The *goals* of Jungian work with children center around returning the child to a normal developmental path. This can correct disturbances in the Self concept (Kalff), deviations from normal Self development (Fordham, Sidoli), behavioral problems, and even some of the more serious pathologies.

Jung (1933, pp. 99–100) thought that children were closely identified with their parents and reflected their pathology:

> In the childish stage of consciousness there are as yet no problems; nothing depends upon the subject, for the child itself is still completely dependent upon its parents. It is as though it were not yet completely born, but were still enclosed in the psychic atmosphere of its parents. . . .
>
> The complex psychic life of the child is of course a problem of the first magnitude to parents, educators, and physicians; but when normal, the child has no real problems of its own. It is only when a human being has grown up that he can have doubts about himself and be at variance with himself.

Jung's position seems extreme. As anyone who works with children knows, it is true that you must often include parents or extended family as adjuncts to child therapy—but Kalff, Sidoli, and others have also worked successfully with individual children from quite early ages.

As discussed in Chapter 6, the Fordham school traces the origin of many adult problems to a failure of the child's caretakers to "humanize" the archetypes for them. These therapists will try to strengthen the child's ego and to promote effective mediation between ego and archetype.

Children, like adults, are assumed to possess an innate tendency toward psychological wholeness and repair. Jungian child therapy fosters the child's development of a secure sense of self in the face of environmental or intrapersonal stressors.

SUBGOALS OF THERAPY IN EARLY ADULTHOOD. Jungian writers traditionally describe the tasks of adolescence and early adulthood as focusing on the achievement of identity relatively independent of the family of origin and grounded in the values of the collective. These are ego tasks involving the Heroic Journey (Beebe, 1991; Hill, 1992, p. 28).

Recently, feminist authors have questioned the assumptions underlying this outline of typical development. A group of women researchers at the Stone Center in Wellesley, Massachusetts, emphasize the role of development within close relationships (Jordan, Kaplan, Miller, Stiver, & Surrey, 1991), and other authors have taken up the theme. Women typically cobble together an identity from disparate parts rather than focusing on a single career (Bateson, 1989). They must develop multiple containers for their multiple roles: many baskets for many eggs.

Jungians as well as other theorists are currently rethinking the goals for young adults. Under Beebe's schema of personality type, we saw that adolescents may identify with their Persona as a result of their efforts to achieve independence. This Persona is too often a False Self developed in response to parental or collective demand. Even if it should be an adaptive mask originating from a position of strength, identification with such an archetype interferes with individuation. In these circumstances, therapy would be directed either toward reestablishing the true "spine" of the personality, or toward some recognition of the individual's inferior function, to enable it to more effectively counteract the inflation of identification with the Persona.

SUBGOALS OF THERAPY IN MIDLIFE. Goals at midlife usually include a shift of emphasis to less-developed aspects of personality that were pushed aside by the demands of earning a living and raising children. The goals for men and women are more similar now than they were in Jung's time, at least in this respect. (See Chapter 6 for an overview of midlife development.)

Jung (1933, pp. 108–109) thought of midlife as the time when all our entrenched values reverse themselves:

> We cannot live the afternoon of life according to the programme of life's morning—for what was great in the morning will be little at evening, and what in the morning was true will at evening have become a lie. . . . For a young person it is almost a sin—and certainly a danger—to be too much occupied with himself; but for the ageing person it is a duty and a necessity to give serious attention to himself.

In the traditional Jungian view, midlife is the point where development in the world passes its noon and starts to descend toward the darkness of death. This is assumed to require a switch of emphasis from extraverted to introverted issues. One loses interest in outside recognition and begins to deal with internal imbalance and the meaning of one's life. This dramatic shift often creates a major crisis among successful professional men and among some women (although women are less likely to invest all their emotions in a single goal).

The severe midlife crisis may not be as inevitable as was once believed. Increased psychological-mindedness may make us less likely to overlook or neglect major aspects of our psyches. Even our recent ecological concerns seem to lead by back lanes to a spiritual interconnectedness that may help to forestall a spiritual crisis in midlife (Sperry, 1983). At the same time, the poor and oppressed may never achieve such a crisis, since they have a lifelong struggle simply to survive.

Recent developments in theories about the biological bases of memory (Edelman, 1990, 1992; Sperry, 1983) imply new goals for therapy at midlife, as follows. First, these theories mesh with research on the importance of narrative in constructing a coherent and flexible self concept (McAdams, 1988). If Edelman is correct in saying that reframing our cognitive grasp of reality creates changes in brain chemistry and neuronal network paths, then "retelling our life narratives is tantamount to performing therapeutic microsurgery on the brain" (D. I. Tresan, personal communication, August 7, 1993).

Knowing this, Jungian therapists can continue with confidence to rely on active listening and can encourage clients to create adaptive patterns through retelling, thereby restructuring, their experiences.

Second, just as brain research adds support to Jung's intuitively stated theories of archetypes and the collective unconscious (see Chapter 10), so does it underline the appropriateness of retaining some archetypal focus in adult psychotherapy. (As Jung said, work with children often involves efforts to *reduce* archetypal influence.)

THERAPY SUBGOALS FOR OLD AGE. Jungian therapists, unlike some pessimistic psychiatrists, do not believe that working with the aged is a waste of time. Development is assumed to continue throughout the life cycle, and a strong, flexible ego produced by long struggles with life events can help old people tolerate a closer relationship to the Self. Old people can bring wisdom and patience to the task of making sense of their lives.

Jane Wheelwright (1984), Bruce Baker (with Wheelwright, 1982), and Allan Chinen (1989) are among the few Jungians who deal specifically with the psychology of the aged. In earlier decades, not many people 70 or older knew much about psychotherapy, and few took advantage of Jungian analysis (Baker & Wheelwright, 1982, p. 257). In recent years, as a later generation ages, this barrier has diminished.

The main *goal* for old age seems to be the attainment of a secure attachment to some concept of transpersonal, Self-related reality. When you are old, if you can feel such a reality in your own body and achieve a concept of life as a seamless whole, then ego concerns about personal survival and loss of identity become less frightening and even irrelevant.

Baker and Wheelwright list seven tasks of aging that they believe start in one's 50s:

1. Accept death as a part of life.
2. Review, reflect upon, and sum up your life; tell your story.
3. Accept limits to what you can accomplish.
4. Let go of the dominance of the ego.
5. Encounter and honor the Self.
6. Articulate your own reason for being.
7. Engage unused potentials: "die with life."
(pp. 266–270)

These steps, if successfully negotiated, lead to a place where the older person can drop the burdens of ambition, Persona, and self-importance in favor of a relaxed, even playful enjoyment of immediate experience. The more completely the individual has been able to live all aspects of life and clear out pockets of "unlived life," the less traumatic will be the approach of death.

SUBGOALS FOR THE LAST STAGE: DEATH AND DYING. Our tendency toward wholeness is not seen as deserting us in the face of imminent death. In fact, the opposite is often true; dying patients can develop new, deeper levels of spiritual insight and serenity. This is not a simple task. Jung (1933, pp. 110–111) said:

> We must not forget that only a very few people are artists in life; that the art of life is the most distinguished and rarest of all the arts. . . . So for many people all too much unlived life remains over—sometimes potentialities which they could never have lived with the best of wills; and so they approach the threshold of old age with unsatisfied claims which invariably turn their glances backward.

Death closes off the last chance to make up for what one has missed, so the best defense against the terror of extinction is to have been thoroughly alive in all one's capabilities. "Dying with life" is "living out one's creative essence to the very end" (Baker & Wheelwright, 1982, p. 272).

A Jungian View of Psychopathology

Various Jungian writers have addressed aspects of psychopathology. They include Schwartz-Salant (1989) and Beebe (1988b) on the borderline patient, Sandner and Beebe (1995) on psychopathology and analysis, Schwartz-Salant (1982) on the related theme of narcissism, and Sullivan (1989) on a feminine approach to neurosis and more serious symptomology. Clarissa Pinkola Estés (1992) has created a best-seller that not only depathologizes but celebrates Animus strength in women.

Jung believed it unnecessary for diagnosis to go beyond separating organic and psychotic symptoms from neurosis. In contrast, today's Jungian practitioners include psychiatrists, psychologists, and other mental health professionals trained to diagnose clients according to the American Psychiatric Association's *Diagnostic and Statistical Manual of Mental Disorders (DSM-III-R)* (1987) in order to perform intake and triage of patients at a hospital or clinic. Beyond indicating the clients' severity of symptoms and distress, however, the use of diagnosis is not central to Jungian practice.

Many Jungians are reluctant to report diagnoses to third-party insurers. The report is seen as a breach of the therapeutic container of privacy and confidentiality, and the *DSM-III-R* terminology is itself pathology-oriented. Under Sandner's classification, dream-centered therapists are perhaps least likely to rely on *DSM-III-R* diagnoses, but they may occasionally provide them as needed for hospitalization or medication purposes. When practitioners who take a regressive or relationship approach are required to diagnose, they are likely to classify symptoms and their origins on the basis of self psychology or object relations theory.

The following discussion is little more than an annotated bibliography of Jungian approaches to differential treatment. The kinds of clients listed here are most frequently customers of private practitioners and are seeking help themselves rather than being referred against their will by probation officers or school psychologists.

These therapy clients can be divided roughly into three classes: the neurotic or "walking wounded," the narcissistic and borderline character-disordered, and the more or less psychotic. Broadly speaking, the *neurotic* person is aware of his or her problems and is unhappy about them but is at a loss on how to remedy them. The *character-disordered* are more intractable to the treatment they seek and to improve must often drop and take up more than one therapist over several years. Persons suffering from *thought disorders* may need medication or periodic hospitalization to keep them functional, but even so, many willingly come for "soul work" in between crises.

Neurotic Clients

Neurotic clients form the bulk of patients who seek out a Jungian analyst for personal growth and transformation. Some may look for practical problem solving as well. As we saw earlier, Jung emphasized the need for personal reevaluation at midlife. Most of Jung's patients were at least middle-aged, as are many of this group of contemporary clients.

Murray Stein (1983) has written a classic book on the origins and treatment of midlife issues. He focuses on the concept of "liminality" or transition and the archetype of Hermes, our Trickster guide to these shadowy regions. (His book is one volume from two useful series of small books—published by Spring Publications and Inner City Books—in which Jungian analysts discuss clinical issues.)

More material relevant to neurotic conflict can be found in Chapters 5, 6, and 8.

Character Problems: Narcissistic and Borderline Disorders

Two books by Schwartz-Salant—*Narcissism and Character Transformation* (1982) and *The Borderline Personality: Vision and Healing* (1989)—relate Kohut's nuclear self to the concept of narcissism, and object relations to borderline symptomology in Jungian psychology. His writing is extremely rich; the ideas in it apply across a great many Jungian issues and are sprinkled throughout the present book.

Narcissistic and borderline problems both result from a poor sense of identity. Schwartz-Salant (1982) emphasizes the multiple nature of narcissistic character problems; like Sullivan (1989), he says that they can originate from any developmental stage, and any personality structure, at any level (pp. 24, 34). He defines it this way: *"The narcissistic character structure is a pattern that is a link between the personal and the archetypal realms.* Accordingly, it is found in any archetypal pattern entering space-time reality, and within any personality structure" (p. 26; Schwartz-Salant's italics).

He also mentions an "evolved" narcissism, in which the individual develops the capacity to observe images from the unconscious without fusing with them (p. 98). This concept supports the value of introversion as a means to pull consciousness down into the body and establish better connections between the unconscious and the exterior world. Such advanced narcissism can lead to "creativity, empathy, wisdom, the capacity for self-transcendence, and humor" (Tresan, 1994, Part II, p. 14).

Borderline issues arise earlier in life and create a much more seriously fragmented state. Schwartz-Salant (1989) concentrates on the origins of these difficulties and the transformations possible through analysis.

Sullivan (1989) takes a stand against the pathologizing of narcissistic or borderline defenses, saying that we all employ such defenses as an appropriate reaction to severe stress. With Schwartz-Salant (1982, 1989), she emphasizes the need for ego strength to contain and channel such "primitive" defenses until the crisis abates and other modes of coping again become available. Sullivan calls her view "feminine" because it does not logically and rigidly classify patients or denigrate their use of the "splitting" defense. She sees such denigration as itself an example of the good/bad "splitting" of objects.

Beebe's (1988b) article on the treatment of borderline patients also employs Kohut's theory to some extent, by assuming the presence of self-object problems in these patients. Beebe, however, considers the Self to be one such self-object. He defines the borderline patient as someone possessed by "an energized complex that will not enter treatment but will not forsake it either," and calls the unconscious attitude resulting from the complex "primary ambivalence toward the Self" (p. 98). His article details a series of steps for therapy with borderline patients.

Thought-Disordered Clients

As Sullivan (1989) reminds us, given enough stress, almost anyone can become psychotic. People with psychotic disorders are not absent from Jungian practice. John Weir Perry (1987) was among the first wave of analysts to write extensively about their treatment.

Many analytical psychologists, besides being reluctant to resort to medication, will try to help these clients ride out severe regressions on an outpatient basis. They may schedule daily appointments and maintain additional telephone contact. If a client must be hospitalized, Perry advocates the least restrictive surroundings possible. Frequent, and if possible, nonmedicated therapy appointments help to hasten the return to outpatient care.

Some analysts view the psychotic process as an ultimately necessary journey of healing through the depths of the psyche. Treating psychosis from this standpoint requires extensive training, plus talent, optimism, patience, and some access to practical safeguards for both patient and therapist.

We turn now from this brief review of Jungian attitudes toward the diagnosis of mental illness to details of the customary Jungian *framework* of clinical practice.

More Detailed Procedures in Jungian Therapy

Underlying the remarks that follow is the assumption that Jungian therapy differs from other modalities mainly by concentrating on inner development over the long haul. Its principles can be applied to shorter interventions, but absent a relaxed time frame, the full spectrum of benefits is less likely to occur.

Authentic Jungian analysis can originate only from certified Jungian analysts. However, therapists with training in Jungian theory who are engaged in personal analysis and who seek out Jungian case consultation can effectively employ Jungian principles in their work.

Some Common Jungian Frame Requirements

For most types of Jungian therapy, the following conditions apply. The seldom-mentioned matter of managing payments from clients is included here as a clinical issue.

THERAPY APPOINTMENTS

1. *Location.* Typically, therapists and patients meet in a semiformal, office setting. Other possible but unusual settings could be a hospital ward or a disabled patient's bedside at home. Jungian therapy is most often individual but can be used with couples or groups.

2. *Duration of the Appointment.* Individual appointments are usually scheduled at one-hour intervals, although client contact usually lasts only 45 to 50 minutes, giving therapists some time to reflect and take notes between clients. Some therapists will go into extra minutes when a client is especially upset

and will schedule extra hours as needed. A therapist may also stop an appointment early for valid reasons. But some keep strictly to the preset "frame," as indicated earlier.

Couples' therapy hours can be the same as or longer than individuals'. Groups often go for an hour and a half or more, and if there are co-therapists, discussion and note taking are scheduled between groups.

3. *Frequency of Appointments.* Some Jungians consider therapy to be "analysis" only if the client comes at least three times a week and lies on a couch during appointments. Others prefer the client to sit more or less facing them, and many say that analysis implies a certain depth of therapy independent of the frequency of appointments. Earlier in this chapter we mentioned the effect of seating arrangements on the transference/countertransference.

4. *Adjustments to Frequency.* The number of appointments per week may shift with the needs of the client, from once a week ordinarily, to more often when important topics surface, and less often when circumstances change. When the client is short of money, it is the therapist's decision whether to meet less often, to adjust the amount or schedule of payments, or to discontinue therapy temporarily or permanently.

Fees for Therapy

Many Jungians ask patients to pay at each session, and some will not accept insurance or its associated reporting requirements, for reasons of privacy, as explained above. Many Jungians use a sliding scale in setting fees, and some will adjust them during ongoing therapy to fit a client's circumstances. Such adjustments invariably involve transference/countertransference issues, which should be discussed as they occur.

FEES AND "MONEY." The preceding remarks concerning fees only scratch the surface of the very deep subject of money. Money has always evoked a complex emotional mixture of love and hate. The Bible (*I Timothy* 6:6) tells us that "the love of money is the root of all evil." In a more contemporary spirit, British novelist Somerset Maugham (1915, p. 304) wrote that "money is like a sixth sense without which you cannot make a complete use of the other five." This pair of maxims presents another paradox, since each is at least partly true. Some kind of currency is needed to survive in most societies, so that its absence can be lethal. Money is also addictive; millionaires are said never to think they have enough money.

Analysts have written books and articles about money (Lockhart et al., 1982; Herron & Welt, 1992), and the entire spring 1991 issue of *Parabola*—a magazine on mythical themes—was devoted to the subject of money. Even the ostensible purpose of alchemy was to change base metals into gold.

In therapeutic circles, few people speak freely about the fees they charge. An article by Muriel Dimen (1994) explores this subject. Dimen wonders what money is, exactly, and then quotes this definition from another source:

> "Money is any material object that performs one or more of the following five functions—a medium of exchange, a standard of value, a unit of account, a store of value, and a standard of deferred payments. While there may be different objects serving each different function in any one society, the first function tends to be controlling; whatever is the medium of exchange likely serves the other functions too. Finally, money itself may be a commodity, as it is in capitalism, where you buy it with what is called interest, that is, with more of the same." (p. 83)

Therapists in private practice, starting with Freud, have been reluctant to associate themselves with commerce, preferring to label the collection of money as "fee for service" rather than "selling my time." Some therapists like to see themselves as motivated by a love for humanity, a trait that Hillman (1972, p. 88) mistrusts when it is substituted for intense personal interest. Lawyer jokes seem to carry this shadow for all professionals, since lawyers are often stereotyped as money-grubbers.

Money and love are frequently seen as mutually exclusive, as in the saying "You can't get it for love or money." Dimen (1994, p. 88) says the two are contradictory and that money is a pact with the devil because

> by reducing everything to a common denominator, it robs everything and every person of individuality and thereby debases what it touches. That is one reason why we like to separate it from love and distinguish the profane, public sphere of work, trade, and politics from the sacred, private space of intimacy, love, and relationship.

Our problem is obvious: Psychotherapy is an intimate relationship, but you can't make a living at it unless money changes hands. The conflict is less pressing if you work on salary for an agency than if you are in private practice—but it is never absent.

Money is a piece of the "frame" of psychotherapy. As Milner (1957, p. 158) says,

> When there is a frame it surely serves to indicate that what's inside the frame has to be interpreted in a different way from what's outside it. . . . Thus the frame marks off an area within which what is perceived

has to be taken symbolically, while what is outside the frame is taken literally.

As I see it, this statement hints at a solution to the dilemma. In the therapeutic container, money is a symbol like any other. But two caveats should be heeded here. First, where love is, there hate will also be, and you need to talk about both emotions. This can get complicated. For instance, patients often suddenly discover they hate you when you insist on full payment, instead of trading at least some of your fee for what they perceive as the "true gold" of their love for you. Clients have also been known to brag about how much they pay for an hour of therapy, deriving reflected glory from being able to afford such a precious commodity, or even from being such a desperate or complicated "case" that therapy requires enormous expense! The transference aspects of money, like other loves or hates, may be treated symbolically.

Second, as in any symbolic (here read "transference/countertransference") issue, the problem is not just the patient's. As a therapist you will also feel anxiety, love, and hate over money matters. How much are you worth per hour anyway—$10, $20, or $100? What about price versus volume? Late payments from clients mess up your own bills; if a long-term client loses a job, can you afford to keep him or her? What about the client who calls you a highway robber for charging your low-end fee of $20, "for just sitting there"? What about the unpromising but wealthy client who wants to know if she should start coming more than once a week? Freud called these clients "goldfish"—not very classy of him (Dimen, 1994, p. 76).

Finally, how much of your feelings about money should you discuss with a client? Probably much less than the client's share of the issue, but sometimes a little frank talk will go far to resolve hidden conflicts over money. When in doubt, ask for consultation from a therapist whom you know to be open about money matters—and *pay* for it.

Other Conventions or Rules

The most important rules are *ethical* and have to do with "dual roles." Ethical therapists do not become involved with clients in business or personal matters outside of the therapy setting. They do not engage in sexual behavior with clients. These rules are standard among the helping professions. Most therapists, including Jungian psychologists, psychiatrists, and social workers, observe extensive codes of ethics administered through their professional associations.

Touch is confined to a minimum, perhaps involving an occasional handshake or a light touch on the shoulder for most therapists. A subcategory of practitioners use bodywork in conjunction with Jungian therapy; this practice has its own professional rules. Most touch is taboo among therapists, probably to protect all concerned from drifting into sexual misunderstandings.

The beginning therapist can stay out of much trouble by paying careful attention to ethical issues and seeking prompt consultation when therapist/ patient boundaries seem endangered in any way. This professional attitude by no means implies that one should act cold and distant with a client, but only that the client's best interests be guarded by maintaining appropriate limits.

READINGS

Chinen, A. B. (1989). *In the ever after: Fairy tales and the second half of life.* Wilmette, IL: Chiron.

Herron, W. G., & Welt, S. R. (1992). *Money matters.* New York: Guilford Press.

Plaut, F. (1993). *Analysis analyzed.* London: Routledge.

Samuels, A. (1985). *Jung and the post-Jungians.* London: Routledge & Kegan Paul.

Sidoli, M. (1989). *The unfolding self.* Boston: Sigo Press.

Stein, M. (Ed.). (in press). *Jungian analysis* (2nd ed.). La Salle, IL: Open Court.

FOUR

Intervention Modes

Three Major Intervention Modes: Narrative Interpretation, Dream Analysis, and Symbolic Approaches

As you have discovered by now, although Jungian practitioners' approaches to therapy vary with their personality type and the patient's needs, a core of theory and action remains, identifying the therapy as "Jungian." For instance, all Jungians rely on the archetypal psyche's tendency to heal itself, so a Jungian therapist will try to facilitate the natural process, rather than impose an out-side standard or pursue a specific goal. Jungian therapy almost always includes a symbolic element, which can be expressed verbally or more experientially.

You should always keep in mind that nobody can go out and practice Jungian therapy after reading this or any other book, or even a whole library. The subtle, nitty-gritty details of therapeutic technique must be learned ex-perientially, with a good supervisor, and cannot be taught through lectures or texts. Even more essentially, one's own troublesome complexes need to be disarmed through personal therapy. Meanwhile, to convey a flavor of the pro-cess, this chapter presents some abstractions from experience. We first review some general criteria for verbal intervention, then shift to dream interpreta-tion. The last section takes a short look at other modalities.

Narrative Interpretation

Therapy is accomplished most often in a verbal, narrative mode. Storr (1988, p. 22) says that the narration of life events, whether done with an analyst or in solitude, in itself leads to healing: "Some kind of rearrangement or sorting-out process often occurs within the mind which brings with it a sense of peace, a sense that the depths of the well of truth have really been reached." As described in Chapter 10, such narration presumably acts physically to reorganize neural networks in your brain, thereby changing the "reality" structure of your cognitions and memory. In time, newer versions of reality that approach current consensual fact can replace distortions acquired earlier.

Principles of Jungian Therapy with Adults

Jungian therapy plunges client and therapist into the alchemical container described in Chapter 7, engages all parts of both psyches, and inevitably creates the entanglements of transference and countertransference. Because of these factors, the therapist is a participant observer, not a spectator of change. Effective therapy facilitates growth in both members of the therapeutic dyad.

HINTS ON TECHNIQUE. There is technique to Jungian therapy, but it is more an attitude than a bag of tricks. You must above all pay close attention to the client—to words, certainly, but also to nonverbal elements such as posture or tone of voice. You may experience helpful countertransference reactions in your own feelings, thoughts, or body. Hillman (1972, p. 88) warns against the distant perspective of a "therapeutic attitude" and advocates personal, emotional caring about each client.

Immediacy of relationship is important in other ways. You should be "in the room with" your client, ready to stop the flow at any time to comment or ask a question about whatever catches your attention as needing further exploration. Many clients have a "tape" they have been playing for years, built from faulty but unquestioned emotional and logical connections. These old structures need to be identified and dismantled if new ones are to develop in their place.

RESPONSIVITY. Jungians often present less of a blank screen than does the classical psychoanalyst. Once a good therapeutic relationship has been established, some Jungian therapists will give limited practical advice, and occasionally even unbend with personal remarks.

As a therapist, whether or not you reveal any of your subjective reactions to the client, you should remember that psychotherapy is always a two-way relationship. Clients pick up your nonverbal responses and also react to your office furniture, your clothes, and other, more unexpected items. Simultaneously, you are affected by clients' appearance, promptness, participation in therapy, and so on, over both the short and the long term.

INTERVENTIONS. The basics of Jungian clinical practice are like any other. You listen attentively to what the client has to say. Your responses may be primarily cognitive, or feeling-based. If a client's statements are contradictory or confused, you can ask for clarification, as in any other therapy. You can attempt mild confrontation when necessary. If the issue is an emotional one, your comments can focus on the affect that the client is struggling to identify or express.

You are unlikely to use double binds, paradoxical interventions, behavioral schedules, or any other technique directed toward what you may perceive as a specific desirable goal. (*Double binds* are psychological predicaments in which clients are given conflicting messages that do not allow them to make an appropriate response. In *paradoxical interventions*, the therapist says one thing to encourage the client to do the opposite. *Behavioral schedules* list the frequency with which some act is performed.) You should always try to map and follow the unique path of the client and be willing to sit with your, and his or her, uncertainty as to where it is leading. Your general goals, as discussed in the previous chapter, should develop from within the therapy process.

PERSONAL INTERPRETATION. The amount of interpretation you provide will vary with the stage of therapy and the psychological-mindedness of the client. It does the new client no favor to indicate that you are more or less successfully reading unexpressed thoughts and feelings between the lines of his or her early, shy confidences.

More seasoned clients can withstand a lot of well-meant interpretation. They have discovered that the therapist is human, too, and must occasionally show off. Nevertheless, it is usually better to let clients discover connections and underlying meanings on their own; they are more likely to accept and remember them that way. If some connection leaps out at you, crying to be mentioned, you can frame it as a query, as in: "I wonder if your dream about a giant gateway could have anything to do with your recent promotion?"

AMPLIFICATION OF ARCHETYPAL THEMES. A Jungian therapist, if steeped in mythology and cross-cultural lore, may occasionally choose to *amplify* some symbol or archetypally related story mentioned by the client, after his or her associations and remarks have been thoroughly explored. This can be done for both therapeutic narrative and dream material.

In most amplification, you tell a brief fairy tale or anecdote that parallels or explains something related to you by the client. Amplification does not involve interpreting such a story; it just adds information or gives a new slant to what was said. Sometimes the solution to a problem is hinted at in other parts of the same myth or fairy tale that describes the dilemma at hand. None of that needs to be said out loud; the symbols carry their own meaning. If your client doesn't "get it," no matter; her unconscious will have picked up the relevant parts anyway.

The purpose of amplification is to help your client recognize similarities between her personal experience and its archetypal configuration. If you remember the holographic analogy concerning Figure 5.1, you can apply it here; the individual experience is like a holographic fragment of the archetypal pattern.

A person feels less isolated and lonely if he realizes that his individual trials illustrate a universal problem. Such recognition helps to relativize the ego; the client can learn to see himself as an appropriately tiny but still integral part of an enormous universe, rather than (say) as the target of persecution by a destructive Fate.

Timeline of Therapy

Jungian therapy will often continue for several years, as successively deeper levels of consciousness are reached. A thorough analysis may take ten or more years. In some ways, the process, once begun, goes on for a lifetime. Therapy may be repeatedly stopped and restarted; many Jungian analysts periodically return to their own analyses.

Long-term therapy can be interrupted by outside life events or by a client's interior decision to consolidate gains before proceeding further. Sometimes it seems desirable to switch from a therapist of one gender to one of the other gender to fill in gaps in the perception of certain issues.

As with most Jungian processes, the parameters of therapy are flexible but often involve the disruption of previous maladaptive cycles by more positive, effective perceptual activity.

Talk and Play Therapy with Children

There are a few special principles for verbal work with children. As with adults, you hope to activate the potential for growth and healing within the child. Fairy tales, myths, and individualized, made-up stories especially help children to recognize mythical motifs that parallel some of their own loves and hates. Sometimes you can help a child hang on to its own true personality "spine" in the face of pressure toward conformity with unreasonable parental or school demands, or you may help a scapegoated child restore personal boundaries and self-respect.

It is often necessary when working with children to guard against the troublesome countertransferential tendency to identify with the child *against* the collective. This is never desirable, for both theoretical and practical reasons. You must maintain reasonably good relations with the adults surrounding the child to maintain your therapeutic equilibrium. Otherwise the child's caretakers may surprise you with a sudden series of canceled appointments.

Children may bring in dreams. Children are unlikely to cope well with complicated interpretation; often it is enough to rely on empathic listening plus some exploration of the symbols. This can occur either verbally or in an expressive modality such as art, dance, or Sandplay. A child having the usual run of dreams will respond well to these approaches, although repetitive night terrors or nightmares require special attention, beyond the purposes of this book.

Children enthusiastically take to Sandplay (described later in this chapter), and to all forms of art, dance, and play therapy, which can be used in a Jungian framework as well as any other.

What Jungian Therapy Is Not

Hypothetical advice on how to do therapy could go on for pages; its effect would be more confusing than enlightening, so I call a halt here, only repeating that Jungian therapy per se does *not* include active manipulative techniques such as paradoxical intervention or behavioral conditioning. Nothing is *done to* the client; you follow the client's need, honoring his or her individuality as equal to your own, no matter how compromised it may be by current symptoms.

We turn now to some details of Jungian dream interpretation with adults.

Dream Analysis

In Sullivan's (1989, p. 3) words, "Dreams can be seen simply as the psyche painting pictures of itself." This is the Jungian attitude toward dream material in a nutshell.

Jungian theory takes neither the behaviorist view that dreams are the "misfiring of neurons" nor the popular view that dream images can be taken literally and concretely; nor does it take the analytical but Freudian view that the manifest-content images all point to repressed and traumatic libidinous conflicts (see Whitmont and Perera, 1989, p. 6). Instead, the Jungian approach views "the dream as an allegoric or symbolic statement about the dreamer's psychological situation, precise and objective, tailored for the consciousness of the dreamer and/or his or her analyst [that is, therapist]" (p. 7). Notice that, as in other expressions of the transference/countertransference field, dreams are concerned with both members of the therapeutic dyad—with the reaction of the therapist to the client's unconscious, as well as with the clients's other concerns.

Before proceeding with details, we will review briefly the history of dream work and look at selected dream theories, then return to the Jungian approach.

Historical Approaches to the Dream

Dreams have been examined and interpreted since the beginning of recorded history. In biblical times, they were treated as messages from God; the dreams of Joseph in Egypt are a good example (Genesis 37–41). Shamans the world over use clues provided by dreams to prophesy the future and to help cure physical and emotional ills of their followers. This is a fascinating subject in itself and can be pursued by consulting other sources (Groesbeck, 1989; Kluckhohn & Morgan, 1951; Morgan, 1932; Radin, 1936).

DREAM LABORATORIES. Dreams were largely ignored as meaningless by mainstream psychologists until the sleep laboratories of Dement (1972) and others provided physiological evidence that individuals prevented from dreaming become increasingly dysfunctional. Along with respiration and temperature, dreaming is controlled by the primitive part of our brain. It occurs mostly during "REM sleep."

REM SLEEP. REM sleep is the stage of rapid eye movement. People report that they were dreaming when awakened during REM sleep, but not when awakened from other stages of sleep. Presumably the eye movements track dream events. Richard Coleman (1986, pp. 104–105) summarizes some aspects of REM sleep as follows:

> Dreams occur 80 percent of the time one is in REM sleep. . . . Oxygen consumption increases and more blood flows to the brain than during wakefulness; blood pressure, heart rate, cardiac output, and respiration rates increase and are more variable than during wakefulness.
>   There are typically four to six REM periods per night, each lasting anywhere from 10 to 45 minutes and constituting about 20 to 25 percent of the total night's sleep.

He adds that "during REM sleep our reflex system is paralyzed, preventing us from acting out our dreams" (p. 125).

Theories About the Structure and Functions of the Dream

Researchers like Coleman believe that dreams may serve an adaptational and emotional purpose by allowing us to process emotional stress, but that nevertheless they originate in random brain activity. Coleman thinks that a main function of dreams may be to tidy up our interior neuronal "computer files" after each day's input. Recent brain research casts some doubt on that explanation (see Edelman, 1992, as well as Chapter 10 of this book).

When looking at relationships between dreaming and various analytical theories about it, sleep lab results have at best been mixed. One problem here is that the subject matter of dreams collected in a lab is more constricted than of those collected at home; people in labs are influenced by their context even though asleep (Coleman, 1986, pp. 111–129).

The meaning of the dream content is also a subject of controversy. Many dreams incorporate the theme of *descent*—to a lower story of a house, to a cave, to the bottom of the sea. They often include an element of timelessness. Alan Ruskin (1994) cited the irony of a dream given by John Hobson in his book *The Dreaming Brain* (1977). Although Hobson's whole point was that dreams are only "neural storms" partly based on residues of the day's events, to which we assign arbitrary meanings, still Hobson's report of one of his own dreams concerns a descent to a basement room and to an earlier time.

Major Psychological Explanations of Dreaming

Each major psychological theory addresses the structure and function of dreaming. Object relations theorists such as Margaret Mahler (1975) say that our early experiences establish significant "historical intersections" of behavior. Under stress, we may return in dreams to those early associations.

Similarly, Kohut's (1971) self psychology maintains that there are nodal points for the organization of the psyche, such as the grandiose self; these critical points may show up in dreams when relevant issues arise in current behavior.

Erik Erikson (1963) sees dreams as reflecting attitudinal ways to engage the environment in the service of interpersonal relations.

In all of these examples, the activity of remembering the dream and discussing its meaning is assumed to produce, if it doesn't already reflect, a reorganization of a person's previously maladaptive cognitions.

Recent research on emotions, memory, and neuronal plasticity seems to support the Jungian view that emotions, as well as cognitions, play a part in memory (including, I would suppose, memories of dreams) (see LeDoux, 1994).

Dreams and Assessment

For Jungian therapists partial to cognitive developmental theory, the Piaget (1954) and Kohlberg (1969) stages are relevant. Therapists can observe the cognitive level or stage evidenced by the client's dream, and also any subsequent transformations during treatment. These changes could be tracked as confirmations of therapeutic progress.

The content and the cognitive level of dreams interact, making children's dreams different from those of normal adults. Young children do "all good–all bad" splitting in their perceptions of adults. So do borderline clients and those with posttraumatic stress disorder; the splits are reflected in their dreams and can be useful for diagnosis (van den Daele, 1991).

The diagnostic usefulness of dreams is also noted by the Jungian writers Edward Whitmont and Sylvia Perera (1989, p. 7), who say that "the dream's images and structure give evidence of ego strength, and may reveal qualities of relationship between various forms of consciousness and the psychological and somatic unconscious." They emphasize, too, that "dreams enhance learning and assist in the completion of personal development" (p. 1).

In any case, Jungian theorists agree that dreams reflect all our predominant preoccupations, whether cognitive or emotional, conscious or unconscious, in a symbolic but relatively straightforward manner.

Current Use of Dreams in Analytical Therapy

The opinions of contemporary Freudian analysts are divided on the usefulness of dreams in analytical work (Rovner, 1992). Half of a national sample reported that in psychoanalytical clinical work the dream is declining in importance. In contrast, another recent study (Roth, 1994) has shown that both in the Jungian literature and among a sample of currently practicing Jungian analysts, the use of dreams is frequent and considered important. What are some possible reasons for this difference, and why do Jungians continue to see dream work as central to therapy?

JUNG'S VIEW OF DREAMS VERSUS FREUD'S. Jung's split from Freud was accelerated by several disagreements over dreams. Jung, unlike Freud, thought (1) that dreams reflect the tendency of the psyche to heal itself, (2) that by symbolically expressing discrepancies between our unconscious and conscious attitudes dreams perform a useful *compensatory function,* and (3) that their *prospective function* can provide clues to future development.

Jung also viewed dreams as using the language of symbols to say what they actually mean, rather than concealing one meaning behind another. He wrote:

I now proceed on the principle that a dream expresses exactly what it means, and that any interpretation which yields a meaning not expressed in the manifest dream-image is therefore wrong. Dreams are neither deliberate nor arbitrary fabrications; they are natural phenomena which are nothing other than what they pretend to be. They do not deceive, they do not lie, they do not distort or disguise, but naively announce what they are and what they mean. . . . They are invariably seeking to express something that the ego does not know and does not understand. (CW 17, para. 189)

Freud, on the other hand, saw dreams as expressing disguised wish-fulfillments. Since he believed libido (motivational energy) to be exclusively sexual, his method of interpretation required the analyst to "strip away" false meanings from the dream images and expose their fundamental sexual connotations. With the rise in popularity of object relations theory, this narrow approach has appeared less fruitful to many therapists.

DREAM WORK IN JUNGIAN THERAPY. Since the earliest days of analytical psychology, Jungians have focused on dreams as a source of information about the psyche. Dream-centered, archetypal therapy was Jung's own preferred modality. Practitioners among all schools of Jungian thought, not just from the classical school of Zurich, frequently examine clients' dreams.

Jung's view of dreams as undistorted and purposeful, having the goal of synthesizing experience in meaningful and creative ways, is supported by contemporary opinion. Fosshage (1983, p. 657), concludes that "the superordinate function of dreams is the development, maintenance (regulation), and, when necessary, restoration of psychic processes, structures, and organization.

THE PROSPECTIVE FUNCTION OF DREAMS. Jung saw dreams as being partly goal-oriented, not exclusively compensatory. He said:

I should like to distinguish between the *prospective* function of dreams and their *compensatory* function. The latter means that the unconscious, considered as relative to consciousness, adds to the conscious situation all those elements from the previous day which remained subliminal because of repression or because they are simply too feeble to reach consciousness. This compensation, in the sense of being a self-regulation of the psychic organism, must be called purposive. (CW 8, para. 492; Jung's italics)

The dream is considered to reveal "a multi-leveled message about the dreamer's current psychic situation seen from a hitherto unknown or unconscious perspective" (Whitmont & Perera, 1989, p. 7). Every dream points to an unconscious complex and to the archetypal dynamism behind the emotionally charged layers of the complex:

> The dream, with uncanny accuracy, depicts the psychological situation confronting the dreamer, exactly as it is. . . . No minor aspect of the dream is extraneous; all build together. . . . In clinical practice, each dream offers diagnosis, prognosis, and appropriate material and timing to address and compensate the dreamer's—and/or therapist's—blind spots. (Whitmont & Perera, 1989, p. 7)

The elucidation of dreams requires the participation of a witness, since dreamers can't recognize their own complexes. Ruskin (1994) examines the dream structure of his analysands to detect examples of dissociative process. If a dreamer experiences two diverse levels of reality at once, that is evidence of the common defense of dissociation. For example, a dreamer being hospitably coaxed to enter a hut in the woods by an old woman wearing a big smile may feel a warmly positive response but at the same time be utterly convinced that her life depends on refusing to go inside. Ruskin's next step would be to ask the dreamer where in real life such a pairing of discordant feelings last arose. The dreamer might then recall an actual situation of neglect or abuse, where everything seemed utterly normal to a casual observer but was totally menacing below the surface.

Ruskin also looks at dreams to learn what they say about the dream process itself (Ruskin, 1994). The dream itself is affected by the presence of an audience, and the acts of telling and interpreting the dream alter it further.

THE INITIAL DREAM. Although some therapists consider the first dream brought into therapy to have a special importance, Charles Roth (1994) found that the majority of Jungian analysts he interviewed saw the initial dream as only of equal importance to other clinical material (including later dreams).

Sometimes an initial dream may reveal the client's attitude toward the safety of the therapeutic *temenos* or container, as illustrated below. A client brought this dream to her second session, but it was the first dream reported.

> A woman came to her second appointment with a female therapist to say goodbye, saying that she had decided that she didn't need therapy, but did the therapist ever go out for coffee with ex-patients? [This was asked in a friendly way, rather than seductively.] The therapist said no, she didn't, and asked if the client remembered having any dreams between sessions. The patient said that she had just dreamed she was in her mother's apartment making coffee in a glass pot. The flame was too high, and the pot cracked.

The therapist made an immediate interpretation; since the patient was planning to end the therapy, she doubted that this interpretation would harm the process and might help. She said to the client that although she might have cracked the analytical container in her dream, she needn't worry, because the therapist was able to maintain it in real life. This interpretation captured the interest of the patient, who continued in therapy to discuss the issue.

Clients' Dreams and the Therapist: Transference Issues

Jung saw the dream world as connected to the day world; since our conscious processes are greatly influenced by subjective factors (selective inattention, for instance), the unconscious helps to integrate such information from the "real" world. Both the conscious ("real") and unconscious (dream) material can be read symbolically and metaphorically.

The aspects of clients' dreams that reflect and distort the "real" world can throw light on corresponding features of their psyche. On the other hand, countertransference problems may be revealed if several clients' dreams comment consistently on a therapist's actions or personality. For example, if several of your clients report dreams in which you are dressed in armor or corsets, you might want to unbutton your therapeutic style a bit.

Recently, philosophically inclined therapists are disputing the existence of any world more objective and real for the therapist than for the client, saying that all worlds are creations of the observer. In this relative view, reality is defined as what we can agree to be "true." But even if we refrain from making judgments about the closeness of dreams to a hypothetical objective psychic reality, attending to messages from clients' dreams can provide a measure of consensus about our perception of shared events.

Practical Considerations in Dream Analysis

We have reviewed some reasons given by many Jungians for paying close attention to dreams. Now, assuming that you want to try using dreams in clinical work, where can you start? The first step is to obtain dream material to work with.

RECORDING THE DREAM: THE DREAM LOG. The client who comes voluntarily to a Jungian therapist is already likely to expect talk about dreams. If no dreams are reported after a few sessions, some therapists will ask clients if they remember any, and will encourage them to write them down.

Therapists differ in their suggestions for keeping dream records, but typically they will ask a client to keep a dream log and to record both the dream and any associations to it that the client may have.

Simple instructions for keeping a dream log may be phrased as follows:

Since dreams are forgotten very quickly, it will be most effective for you to keep a small notebook and a pen or pencil next to your bed, near a lamp or flashlight. When you first wake up, take a moment to jot down the following information:

1. Date; 2. Time of dream; 3. A brief narrative of events; 4. A list of the main characters (Do any remind you of someone? Who? How?); 5. Setting; 6. Over-all emotional tone; and 7. Any other important aspects of the dream that occur to you. (Harris, 1988)

Some therapists request a copy of the dream log, while others merely listen to the dream report and may or may not take notes during or after the appointment.

If unconscious processes interest you, keeping your own dream journal can be informative, especially if you discuss your dreams with a qualified Jungian therapist. Perhaps the psyche "appreciates" the attention a dream log provides and may be extra helpful as a result. Even without that, reading through dreams from earlier years can reveal developments in your psyche of which you were not previously aware.

Not all therapists are typologically suited to work with dreams; some possess the needed qualities and some do not. In the last chapter you saw Sandner's suggestion that therapists who have intuition as their top personality function will be most interested in dreams. Also, you saw in Samuels's grid of Jungian schools that archetypal or classical Jungians are more likely to concentrate on archetypal and symbolic imagery than are therapists of a developmental bent. If you have the needed personality features to any degree, you can develop them further through training and practice.

DREAM INTERPRETATION: SOME GENERAL POINTS. Dream images are usually multileveled and carry personal as well as archetypal meanings. For instance, if I dream about a maple tree, it might represent the tree in my back yard, the tree of life in the Garden of Eden, ecological issues, or a shelter from unfriendly elements. It can mean all of these and more at the same time and will carry different connotations for me than it does for my therapist.

To evoke meanings from a dream, you need to *circumambulate* it. This means that you will (symbolically) walk all around it, looking at it from all sides, and will not simply translate it in a flat or linear way. You can also use the circumambulation to determine which aspects of a dream carry the most feeling for the dreamer—and follow up those clues. Details add meaning; if your questioning revealed that I dreamed of a *red* maple, new connotations could emerge.

Once the dreamer's information has been obtained, you may choose to make an interpretation of the dream. These interpretations can be offhand or more carefully introduced. In any case, several considerations are important.

The interpretation is only a *hypothesis*, not a statement of "truth." It should always be *brief*—a sentence or two, not a verbal essay. It should translate the dream language in terms related closely to the information at hand, and in language understood by the dreamer. The dreamer may make modifications or corrections to the interpretation. Ideally, as a dream interpreter you will discuss or accept any client's objections to an interpretation, and not see them simply as evidence of "resistance."

Finally, no interpretation is correct until it is accepted by the client! Verify it. This does not mean accepting a dreamer's sullen acquiescence, or passive acknowledgment. If an interpretation hits pay dirt, usually the dreamer will appear struck by it in some way, and often will immediately provide further instances confirming it.

For example, if your query about the enormous gateway and the recent promotion (above) hit a nerve, the dreamer might reply enthusiastically, "Oh, yes! That gate looked just like the door to the big conference room!" If you are off base, the response might be more like, "Uh, I guess so, but it didn't look like anything *I* ever saw . . ."

Interpretation is not always necessary. Sometimes the dream can be received in silence and "reverberate into the unknowable depths of the psyche" (Whitmont & Perera, 1989, p. 9). What you do with a dream always depends on the particular circumstances—and whether the reaction to an interpretation proves it to be a stroke of genius or a big mistake, your best internal stance is, "It seemed like a good idea at the time."

INTERPRETIVE MODALITY AND TYPOLOGICAL DIFFERENCES. When working with dreams, both you and your client need to be able to vary perspectives among "affective, body, mythological, allegoric, symbolic, and rational awareness," and you must "shift from one situationally relevant typological function to another" (Whitmont & Perera, 1989, p. 3). In other words, whatever your own personality type, it helps to temporarily "rotate" your personality to empathize with your current client's type, whether it be thinking, feeling, intuition, or sensation.

In addition, Sandner (1994) says that introverts' dreams are easier to interpret than extraverts' dreams: Images come from the introverts' inner life, so their references are clear. Extraverts dream about real people, so it's hard for you to know what they stand for (symbolize).

Context is necessary to build the understanding needed for therapy with dreams; context has multiple levels. For the purposes of some kinds of dream research, one can *abstract* from context—do some naming, counting, or comparing of themes between dreamers or dream series. To survive the abstracting process and still show meaningful differences, these aspects need to be robust and unsubtle.

In the intricacies of therapy, as contrasted to research, you should develop detailed context for each dream; you explore with the dreamer the material in which the dream is embedded. For instance, you will want to find out more about the persons in your extraverted clients' dreams. Context can be developed by *personal associations,* by *archetypal amplification* of the dream images, or by considering *environmental events* relevant to the image.

PERSONAL INTERPRETATION OF DREAMS. The *structure* of a dream is important. It includes the setting of the dream, the initial situation, and the characters. You should pay attention to plot development; favorable or unfavorable change reflects the feeling of the dreamer about the material. Finally, the presence or absence of a resolution to the action is significant. From these factors, the degree of complexity and apparent level of the dreamer's ego development can be derived.

The dream images can be considered in both their *objective and subjective aspects.* How do they relate to actual persons or events? On the other hand, how do they represent elements of the dreamer's own attributes?

Is this dream serving a *compensatory function* relative to the dreamer's conscious attitudes? Does it relate to a known problem or complex? Would it be more useful to address *reductive or constructive* aspects of the dream, relative to the dreamer's psychic development? In other words, does it relate more to the dreamer's childhood and its complexes, or to significant current problems of living? The dream can compensate by *opposing, modifying,* or *confirming* the relevant conscious position (see Mattoon, 1984, pp. 48–49).

ARCHETYPAL AMPLIFICATION OF DREAMS. After the personal associations have been completed, you can explore *archetypal parallels* to the dream. This requires an introverted attitude (Beebe, 1993c) and will be easier or harder to do, depending on your personality type—and that of the client. It is often possible to start with other aspects and work around to the archetypal in the course of circumambulation.

You may want to consider myths or fairy tales evoked by the dream events. Is there a symbolic element in the dream, such as a dragon, helpful animal, or strangely transformed object? What significance does the dreamer assign to this image? Sometimes you may choose to amplify an archetypal association, story, or attribute of an image, just as for images and events derived from other sources.

DREAM SERIES. A single dream provides minimum context and illuminates the dreamer's psyche less than does a series of dreams. A long series enables you to identify frequent themes, characters, and symbols, and to track shifts in the dreamer's attitude or mood. Archetypal images most frequently occur in long series of several hundred dreams.

DREAM GROUPS. Dream work is sometimes done by itself in a quasi-therapeutic modality. Such dream work can be done one on one or in a group. Dream groups have become popular recently, and even appear on "online" computer networks. Members of such groups (on- or off-line) take turns reporting a dream, and the other members give their reactions and associations. As the group continues, the series of dreams builds up context for each dreamer, making later dreams more easily understood relative to preceding ones.

These groups may or may not have a trained, professional group leader. If you join a dream group, or decide to lead one, be sure the leader, whether yourself or another, knows enough about the process to stay out of trouble. It never hurts to arrange regular consultation with an expert when you try a new therapy modality.

Consult Whitmont and Perera (1989) for an excellent, detailed treatment of the use of dreams in Jungian therapy, well beyond the scope of this introductory text.

Active Imagination and Dreams

Active imagination is a process closely related to dreaming and to sandplay. James Hall (1986, p. 105) has provided a clear definition: "Active imagination is a technique devised by Jung for direct interaction with the unconscious through a controlled imaginal state while one is awake. It is a form of meditation that in some ways resembles self-hypnosis." Barbara Hannah's classic book, *Encounters with the Soul: Active Imagination as Developed by C. G. Jung* (1981), provides both theory and a series of case studies.

HISTORY AND GUIDELINES OF ACTIVE IMAGINATION. Jung stumbled across the process of active imagination while recovering from his break with Freud. His ensuing "visions" matured into active imagination as we know it. As Hall (1986, p. 80) succinctly puts it, "Early in life, [Jung] had active imagination conversations with his personified anima in order to get in touch with his inferior feeling."

Jung carefully distinguishes between a state in which "you dream with open eyes" (CW 14, para. 706) and true active imagination, in which you make the "transition from a merely perceptive, i.e. *aesthetic* attitude to one of judgment" (CW 14, para. 754; Jung's italics). (He similarly refused the aesthetic view of his paintings as "art.") He advocated a careful record of the events of active imagination through written notes and pictures, in order to anchor them in consciousness (CW 14, para. 706, para. 754).

Hall (1986, pp. 105–106) gives two fundamental rules and a corollary that distinguish active imagination from fantasy and daydreaming:

> 1. The attitude of the ego (the "imaginal-ego") in active imagination must be the same as if the imagined situation were a real one. That is, the moral, ethical, and personal rules that apply to a situation in waking life must be followed in the imaginal sequence as well. This prevents the psyche from splitting and elaborating fantasy images that "don't count" because they do not come into contact with the complexes that are troublesome to the waking-ego.
>
> 2. When situations or persons *other than the imaginal-ego* react to the ego in active imagination, they must be permitted to react *with no active interference whatsoever from the ego.* This seemingly easy rule is very hard to follow, for it is tempting in active imagination to "fix" a difficult situation as one would in fantasy.
>
> 3. The rule is that *you should not do active imagination involving real people.* There are two reasons. . . . The practical reason is that . . . it may give only a symbolic solution to the problems with that person, while short-circuiting interaction with the real person and inhibiting an actual solution in the everyday world.
>
> Doing active imagination involving a real person can also be seen as [an] attempt to change a person through interaction with an image of that person.

Not everyone appreciates the distinction between active imagination and daydreaming. Kerr (1993) consigns active imagination to a dust heap he calls "reverie," saying of Jung that "reverie constituted a temptation for this particular man beyond what it poses for most people" (p. 330). He is equally dismissive about Jung's discovery of the personified Anima mentioned by Hall: "Jung continued to be intermittently troubled by depersonalization episodes and frank hallucinations. . . . It was while he was engaged in [writing down his experiences] that he first encountered the 'anima' archetype" (p. 503). Kerr goes on to connect the origins of this anima to Sabina Spielrein, whom we discuss further in Chapter 11, but nowhere does he acknowledge any positive result from Jung's encounter with and elucidation of the anima concept.

You may agree either with Hall and Jung or with academic rationalists like Kerr (1993) and Noll (1993) on the value of the archetypes of active imagination and their domicile, the collective unconscious. This is probably a good litmus test of whether you would be comfortable as a classical or archetypal Jungian therapist; Jungians of the developmental school might be less affected.

ACTIVE IMAGINATION VERSUS HYPNOSIS OR GUIDED IMAGERY. Active imagination is usually initiated by the client, perhaps at the suggestion of the therapist, near the end of an analysis. By using active imagination, a client can consult his or her own versions of significant archetypal figures for help in carrying out further developmental tasks in the absence of a therapist. Sometimes a therapist may introduce the technique to a client by using guided imagery in the office.

Hall (1986, p. 116) makes the point that under hypnosis, in contrast to active imagination, "the suggestions of the therapist come from outside the patient's own mind." Guided imagery is close to hypnosis; you invite the client to relax, perhaps through muscle-relaxation exercises, and then suggest going in imagination to a safe environment, or following a suggested scenario.

A client can learn to do active imagination alone, without any more suggestion from a therapist than perhaps "I wonder whether, if you spoke directly to that dream figure, it might give you further clues to . . ." whatever the situation might be. The actual process could occur on the spot, or later at the client's home.

Once you have sufficient Jungian training, and have dealt adequately with Shadow aspects of the work, you may want some clients to learn active imagination independent of your suggestions and presence. This can develop their capacity to do active imagination outside of or after therapy. Once they have learned the process, they can use active imagination for the rest of their life.

The symbolic activities of dreaming, active imagination, and the modalities described in the next sections all speak a language with its own illogical rules. Like the Greek messenger Hermes, they lead us down to the world of shadows and the cool light of lunar consciousness.

Symbolic Approaches

Not all therapy is "talking" therapy. In your own mundane crises, you know that a kind look, a roll of the eyes, or a hug may do better than any verbal response. Therapists must restrain some of their similar reactions, but nonverbal messages are important in the consulting room, too.

Some Jungians concentrate on mostly nonverbal activities for therapeutic intervention. These techniques include art, dance and play therapy, and—best known to Jungian therapists—Sandplay.

Sandplay

A projective technique called *Sandplay* was developed in the 1950s by a Swiss Jungian therapist named Dora Kalff. It originated as a therapy for children, but has proved useful with clients of all ages.

THE PRACTICE OF SANDPLAY. In Sandplay the client (adult or child) creates a three-dimensional scene by arranging miniature figures in a tray approximately 30 × 20 × 3 inches in size, half filled with wet or dry sand. The arrangement and use of the miniatures create a symbolism of relationship in addition to the individual connotations of the figures.

JUNG AND SANDPLAY. In 1913, after his painful and disorienting break with Freud, Jung himself utilized a self-healing technique reminiscent of Sandplay. He felt compelled to build a miniature stone town on the shores of Lake Zurich. At the end of this activity he felt that he was finally on the way to discovering his own myth, and the flowering of his subsequent work reflected that introverted experience (Jung, 1961a, pp. 174–175).

JUNGIAN SANDPLAY THEORY. The central tenet of the Jungian view of Sandplay therapy is that like dreams, art, or active imagination, sandtrays allow a client to produce pictures of situations that have been less than consciously experienced. In this virtually nonverbal process, earlier and deeper preverbal issues may find expression.

Sandplay with children is often confused with non-Jungian play therapy. In schools, clinics, or private practice, therapists of a non-Jungian bent who own sandtray equipment encourage child patients to use the materials as just another kind of sandbox or dollhouse. This can be quite effective play therapy, but it is not classic Sandplay therapy.

For further particulars of Jungian theory relevant to the Sandplay process, see Ammann (1991), Bradway et al. (1990), Kalff (1981), Ryce-Menuhin (1993), Weinrib (1983), and the *Journal of Sandplay Therapy*.

Art Therapy and Dance Therapy

These procedures do not seem to be as publicized in Jungian therapy as Sandplay, but they are used with both children and adults. Art therapy is especially suited for schools and clinics, as it requires only some paper and colors, and can be done in a limited space.

ART THERAPY. Symbols expressed on paper or in clay express meaning much the same way as do dreams, or Sandplay, or active imagination. The symbolic products may be spontaneously generated by the client, or can be suggested by the therapist, as is done in various diagnostic projective drawing techniques.

Jungian therapists are likely to refrain from suggesting subjects for art, and will explore an artifact's wider meaning with the client, rather than offer interpretations or make diagnostic inferences.

Art therapy is a field to itself, and I will not venture more deeply into it here. There are several good books on the subject. John Allan (1988) has written about Jungian art therapy with children, and Elinor Ulman and Penny Dachinger (1975) edited a classic collection of papers on art therapy.

DANCE THERAPY. Movement and dance therapy are body-centered ways of expressing symbolism. Generally speaking, a movement therapist, like a Sandplay therapist, will silently witness the client's self-generated patterns and modalities of movement. Perhaps the therapist will suggest further exploration of a certain posture or sequence in order to free up less conscious images or memories. Some therapists may even "position" the patient; these "suggestions" are like the suggestions of guided imagery, but they are carried out by the body rather than in the mind. Joan Chodorow (1991) discusses a Jungian approach to movement therapy.

Interrelationships of Symbolic Modalities

Jung (1961, pp. 161–162) called dreams a natural and necessary expression of the life force:

> To me, dreams are a part of nature, which harbors no intention to deceive, but expresses something as best it can, just as a plant grows or an animal seeks its food as best it can. . . . Long before I met Freud I regarded the unconscious, and dreams, which are its direct exponents, as natural processes to which no arbitrariness can be attributed, and above all no legerdemain.

Jung also said that dreams synthesize past and present, personal and collective experiences. Thus they reflect matters outside time and space as we normally experience them.

Some aspects of the Sandplay process are like reflections on dreams, but they are not identical processes. On the one hand, Sandplay is limited by its structure: The actual arrangement of sandtray scenes occurs in "real time," and the symbols involved are objects offered by the therapist's collection.

On the other hand, during the creation of a sandtray, although therapists have no access to the client's thoughts, they are present and observing the client, who is usually operating in a mildly altered state of consciousness, or "waking dream." Therapists observe the assembly process and the final gestalt of the objects in the tray. These aspects of the tray require neither remembering, nor translation into the grammar of spoken language, and so their expression is more complete and evocative than are the writing down and telling of a dream.

Sandplay writers such as Kay Bradway (1985) often mention "bridging" the gap between conscious and unconscious. The process of creating a sand scene may itself lie somewhere between dreaming and waking, like active imagination.

The techniques of therapy covered in this chapter all center around the importance of symbols. Their goal is to bring conscious and unconscious processes into better harmony, and symbols provide bridges between the two. Unraveling some of the meaning of the symbols with the client may result in practical changes in "real life," but the creation of pragmatic results is not the primary intent. Symbols provide a way for clients to express feelings and situations inexpressible in words.

Symbols are central to most Jungian therapy. As we saw earlier, if you have an intuitive personality configuration you are likely to emphasize symbolic material in verbal therapy; if you are a sensation type, perhaps Sandplay, art, or dance therapy would be more appealing.

There is room for wide variation within Jungian approaches, but it should be obvious by now that to be an effective Jungian therapist, you must at least be aware of the presence of symbolic material in therapeutic exchanges—and it's even better if you enjoy playing with the symbols.

READINGS

Allen, J. (1988). *Inscapes of the child's world: Jungian counseling in schools and clinics.* Dallas, TX: Spring Publications.

Ammann, R. (1991). *Healing and transformation in Sandplay: Creative processes become visible.* La Salle, IL: Open Court.

Bradway, K., Signell, K. A., Spare, G. S., Stewart, C. S., Stewart, L. H., & Thompson, C. (1990). *Sandplay studies: Origins, theory, and practice.* Boston: Sigo Press.

Chodorow, J. (1991). *Dance therapy and depth psychology: The moving imagination.* London: Routledge.

Kalff, D. M. (1981). *Sandplay: A psychotherapeutic approach to the psyche* (2nd ed.). Boston: Sigo Press.

Ulman, E., & Dachinger, P. (Eds.). (1975). *Art therapy in theory and practice.* New York: Schocken Books.

Weinrib, E. (1983). *Images of the self: The Sandplay therapy process.* Boston: Sigo Press.

Whitmont, E. C., & Perera, S. B. (1989). *Dreams: A portal to the source.* New York: Routledge.

FIVE

Current Issues
in Jungian Psychology

CHAPTER 10

Jung, the Transpersonal, Religion, and Science

THE SCIENTIST'S NIGHTMARE

The astrophysicist Robert Jastrow, in his book *God and the Astronomers*, described . . . the scientist's nightmare: "He has scaled the mountains of ignorance; he is about to conquer the highest peak; as he pulls himself over the final rock, he is greeted by a band of theologians who have been sitting there for centuries." (Smoot & Davidson, 1993, p. 291)

This nightmare seems more and more likely to come true, especially if Jungian psychologists are included among the band sitting at the top.

Most psychologists in the United States have been trained in an objectivist tradition, which emphasizes laboratory or field measurements of observable behavior. Many social workers and family/child therapists have undergone similar training. Irwin Z. Hoffman (1992, p. 289) defines this as a model in which the therapist

applies what he or she knows on the basis of theory, research, and previous clinical experience in a systematic way to achieve certain immediate and long-term results. The approach is implicitly diagnostic and prescriptive. Based on an assessment of the nature of the patient's psychological disturbance or immediate state of mind, the [therapist] implements a prescribed approach or specific intervention within one or another theoretical framework.

This tradition rejects introspection as a source of knowledge, and even more strongly rejects, as being outside the realm of science, any speculations about the great unanswerable questions of our lives. Besides being diagnostic and prescriptive, traditional scientific psychology has been reductionist; it has imitated the physical sciences by seeking to break complex issues into ever smaller, testable components.

Meanwhile, in the last few decades, puzzling results from experiments on particles, waves, and quanta (always a source of confusion to tidy minds) have forced some physical scientists to abandon their traditional reductionism. These changes support Jung's theories. Some of those results will be outlined below. As you proceed through this chapter, you should gradually understand more about what science, religion, and analytical psychology might have in common.

Jungian Therapy and Religion

Noll (1994) claims that Jung consciously founded a charismatic religious movement. This apparently bizarre interpretation of Jung's interest in the transpersonal is less unusual than we might expect. In this section we look at some possible reasons for such assertions.

The Transpersonal and Jung's Fantasy Activities: Beyond Objectivity

As a young man, Jung rebelled against codified religion. He saw that it had lost its meaning for his father, the Protestant minister. His interest in the spiritualism of his mother's family led first to séances with his cousin Helene Preiswerk, and eventually to his doctoral dissertation on the "so-called occult phenomena" of hypnosis and multiple personality (see Chapter 2). In later years Jung's interest in matters beyond the individual ego deepened and diversified.

Following the break with Freud, Jung engaged in vigorous fantasy both by building a miniature village on the shore at Bollingen and by engaging in dialogues of active imagination with visionary images that originated in what he called archetypes of the collective unconscious. The forms taken by his images were apparently influenced by his study of the symbolism of the Mithraic religion, and included a rather negative view of the feminine principle, which appeared to Jung in the guise of Salome (Noll, 1992). It is perhaps our good fortune that psychotropic medication to suppress such phenomena had not yet been invented, so that Jung was forced either to go mad or to enter into a dialogue with his visions.

Objectivist psychologist John Kerr (1993) insists that the resulting concepts are suspect products of near-psychotic, introspective "reverie." Noll (1992, 1994) accuses Jung of suffering from a psychotic paranoid inflation expressed through identification with the god Mithras and through a desire to found his own religious cult. More reasonably, physicist F. David Peat (1987, p. 14) asks:

> What exactly happened to Carl Jung during this period of breakdown? To say that he was mad explains nothing, for . . . his voyage into the unconscious . . . was by no means chaotic but exhibited its own interior order . . . so that the psychologist was able to return to the surface of "normal sanity" bringing profound insights and discoveries that formed the basis for all his later work.

Luckily Jung's ego proved strong enough to contain and harness the irruptions of his unconscious. He was able to organize its messages into an extremely innovative and useful collection of psychological insights.

Jung and Traditional Religions

Jung's interest in religion was eclectic. J. J. Clarke (1992, p. 55) says that Jung saw even the most diverse religions "as so many different manifestations of underlying unconscious impulses that were common to mankind and pointed to their underlying unity." Jung's early interest in Mithraism—a mystery cult that flourished in the late Roman Empire—later gave way to his use of Gnostic and alchemical metaphors.

The late Joseph Campbell (1976, 1988) brought comparative religion to a wide audience through his books and public lectures lavishly illustrated by slides of conceptually parallel religious artifacts widely scattered in space and time. His books and films provide a vivid visual experience of the sources of Jung's ideas.

THE SELF, RELIGION, AND SPIRIT. A number of analysts have written about the relationship between analytical psychology and spirituality (see Jaffe, 1990; Whitmont, 1969). These authors say that Jung's concept of the Self corresponds to a Godhead of some sort. They agree that the specific doctrine of a codified religion is less important than the assumption that a purposive Power guides the universe. Jung's own writings support this view; for example:

> Far from being a negation, God is actually the strongest and most effective "position" the psyche can reach. . . . The strongest and therefore the decisive factor in any individual psyche compels the same belief or fear,

submission, or devotion which a God would demand from man. Anything despotic and inescapable is in this sense "God," and it becomes absolute unless, by an ethical decision freely chosen, one succeeds in building up against this natural phenomenon a position that is equally strong and invincible. . . . Man is free to decide whether "God" shall be a "spirit" or a natural phenomenon like the craving of a morphine addict, and hence whether "God" shall act as a beneficent or a destructive force. . . . It is merely incumbent on us to *choose* the master we wish to serve, so that his service shall be our safeguard against being mastered by the "other" whom we have not chosen. We do not *create* God, we *choose* him. (CW 11, para. 142–143)

Here as always Jung emphasizes individual choice over passive conformity to an undifferentiated collective influence, even when it is defined as the Self or "God."

Other writers like June Singer (1991) prefer to conceptualize the Self in terms of "spirit" rather than "God." Either term refers to what Jung once called the "mycelium" underlying the individual mushrooms of personal identity.

A familiar Buddhist and also Gnostic analogy describes each life as a point of light derived from the omnipresent light of the universe. The schematic diagram given in Figure 5.1 shows another approach. The fundamental assumption common to all is the *reality of the psyche*—the concept that the individual ego emerges from a pervasive and compelling enigma.

JUNG AND THE GNOSTIC TRADITION. Singer (1991) has detailed correspondences between Jung's thought and Gnosticism. She tells us that Jung

first used the word *transpersonal* in connection with psychology when he spoke of the collective or "transpersonal" unconscious in 1917. The transpersonal perspective is a view of people and their relations to the larger world that is compatible with the new world view that sees the universe and everything in it, including human beings, as a series of interconnecting, interacting, and mutually influencing systems.

Transpersonal psychology approaches human beings in the context of the wider world, including the invisible world of spirit. . . . In the transpersonal view, the only way the spiritual world can manifest is through ordinary people in the visible world. (pp. 142–143)

Jung's theory did borrow a great deal from the Gnostic tradition. This is documented by Robert A. Segal in *The Gnostic Jung* (1992) and summarized in a review of the book and in Michael Howard's (1994, pp. 47–65) interview with Segal in the *San Francisco Jung Institute Library Journal*. Gilles Quispel (1994, p. 48), the reviewer of Segal's book, defines Gnosticism as follows:

> Gnosticism is the third component of Western civilization. It originated in Alexandria just before the Common Era, and in its Hermetic, Jewish, and Christian ramifications it profoundly influenced our religion and culture. . . . Until this day the churches preach the faith and the philosophers believe in logos, but the Gnostics trust their inner experiences and express them in imaginative symbols.

Jung's psychology departed significantly from Freud's in including transpersonal elements of this kind. After his break with Freud, Jung was free to pursue these interests more intensively. His concepts of the Pleroma and the Creatura were derived from Gnosticism and first appeared in the *Seven Sermons to the Dead* (Jung, 1967c).

The interview with Segal (Howard, 1994) debates whether Jung's interpretation of Gnosticism was entirely accurate. Jung's main departure seems to be that he saw life's goal as a balance between spirit and matter, whereas the Gnostics advocated the total freeing of spirit from matter.

GNOSTICISM AND THE FEMININE DEITY. The two finds of Gnostic books at Nag Hammadi, Egypt, in 1945 and 1975 added greatly to previously sketchy Gnostic religious history. Jung, of course, had not read them. They demonstrate that the Gnostic writers paid much more attention to the idea of feminine deity than we are accustomed to in Western religious traditions (Singer, 1991, pp. 78–102).

Gnostic Roots of the Feminine Principle

Jung's Gnostic, mystical interests make his psychology less male-oriented than Freud's. Originally, the Gnostic religious tradition assigned the patriarchal creator God only the second or third place of influence. First came the unnameable One, who is either both Mother and Father or totally gender-free. From the One emerged a Goddess—known by several names, including Sophia, Psyche, and Eve—in whom the spirit of the One became incarnated, creating the material universe.

In the Gnostic myth, this Goddess was shown going through multiple rebirths and actively mingling with the created world, unlike in the patriarchal, biblical creation. The patriarchal version created a power hierarchy absent in the Goddess creation myth.

Whether or not you believe in a deity, you can examine religious scenarios for their reflection of cultural values. In recent years Jungian authors such as Betty Meador (1992), Jean Shinoda Bolen (1984), and Sylvia Brinton Perera (1981) have examined ancient women's myths and applied them to contemporary psychological systems. They advocate a renewed trust in depths

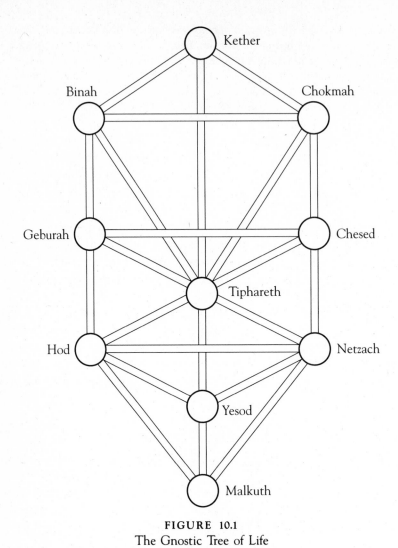

FIGURE 10.1
The Gnostic Tree of Life

traditionally considered "feminine," "regressive," the "watery unconscious," and so on.

The patriarchal God of Judaism, Islam, and Christianity was Sophia's creation, and flawed to boot. This upstart "demiurge" claimed power for himself (read: developing patriarchal culture attributed power to him) and with his ascendancy Sophia, along with the Gnostic "heresy," fell out of favor. Gnosticism went underground and the books were hidden away. Even after their discovery and translation they were only recently made available for general study.

As you may imagine, the Gnostic Gospels are of great interest to feminists, as newly illuminating some ways the role of the feminine in religion has reflected cultural changes.

Grace from Above Down—or Vice Versa?

Jung contrasted alchemy and Christianity, saying, "The alchemical drama leads from below upwards, . . . the Christian drama, on the other hand, represents the descent of the Kingdom of Heaven to earth" (CW 14, para. 124). This parallels the contrast between Jung's acceptance of the Platonic ideal of an ineffable One (the Self) who directs our lives (a descent), and the views of contemporary neuroscientist Gerald Edelman (1992, p. 153), who maintains that brain function evolved from biological processes and that the idea of Platonism itself evolved with it through the process of synthesis.

Interestingly, the alchemists' sequence of stages seems closer to Edelman's view of mental development than does Jung's, although even Edelman must assume the a priori presence of what he terms *qualia* or values, thus letting Plato enter the picture again through an unprovable assumption. Edelman calls this a "poignant paradox" (p. 114).

Jung and the Cabbala

Jung did not neglect Jewish mysticism (see CW 14, *Mysterium Coniunctionis*). He noted the connections among the Cabbala, Christian Gnosticism, and alchemy: "Directly or indirectly the Cabala was assimilated into alchemy" (para. 19).

The Jewish mystic tradition, like the Gnostic gospels, posits a feminine or bisexual Being that precedes the later, masculine God. This most general One (called En Soph) was unknowable. The revealed part of En Soph enters our world as a lightning flash of energy through the Sefirot of the Tree of Life (S. Rubin, personal communication, February 1994). En Soph preceded and produced the universe, called Adam Kadmon, who is both one and many. Jung says, "He [Adam Kadmon] is thus something like a schema of the psychic structure" (para. 594).

The Cabbala features the symbolic Tree of Life (Scholem, 1974, pp. 87–189), which Jung relates to Gnostic and later Christian symbolism in numerous ways. One example: Jung, discussing the Cabbala symbol of the Crown, notes, "In the Cabala the highest Sefira [on the tree] (like the lowest) is called Kether, the Crown. In Christian allegory the crown signifies Christ's humanity" (CW 14, para. 6, Note 32).

The Tree of Life with its individual centers or Sefirot is also a central symbol in the Tarot card system of divination, discussed below.

Jung's Interest in Buddhism, the I Ching, and the Tarot

Jung's wide-ranging curiosity led him to the study of other non-Christian religions. He commented on the Tibetan *Book of the Dead* and related writings and noted correspondences between the Indian *Upanishads* (CW 11, para. 140, p. 82) and the properties of mandalas, circular symbols of wholeness found in Eastern religion.

His interest in synchronicity (see below) attracted him to the Chinese *I Ching*, a religious/prophetic manual for which he wrote a foreword (1967b, pp. xxi–xxxix). In it Jung reported his own use of the *I Ching*:

> The method of the *I Ching* does indeed take into account the hidden individual quality in things and men, and in one's own unconscious self as well. I have questioned the *I Ching* as one questions a person whom one is about to introduce to friends: one asks whether or not it will be agreeable to him. In answer the *I Ching* tells me of its religious significance, of the fact that at present it is unknown and misjudged, of its hope of being restored to a place of honor—this last obviously with a sidelong glance at my as yet unwritten foreword, and above all at the English translation. (pp. xxvii–xxix)

Several authors have written about links among Jungian theory, the Tarot, and astrology. To this day, popular books on the Tarot include pictures of the Cabbalistic Tree of Life (Gray, 1970, p. 204). Jung himself was not closely associated with these phenomena, although he carried out a much-criticized experiment on astrology and synchronicity in 1952 (CW 8, para. 872–915; Samuels et al., pp. 146–147).

Jung's work on synchronicity, which he defined as "an acausal connecting principle," rests on the line between religion and science, and between mind and body.

Synchronicity and Science

> Time present and time past
> Are both perhaps present in time future,
> And time future contained in time past . . .
> What might have been and what has been
> Point to one end, which is always present.[1]

[1]Excerpt from "Burnt Norton" in *Four Quartets*, copyright 1943 by T. S. Eliot and renewed 1971 by Esme Valerie Eliot, reprinted by permission of Harcourt Brace & Company.

Jung's Concept of Synchronicity

Storr (1983, p. 26) tells us that

> throughout his life, Jung had been impressed by clusters of significant events occurring together, and by the fact that these events might be physical as well as mental. The physical death of one individual, for instance, might coincide with a disturbing dream referring to that death in the mind of another.

Jung named that kind of meaningful coincidence *synchronicity*. The events carry meaning and happen near each other in time, but not necessarily in space, and vice versa. It is impossible to say that one "caused" the other, based on experience, or to predict that the association of those events is ever likely to occur again.

Occasionally, and more for some people than others, events seem associated in a noncausal but also nonrandom way. Von Franz (1980) gives many examples of synchronistic occurrences in her book on the subject. She says, "The question is not why has this come about, or what factor caused this effect, but what *likes* to happen in a meaningful way at the same moment? The Chinese always ask: 'What tends to happen together in time?'" (p. 8; emphasis added).

Peat (1987, p. 65) reports that the science/philosophy writer Arthur Koestler also thinks that "certain things like to happen together." For von Franz (1988, pp. 193–194), this "liking" is related to number theory and also to the idea of the *Sapientia Dei* (Wisdom of God), which is "the psychic total interconnectedness of the universe through a spirit of love. This feminine creative spirit of God's love, personified by Fatima, plays a major role in Islamic mysticism. . . . In the Christian world, she was identified with Mary."

Not everyone in Western culture is content to drop the search for nonmystical reasons why things have such an affinity for each other. However, when Peat's scientific mind approaches the problem, his answer is not markedly different from that of a philosopher or mystic: He says that synchronicity is a consequence of the existence of an underlying unity (the Self, or Pleroma, in Jung's terms) where time and space are absent.

J. R. van Eenwyk (1991a, 1991b), June Singer (1991), Louis Zinkin (1987), and F. David Peat (1987), among others, have correlated Jung's writings with recent developments in physics. An overview follows.

ACAUSAL CONNECTIONS. In his writing about synchronicity, Jung anticipated contemporary concepts of a region beyond space and time:

> Synchronicity in space can equally well be perceived as perception in time, but . . . we cannot imagine any space in which future events are objectively present. . . . But since experience has shown that under certain conditions space and time can be reduced almost to zero, causality disappears along with them, because causality is bound up with the existence of space and time and physical changes, and consists essentially of the succession of cause and effect. For this reason synchronistic phenomena . . . must necessarily be thought of as acausal. (*CW* 8, para. 855).

When we seek advice from the *I Ching*, the Tarot, or astrology, we assume the existence of some kind of acausal connections among events, as do practitioners of other forms of religious divination. If I am not religious or "superstitious" but put my finger at random in a text or turn over a card, and am struck by the aptness of that text or symbol for my situation, I can either brush it off as coincidence or tell myself, "That's synchronicity."

This is not a usual mode of thinking. In our normal existence within the realm of space and time, we perceive cause and effect as the link between events: Sometimes I trip over my cat in the kitchen; after a few repetitions I assume that she complains *because* I kicked her.

Causality is not proved by logic, however, but is merely an historical precedent from repeated observations. The 18th-century philosopher David Hume established this for the Western world when he wrote *An Enquiry Concerning Human Understanding* (1777/1965, p. 63), which developed the proposition that "the knowledge of this relation [of cause and effect] is not, in any instance, attained by reasonings a priori; but arises entirely from experience, when we find, that any particular objects are constantly conjoined with each other."

Alfred North Whitehead (1967), another philosopher, concluded that since we can't explain cause and effect, it must not exist: The universe must be an organic system in which objects do not occur in space at particular moments of time. Instead, he saw the cosmos as a unity or a patterned process of events, a functional organism rather than a collection of clockwork parts. Whitehead believed that cause and effect originate in our minds, as we impose our perceptual structures on the universe. Recent developments in the sciences echo the philosophies of Hume and Whitehead.

BEYOND SPACE AND TIME. In this hypothetical region, all events of the past, present, or future coexist: David Bohm (see below) would say that they are enfolded together. In the absence of time, there can be no causality, because no event precedes any other. This, as Whitehead saw, must pacify Hume: We need not try to prove causality, since connected events can only be linked *acausally.* Furthermore, these highly significant but rare pairings of events not linked by repeated association in our everyday experience are connected only by the *meaning* we see in them.

Science, Quantum Theory, and Synchronicity

As science uncovers new insights, Jungian writers translate Jung's theories into current terms, to show how modern science is prefigured in Jungian thought (May & Groder, 1989; van Eenwyk, 1991a, 1991b).

Jung and physicist Wolfgang Pauli worked out a diagram to show how synchronistic meaning balances causality, just as the Pleroma balances our space-time continuum. The concept of synchronicity is not meant to "disprove" or replace causality; one merely complements the other. Peat (1987, p. 37) says that quantum theory creates a place for acausality *beside* the former scientific view of the world as completely predictable and built on cause/effect sequences:

> Quantum theory will not allow the individual event to be pinned down in any exact way. Moreover, the theory asserts that this breakdown in predictability has nothing to do with an ignorance about the fine details of the system, . . . rather it is a fundamental and absolute indeterminism.

Here Peat refers indirectly to *Bohm's law.* This states that some ignorance about an event exists as a matter of principle, rather than there being an irreducible element of chance. Thus Bohm's system is unpredictable but fully determinate (Albert, 1994).

Bohm found a solution to the problem of how to measure subatomic events, and physicist John Stewart Bell used it to prove that reality cannot be local (Herbert, 1988). Bell produced a pair of "twin" photons, then sent them off in different directions. A subsequent event that affected one of them also affected the other. Bell reported that this will occur no matter how distant from each other the particles may be. These "nonlocal influences"

> are not mediated by fields or anything else . . . do not diminish with distance . . . act instantaneously. The speed of their transmission is not limited by the velocity of light. . . . [They link] one location with another without crossing space, without decay, and without delay. A nonlocal interaction is, in short, *unmediated, unmitigated, and immediate.* . . . *Nonlocal connections are ubiquitous because reality itself is nonlocal* (Herbert, 1988, pp. 318–319; Herbert's italics).

Peat (1994) amplifies this explanation, saying that the nonlocal correlation vanishes as soon as you interfere in any way—reality is nonlocal but the field is sensitive to interference. It is unaffected by distance because the field carries information rather than energy; the electron "reads" the form and is guided by it.

Bell's and Bohm's theories assume that waves are physical things like gravitational and magnetic force fields. When faced with two possible paths, a particle will take one path or the other, but its *wave* splits and takes both paths. The part of the wave that has no particle in it is "empty" and undetectable by any measuring instrument.

Bell's theory implies that we must either support the concept of nonlocality or endorse the supposition that there are many parallel worlds or minds, in which all possible outcomes occur (Albert, 1994, p. 67). Physicists writing articles for *Scientific American* on these issues seem to find nonlocality more plausible than parallelism.

These complexities are touched on here to show correspondences between simple physical and complicated human events. In an interview, Bell (1988, p. 304) commented on some Minnesota research on human twins, saying that "in the case of twins separated from birth giving their dogs the same name, telepathy is less implausible than genetic predetermination."

Data like twin reports need extensive substantiation to be convincing, because it makes a difference if we look at large rather than small numbers. In both Bohm's theory and classical quantum mechanics, the effects of indeterminism "are lost when averaged out over the law of large numbers that applies in the everyday world" (Peat, 1987, p. 38). Let's give the last word to poet W. H. Auden (1975, pp. 319–320):

> Lovers of small numbers go benignly potty
> Believe all tales are thirteen chapters long,
> Have animal doubles, carry pentagrams,
> Are Millerites, Baconians, Flat-Earth-Men.

> Lovers of big numbers go horridly mad,
> Would have the Swiss abolished, all of us
> Well purged, somatotyped, baptised, taught baseball:
> They empty bars, spoil parties, run for Congress.[2]

It's a stand-off.

[2]From *Collection Poems* by W. H. Auden. Copyright © 1951 by W. H. Auden. Reprinted by permission of Random House, Inc.

Jungian Psychology and the New Science

In the previous section we saw how Jung's concept of synchronicity anticipated current developments in science. This section examines the relationship of other elements of Jung's theory to chaos theory, holograms, and the evolutionary development of living systems, bringing us around to another view of synchronicity.

Chaos Theory and Fractals

Physics can predict the interactions of complex elements well enough to send a rocket to Venus. What it cannot do is predict tomorrow's weather. Here large numbers are at the mercy of small numbers.

The topics of chaos theory and fractals are related through the discipline of nonlinear dynamics, in which a few simple processes interact to create totally unforeseeable outcomes. Nonlinear dynamics is another unpredictable but determinate process like Bohm's law, discussed earlier.

The Butterfly Effect

The modern study of chaos began with the creeping realization in the 1960s that a simple mathematical equation could model systems every bit as complex and turbulent as, say, a waterfall. Tiny differences in input quickly became overwhelming differences in output—a phenomenon given the name *sensitive dependence on initial conditions* (SDIC). In weather, for example, this translates into what is only half-jokingly known as the *butterfly effect*—the notion that a butterfly stirring the air today in Beijing can transform storm systems next month in New York (Gleick, 1987, p. 8).

A meteorologist named Edward Lorenz made this discovery by accident in 1961. Intending to duplicate a computer run of a weather pattern, he punched in numbers from his previous experiment to three decimal places. Astoundingly, by the time he returned from getting a cup of coffee the second run had diverged enormously from the first. After much checking of his equipment to make sure it wasn't broken, Lorenz realized that rounding the first figures from six to three decimal places (a difference of only one part in a thousand) had produced a butterfly effect in his cyber-weather system: A tiny initial difference had become magnified over time (Gleick, 1987, p. 16).

Lorenz went on to demonstrate the sensitive dependence on initial conditions in such diverse areas as convection effects in heated fluids, and the simple device of a waterwheel with leaky buckets that any of us could build.

He developed equations to describe these effects, which became known as the *Lorenz attractor*. When diagrammed, it resembles an owl's mask or butterfly's wings (Figure 10.1). More specifically, the attractor diagram shows

> the fine structure hidden within a disorderly stream of data. . . . Because the system never exactly repeats itself, the trajectory never intersects itself. Instead it loops around and around forever. Motion on the attractor is abstract, but it conveys the flavor of the motion of the real system. For example, the crossover from one wing of the attractor to the other corresponds to a reversal in the direction of spin of the waterwheel or convecting fluid. (Gleick, 1987, p. 29)

Gleick's 1987 book recapitulates the development of chaos theory and describes some of the other attractors developed by subsequent investigators. If you would like to explore these topics further, you'll find the book thought-provoking.

ARCHETYPES AS ATTRACTORS. Van Eenwyk (1991a, 1991b) wrote two articles summarizing his interpretation of the possible application of chaos theory to Jungian theory. He concludes that the Self can be viewed through the metaphor of a *strange attractor*. Attractors may be static (fixed) or dynamic (constantly changing) and may have many dimensions. All chaotic attractors are nonlinear:

> The term "attractor" is used in mathematics and physics to specify the pattern into which a particular motion will settle. For example, a pendulum that is subject to friction will eventually stop swinging. The point directly underneath the pendulum when it stops is called a single-point attractor, as it appears to attract the motion of the pendulum during each successive swing, bringing it to a state of rest over that point. . . . There are other kinds of attractors. (Van Eenwyk, 1991b, pp. 6–7)

Strange attractors describe the pattern into which the graphs of chaotic events will fall. They are "strange" because they: "never retrace the same path twice, even though they do achieve patterns that are recognisable. . . . Unlike regular attractors, which settle into repetitive cycles of limited size, strange attractors contain 'isolated orbits . . . [that display] no orbital stability'" (p. 7).

Lorenz's attractor, shown in Figure 10.2, is an example of a strange attractor. Although it appears on the page in only two dimensions, even this relatively crude diagram shows both the recognizable pattern and the path that never repeats itself.

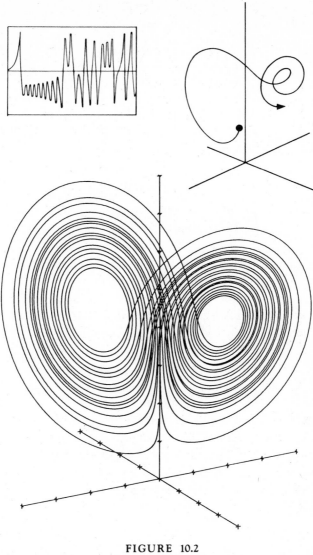

FIGURE 10.2
Lorenz Attractor[3]

FRACTALS. Fractal patterns result from the action of attractors in both animate and inanimate nature. Like attractors, fractals are an aspect of nonlinear dynamics. Scientists have not yet fully established the connections between the mathematics of fractals and nonlinear dynamics. But I was

[3]From *Chaos: Making a New Science*, by James Gleick, 1987, p. 28. Penguin USA. Reprinted by permission of the William Morris Agency on behalf of James Gleick.

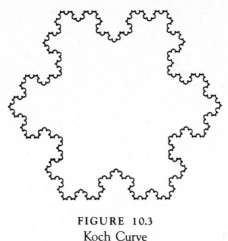

FIGURE 10.3
Koch Curve

fascinated to see that both the minute pattern of a fern leaf and the enormous patterns of the geography of coastlines or mountains can be duplicated from the mathematics of fractals. The *Koch curve* shown in Figure 10.3 is a simple example of a fractal line with a finite boundary but infinite length.

You can produce fractals on your home computer if you have the right formula (see Lauwerier, 1991). Many of the wilder bits of scenery in sci-fi movies are fractals generated by the special effects department. Nature works in a similar way: "Fractal structures are often the remnants of chaotic non-linear dynamics. Whenever a chaotic process has shaped an environment (the seashore, the atmosphere, a geologic fault) fractals are likely to be left behind (coastlines, clouds, rock formations)" (Goldberger, Rigney, & West, 1990, p. 44).

Many organ systems, including coronary arteries and veins, connective tissue, cardiac muscle, and the His-Purkinje cardiac nerve system, appear to have developed by a fractal process. These systems arise from the "slow dynamics of embryonic development and evolution," as Goldberger et al. (1990, p. 46) point out. The fractal organization creates a pattern of diversity, allowing the organism to survive unexpected events. Chaotic effects are evident in electrical patterns generated by the heart and brain and in the "apparently chaotic fluctuations" of hormone levels in healthy human subjects (p. 49).

Research is showing that chaos in bodily functioning signals health, whereas more regular, periodic behavior can foreshadow disease (p. 44). Less-healthy organisms show a loss of variability and increasingly periodic behavior. These effects have been detected in epilepsy, Parkinsonianism, and manic depression, as well as in heart disease (p. 49). Most recently, researchers are beginning to "drive" body systems back to healthy chaotic functioning by introducing weakly chaotic signals that interrupt the pathological regularity.

GENETIC AND NEUROLOGICAL SUPPORT FOR JUNG'S VIEWS. Jung has been much criticized for his "Lamarckian" supposition that thousands of years of experience had impressed archetypes on our brains. Nowadays even such a staunch reductionist as Francis Crick (1994, p. 10)—(the DNA Nobel laureate)—speaks of the effects of experience on our genes and neurology: "The genes we received from our parents have, over many millions of years, been influenced by the experience of our distant ancestors." He adds that "the *details* of the neuron's connections . . . are greatly influenced by its experience" (p. 236; Crick's italics).

Other investigators have described the process by which experience influences neural connections. Peat (1987, p. 178), reporting the findings of neurologist Eric Kandel, says:

> Information about the environment has an active effect upon the material processes of the animal's nervous system and in a sense creates its "brain" afresh. In turn this new "brain" will gather fresh information about its environment and build a revised image of its environment.
>
> Therefore, during each moment of the day the brain is structurally unfolding from a background of active information which is present both in its own structure and in the external environment. In turn, the eternally fresh brain acts upon the environment to change it and to create a new "reality." This reality will, of course, act back upon the brain through a constant process of formation and information.

Research has begun to bridge the gap between Kandel's early sea slugs, mammals, and human beings (Kandel & Hawkins, 1992; Dudai, 1989). A recent article (LeDoux, 1994, p. 36) mentions these effects in relation to memory:

> Norman N. Weinberger and his colleagues at the University of California at Irvine have performed elegant studies showing that neurons in the auditory cortex undergo specific physiological changes in their reaction to sounds as a result of conditioning. This finding indicates that the cortex is establishing its own record of the event.

How do all these developments relate to Jungian psychology?

These effects seem to provide the very link between learning and evolution needed to justify Jung's theory of the acquisition of archetypes. The surprise here is that the brain restructures itself over both the short and the long term. Psychologists had previously heard a good deal about how brain chemistry restructures *perceptions* about the world (see Eccles, 1989)—but only recently about changes in actual physical structure in response to stimuli.

THE USEFULNESS OF THESE PARALLELS. We have seen how both nonlinear dynamics and biological research seem to reinforce Jung's intuitions about the relationship between archetypes and our biological dispositions of thought. Perhaps we could summarize the chaos analogy by saying that the "slow dynamics" of evolution, through iteration or reverberation of events over time, appear to produce ordered wholeness by way of a teleological process of growth. In any case, we can see why it is often useful to tolerate disorder long enough to allow its underlying pattern to become apparent. For therapists, this means not being too quick to medicate, and not taking premature shelter in simple approaches to complex psychological problems. Jung believed this on an intuitive basis; science seems to support his intuition.

Having polished off attractors and fractals, let us now take up a different metaphor: the hologram.

Holograms

Chapter 5 touched on the possibility that our human psyches may be seen as symbolic holograms of the Self. This section elaborates some details of that analogy.

Proponents of the holographic paradigm include neurobiologist Karl Pribram (1971), physicists David Bohm (1980) and Robert Sperry (1983), and Jungian analyst Louis Zinkin (1987). Zinkin has given an especially clear definition of what a hologram is, and of its usefulness as a Jungian metaphor. He reports that the hologram was invented by Dennis Gabor; it uses a laser beam and mirrors to create an interference pattern in light waves. Zinkin (1987) explains the result as follows:

> To understand how it is possible for a small part to contain the information of the whole it is helpful to use another analogy. Imagine a pebble thrown into a still pond. A few moments later, a second pebble is thrown in. As the waves of the two pebbles radiate outwards across each other the water is suddenly frozen. Any piece of ice contains the complicated wave patterns made by the two pebbles so that the whole pond, the exact place in which the pebbles fell, and the time interval between them can be read off from this small piece, provided the pattern of the crossing curves can be decoded. (p. 3)

Zinkin reports that Pribram describes the functions of the human brain in holographic terms. Briefly, Pribram contends that *we create order* in the universe as our neurological system receives and sorts impressions of events in the world. We decode what Pribram calls the *frequency domain* (which lies outside space and time, like Jung's Pleroma) as the ripple pattern of a hologram is decoded, into space and time. Thus we create our individual images, whether conscious or unconscious. This sounds remarkably like Bohm's description of unfolding the implicate order into the explicate order.

BOHM, HOLOGRAMS, AND THE IMPLICATE ORDER. Zinkin (1987) and Singer (1991) tie Bohm's (1980) notion of the "implicate order" to Jung's theory. Zinkin (1987, p. 6) gives Bohm's modifying view of the hologram:

> The pattern on the holographic plate . . . is only a static record of the movement of light. What is caught is light waves in movement. . . . Enfolding and unfolding is . . . the primary reality and this is called the "holomovement." Object and image, therefore, result from an unfolding into the explicate order. . . . There are no absolute or fixed separate entities, though there are relatively stable and autonomous entities, which are like the vortex [for example, a whirlpool in water], which is a stable form though a result of the movement of a fluid.

Bohm (1980) was one of the first to emphasize *"undivided wholeness, in which the observing instrument is not separable from what is observed"* (p. 134; Bohm's italics). Spencer (1988) says about Bohm's implicate order:

> *Structures enfold each other so that one structure can be simultaneously internal and external to the other.* Since all forms unfold out of the same ground, there is no need to postulate the existence of forces between them; their whole dynamic is a function of the unfolding of explicate forms, and they have non-local causation. (p. 154; Spencer's italics)

This approach is controversial. The brain/hologram analogy may nevertheless remain useful, like the pond/hologram analogy, until we discover more about the details of brain function. For now it is enough to suggest that the hologram metaphor provides one way to relate brain theory to Jung's concepts of the Pleroma, the Ego and the Self, and synchronicity, as well as to Bohm's "implicate" and "explicate" orders.

Morphic Resonance

We should also mention Sheldrake's (1981) concept of morphic resonance, although he has ventured much farther out on the fringes of accepted science than Bohm has. Sheldrake hypothesizes that fields of influence (morphogenetic fields) affect the ease of discovery of new principles, whether they concern monkeys washing their food or human discoveries in science. He says that once the first individual has pushed through a new insight with great effort, people (or animals) anywhere in the world will find it easier to develop independent, parallel insights.

The interaction of morphogenetic fields with learning and genetics would help to explain how, in Jung's language, archetypal principles arose in widely separated societies.

Writers such as Michael Conforti (1994), Fred Wolf (1989, 1994), and Ernest Rossi (1992) have developed many of these ideas in the pages of *Psychological Perspectives*, of which Rossi was for a long time the editor.

Relevance of the New Science to the Jungian Individuation Process

The Jungian individuation process seems closely related to the phenomenon of synchronicity. It may be useful to think of individuation as a dynamic of development in the psyche that proceeds much faster than species development. Synchronicity plays a role since individuation includes the gradual emergence of meaning from neutral, objective data, caused in part by the repetition of synchronistic events over time.

The pattern of a life develops as one performs countless iterations of an orbit around the attractor of the Self. Meaning accrues for the paths as they gradually provide mutual context. In both synchronicity and individuation, apparently unrelated events are associated through the meaning one can infer from them. The choice of objective explanations depends on one's personality type, complexes, and knowledge:

> The old common sense picture of the world associated with Newton and the idea of a clockwork universe has given way to one in which, not only is uncertainty intrinsic to nature at the subatomic level, but our very attempts to understand it lead to . . . a world in which "intuition deserts us, and seemingly absurd or miraculous events can occur. . . . The language I speak," wrote Jung, "must be ambiguous, must have two meanings in order to do justice to the dual aspects of our psychic nature." (Clarke, 1992, p. 25)

The paradoxical nature and content of Jung's speculations were not naive. Jung's acquaintance with both Albert Einstein and Wolfgang Pauli enabled him to learn something about modern physics. His statements were indeterminate rather than precise but can be seen as anticipating scientific developments down to the present.

The less "scientific" observer, when tempted to seize scientific findings and apply them to psychological events, as I have been doing, should remember that such application requires a most unscientific leap from matter to metaphor.

READINGS

Campbell, J. (1976). *The masks of God.* (Vols. 1–4). New York: Penguin Books.

Eccles, J. C. (1989). *Evolution of the brain: Creation of the self.* New York: Routledge.

Edelman, G. M. (1992). *Bright air, brilliant fire.* New York: Basic Books.

Gleick, J. (1987). *Chaos: Making a new science.* New York: Viking Penguin.

Lauwerier, H. (1991). *Fractals: Endlessly repeated geometrical figures.* Princeton, NJ: Princeton University Press.

Peat, F. D. (1987). *Synchronicity: The bridge between matter and mind.* New York: Bantam Books.

Singer, J. (1991). *Seeing through the visible world: Jung, Gnosis, and Chaos.* New York: HarperCollins.

Smoot, G., & Davidson, K. (1993). *Wrinkles in time.* New York: Morrow.

Wolf, F. A. (1989). *Taking the quantum leap: The new physics for non-scientists* (Rev. Ed.). San Francisco: Harper & Row.

CHAPTER 11

Three of Jung's Major Limitations

Jung was a towering intellectual, but, like any other person, subject to imperfections. In addition, his views were colored by context; a male psychiatrist, he wrote in Switzerland, mostly in the first half of the 20th century. Some of Jung's original writing distresses modern readers, especially for what it reveals about his attitudes toward the Nazis during World War II. His relationships with some women patients were also questionable by current standards, as were many of the assumptions he made about gender. Discussion of these three issues is provided here as an inoculation against rumor and exaggerated criticism. (Objections to Jung's interest in the transpersonal were touched on in several earlier chapters and so are omitted here.)

An informed discussion may help you to separate the theory from the man who originated it. If you understand Jung's personal deficiences, you may better decide for yourself how much his work was affected by them, and how much of the current criticism should be taken with a grain of salt.

The Anti-Semitism Issue

Jay Sherry (1989) provides a balanced discussion of a three-day meeting of Jungian professionals on the issue of Jung's anti-Semitism, where prominent analysts differed in their opinions. Their conclusion was bleak; most agreed that on a deep feeling level Jung failed to appreciate Hitler's evil. Sherry reports that Philip Zabriskie said that " 'Jung exhibited a profound failure of feeling' "

(p. 39). She quoted more from Zabriskie: "'The medical and political neutrality that [Jung] claimed in the 1930s was unfortunately accompanied by a *moral* neutrality as well, which helps to explain the ambiguous tone of his contemporary comments'" (p. 4).

On the other hand, Aryeh Maidenbaum, in 1989 the executive director of the C. G. Jung Foundation of New York, is reported as saying that

> "Jung was neither a Nazi sympathizer nor an explicit anti-Semite. It is a matter of record that Jung had sponsored rule changes to accommodate Jewish members expelled from the German section of the International Society and that he did help Jewish refugees." (Sherry, 1989, p. 36)

By 1946 Jung could observe:

> Like the rest of the world [the Germans] did not understand wherein Hitler's significance lay, that he symbolized something in every individual. He was the most prodigious personification of all human inferiorities. He was an utterly incapable, unadapted, irresponsible, psychopathic personality, full of empty, infantile fantasies, but cursed with the keen intuition of a rat or a guttersnipe. He represented the shadow, the inferior part of everybody's personality, in an overwhelming degree, and this was another reason why they fell for him. (Broadcast talk 1946, "The Fight with the Shadow"; *CW* 10, para. 454)

However, Maidenbaum also confirmed that from "'December 1944, the Analytical Psychology Club in Zurich instituted a rule that Jewish membership was not to exceed 10 per cent'" (Sherry, 1989, p. 36). This rule was in the form of an appendix to the bylaws of the Analytical Club and was never made public. It was not rescinded until 1950. On the more positive side, when Aniela Jaffé, who was Jewish, had problems at the club, Jung threatened to resign (p. 37).

Micah Neumann, a psychiatrist and Erich Neumann's son, said of the relationship between Jung and the senior Neumann: "'On a personal level Jung was connected, but . . . he was unconnected on the collective level'" (p. 37). Neumann added that

> "although there was no trace of anti-Semitism in that relationship [between Jung and Erich Neumann], Jung was nevertheless anti-Semitic in the full sense of the word until after the war and . . . he never integrated this shadow experience into his life." (p. 38)

Sherry attributes most of these difficulties to Jung's troubled relationship with Freud:

Most [speakers] referred to the crucial role of his relationship with Freud as the source of these unacknowledged feelings. Unfortunately, the effects of this relationship were more referred to than analyzed. I think it caused a deep resentment in Jung, a narcissistic rage, which blinded him to those who cautioned him about his remarks and left him feeling entitled to seek redress through public pronouncements of dubious scientific integrity. (p. 40)

A criticism related to that of anti-Semitism is that Jung was elitist. Sherry includes this 1947 quotation from Jung, writing about application of the analytical method:

One can apply this method with reasonable hope of success only to in-dividuals endowed with a certain degree of intelligence and sound sense of morality. A marked lack of education, a low degree of intelligence, and a moral deficit are prohibitive. As 50 per cent of the population are below normal in one or another of these respects, the method could not have any effect on them even under ideal circumstances. (CW 18, para. 1392; quoted in Sherry, 1989, p. 35)

Sherry felt that the issues were complicated by the fact that

Jung and the Nazis shared a common vocabulary derived from the German Romantic tradition with its emphasis on the irrational side of the psyche. Both sought to revive the Romantic emphasis on the soul and shared a contemptuous rejection of the materialistic philosophy of the last half of the nineteenth century. The differences were equally important, however: the Nazis advocated a retreat *from* rationality while Jung sought to establish a psychology *beyond* rationality. (p. 40)

Although the distinction between "establish beyond rationality" and "retreat from rationality" is subtle, the central point is that Jung saw a pressing need to increase our consciousness of our irrationality.

Corinna Peterson (1989) says that Gerhard Wehr's 1987 book on Jung clarifies Jung's difficulties with Nazism, when Wehr

finally endorses Aniela Jaffé's verdict that [Jung] came up against his own shadow and made a serious mistake by speaking out unnecessarily on occa-sions in ways which could be misinterpreted, e. g., his statement that "The Aryan unconscious has a greater potential than the Jewish." At the same time we are reminded that the Berlin Rabbi, Leo Baeck, was able to discuss the whole question with Jung at a later date and felt sufficiently reassured to accept a subsequent invitation to Eranos. (p. 302)

The analyst David Tresan (1992, p. 106), writing elsewhere, summed up this issue as follows: "Irrespective of when he straightened up his thinking around Nazism, Jung's failure to register and communicate an immediate experience of outrage made his deficiencies apparent to the world."

Samuels published a two-part "critical study of the intellectual relations of analytical psychology and National Socialism" (1992a, p. 26). He criticizes Jung for being the proponent of a national psychology (1992a, p. 23) and concludes with a plea for analysts to broaden their scope as well as their concepts:

> We need, I think, to sit down with the materially disadvantaged and the socially frightened, as well as with educated analysands. . . . We may have to question the very way we work, for private practice with a privileged clientele is not politically neutral. We may have to question . . . rejecting multidisciplinary work as "un-psychological." (Samuels, 1992b, pp. 144–145)

One lesson to be derived from all this is that analytical psychology, like all healthy systems, must keep growing and changing with the times.

Jung's Personal Relations with Women Patients

Jung's relationships with women were problematic for most of his life for much the same reason that he encountered political problems: His *feeling function* was relatively undeveloped. Jung was a dyed-in-the-wool thinker. (See Chapter 5 to review the "functions" of personality.)

Tresan (1992, pp. 86–87) said about the women in Jung's life:

> From 1895 to 1912, from age twenty to thirty-seven, Jung was involved with three women who were his patients. . . . The first was Helene Preiswerk, his cousin and the subject of his doctoral dissertation on occult phenomena. . . . Jung's total unawareness of her obvious love for him . . . gives a clear picture of the insensitive state of his anima and feeling at that time.
> The seances [with Preiswerk] occurred probably from 1895 until 1899, and Jung's dissertation was published in 1902 when he was twenty-seven years old. He married [Emma Rauschenbach] the next year. . . . [In] 1904, he began to treat Sabina Spielrein and became very emotionally embroiled with her. . . . Jung's meetings with Spielrein ended in 1909, but he wrote to her until at least 1913, and she to him until probably 1918.

Interested students will find a long, detailed account of the Jung-Spielrein relationship in Kerr (1993). The book is especially critical of Freudian theory but also focuses on defects in Jung's emotional nature and attachments.

Spielrein and Jung both sought consultation with Freud over their mutual difficulties, and she later left Jung's practice to analyze with Freud. Some have persuasively charged Jung and Freud with "stealing" Spielrein's concept of destruction or sacrifice as a condition of love (Carotenuto, 1980; Kerr, 1993). Spielrein was a gifted thinker, and their analytical sessions were a mixture of therapy and intellectual debate, as was often true in the early days among analysts of all persuasions (and sometimes happens still). An English translation of her original paper on the subject has now appeared (Spielrein, 1994).

Tresan's article on Jung continues, "In 1910, now thirty-five years old, Jung began to see Toni Wolff as a patient, and, in 1912, he began his personal relationship with her" (p. 87). Wolff, later a famous Jungian analyst, consulted Jung when she was young and deeply troubled. During her recovery, she developed into a full-blown anima figure for him, then advised him on his writing, produced theory herself, and most notoriously, became Jung's mistress for many years, with the apparent knowledge and tolerance of Emma Jung, who had also become an analyst, well respected for her clinical abilities and for her writing.

Although the inception of this relationship coincided with the break between Jung and Freud and probably contributed to Jung's emotional turmoil, the established *ménage à trois* seems to have provided invaluable support for Jung both emotionally and intellectually. Tresan remarks that "in these three women—Preiswerk, Spielrein, and Wolff—there is a progression from what appears to be gross unconsciousness of eros to a seemingly mature relationship of a married man to his mistress" (p. 87). This "progression," although in some ways a positive development for Jung, had its questionable side: "What it does to the development of [a male] analyst and to his anima to live out his eros longings is not well known even today; we better understand the dangers to the analysand" (p. 87).

In addition to these complexities, Jung was surrounded for all of his mature life by a devoted group of women, his current analysands and "graduates," many of whom became analysts themselves. (In the early days, after an undetermined amount of work with Jung, it took only his permission for student-analysands to start an analytical practice of their own.) Three of these women (Eleanor Bertine, Esther Harding, and Kristine Mann), all medical doctors, introduced Jungian analysis to New York (Hannah, 1976, p. 141) and founded the New York Analytic Club in 1936 (p. 164).

Jane Wheelwright, a senior American analyst, said in *Matter of Heart* (one of the films on Jung) that it was repellant at first to observe the "goofy" devotion of the women surrounding Jung, but that she, of course, also developed a strong positive transference during her analysis with him.

Women in Jung's Theory: Feminism and the Animus

Jung's writing about the animus suffers limitations similar to those affecting his personal relationships with women. His descriptions of contrasexual aspects of the Anima/Animus in men and women are biased by his personal character type and by cultural assumptions, distorting his treatment of rational functioning in women and emotional processes in men.

Some Cultural Limitations of Jung's Anima/Animus Theory

Contemporary women and men take serious issue with Jung's descriptions of the Anima/Animus archetype. A short excerpt from Jung should illustrate the problem:

> In intellectual women the animus encourages a critical disputatiousness and would-be highbrowism, which, however, consists essentially in harping on some irrelevant weak point and nonsensically making it the main one. Or a perfectly lucid discussion gets tangled up in the most maddening way through the introduction of a quite different and if possible perverse point of view. Without knowing it, such women are solely intent upon exasperating the man and are, in consequence, the more completely at the mercy of the animus. "Unfortunately I am always right," one of these creatures once confessed to me. (CW 7, para 335)

For a long time, Jung expressed a negative attitude toward the Anima, illustrated by his vision at midlife of the Anima as Salome. Tresan (1992, p. 94) remarks on the paradox inherent in this attitude:

> From 1912 until 1944, from ages thirty-seven to sixty-nine, thirty-two adult years, Jung's personal psychology and the psychology he expounded centered about a process of confrontation between ego consciousness and the unconscious. . . . The paradox is this: the anima, the very symbol for Jung of the collective unconscious, is treated consistently by him, that is by his ego-consciousness, like a most dangerous and decidedly untrustworthy figure hardly available for an enduring reconciliation. So, too, to an avowed degree women in general, whom he identifies repeatedly with the anima.

In 1944, following a severe heart attack, Jung had a series of visions that changed his attitude by providing a "coniunctio experience" (in alchemical terms) and an end to his illusions of personal power. Eleven years later, shortly after Emma Jung's death in 1955, Jung's final anima vision occurred in a dream about her. This dream consolidated the anima qualities of Aphrodite and Psyche, of lover and mother, in a way Jung had not achieved earlier.

By the end of his long life Jung had largely overcome his cultural and personal biases about women and about the anima in men. His writings, published earlier, remain to irritate the contemporary reader, and must be seen as reflecting a less-than-ideal stage in the development of Jung's character.

Recent Developments in Jungian Thought on the Anima/Animus

Recently, writers have been trying to reach a relatively gender-free concept of these archetypes and to reframe them as being present in the psyches of both sexes. (See, for example, Schwartz-Salant & Stein, 1992.)

A useful way of dealing with the contrasexual issue is to imagine that all individuals incorporate aspects of an archetypal "other." Often this "other" is visualized, and appears in dreams, as a person of the other gender. This approach has been complicated by the recognition that homosexual individuals must be included in psychological formulations of the psyche. Does the statement that the Anima/Animus describes our "contrasexual" aspects follow the same principles for straight men, straight women, gay men, and lesbian women? And how about the bisexuals? Does sexual identity depend at all on the Anima/Animus, or is it grounded in the Self?

These issues are some of many leading to the acrimony at Ghost Ranch (cited earlier and reported in Schwartz-Salant & Stein, 1992), when Jungians tried to agree on acceptable ways to describe the masculine and feminine principles. Another meeting treated aspects of the same subject (*Who Do We Think We Are? The Mystery and Muddle of Gender*, 1993). Opinions are still divided.

Gender Versus Sex

Exploratory steps taken by Polly Young-Eisendrath (1992) and Gareth Hill (1992) tracked differences between biological sexual identity and gender identity. These are most often congruent: Most of us are born with clearly identifiable sexual characteristics and are assigned a gender role in our society on that basis.

Unless we are one of the few who choose to have a sex-change operation, our physical sex remains the same for life. But gender roles differ from one group to another, and even over time within a group. Thus in the United States we no longer expect that most mothers will quit their jobs to care for their children on a full-time basis. Economics on the one hand, and better employment opportunities for women on the other, have changed the context.

In a further step, some writers separate the archetypal masculine or feminine *principles* both from gender roles and from sex. This leads to much confusion in terminology. Our language and myths are loaded with conventional terms closely tied to the assigned sex of the symbol described. To give a simple example, an "heroic" effort sounds different from a "heroine-like" effort; the term sounds more awkward for women. In most contexts, including that of science, people automatically envision different scenarios for the two sexes (Shepherd, 1993). These sex-toned associations, though often inopportune, are so strong that we could call them archetypal.

Hillman (1985) was especially insistent on the presence of both principles in every individual. My personal solution would be to use Hillman and Jung's term *syzygy* to describe the polarities of Anima/Animus differences as well as those between other archetypes, thus altogether avoiding the terms *masculine* and *feminine*. Obviously, no simple solution will prevail any time soon, and we can expect many more intense discussions before the issue is settled.

Reprise: The Man and the Theory

It is unfortunate but not surprising that Jung's own relationships with women add a questionable twist to his theorizing about women's psyches. I venture to say that if he were alive and still developing today, Jung would be reworking his theories into closer accordance with current belief, much as a new generation of Jungians are attempting to do.

In the early days of analysis, the various patient/therapist limits we now take for granted were kept loosely, if at all. Both Freud and Jung played multiple roles with their analysands. Indeed, the two doctors played analyst to each other, examined each others' dreams, and fell into transferential quarrels as a result.

Both Jung and Freud analyzed their immediate families; Freud analyzed his daughter Anna (with ill-fated results—she never married and achieved no close relationship until the latter part of her life). Jung analyzed himself, his wife, and his lovers.

With the wider development of the field of psychoanalysis, personal judgment about these and other therapy decisions proved unreliable. As the numbers of analysts and analysands multiplied, senior analysts instituted formal training procedures and outlined rules of conduct. Nowadays it is considered unprofessional and unethical to see in therapy any friend or relative. As a pioneer, Jung could not know the effects of ignoring these boundaries— and his work itself led to the discovery of the boundaries.

Kerr (1993) ridicules and discounts Jung's theories in terms of his personal difficulties. More moderately, Tresan (1992, p. 106) remarks, "I can only conjecture that a world-class figure must endure a world-class corrective for his blind sides." Tresan believes that one such corrective was administered by the public condemnation of Jung's position on the Nazis.

Sherry (1989, p. 42), concludes that "if Jungians are to do more than pay lip service to 'wholeness' then the discomforting fallibilities of their founder must continue to be faced squarely, casting more light on lingering shadows."

I can only hope that beginning Jungian students will do the same.

READINGS

Carotenuto, A. (1982). *A secret symmetry.* New York: Random House.

Hannah, B. (1976). *Jung: His life and work—A biographical memoir.* New York: Putnam.

Hillman, J. (1985). *Anima: An anatomy of a personified notion.* Dallas, TX: Spring Publications.

Schwartz-Salant, N., & Stein, M. (Eds.). *Chiron: Gender and soul in psychotherapy.* (1992) Wilmette, IL: Chiron.

Shepherd, L. J. (1993). *Lifting the veil: The feminine face of science.* Boston: Shambhala.

Young-Eisendrath, P. (1992). *Hags and heroes: A feminist approach to Jungian psychotherapy with couples.* Toronto: Inner City Books.

SIX

The Beginning Clinician
and Jungian Therapy

CHAPTER 12

The Context of Jungian Practice

This chapter covers working conditions in both public clinical settings and private practice. You are most likely to begin your practice of therapy in a public setting, and only gradually, if ever, establish a full-time private practice. You may eventually work in many different settings either simultaneously or sequentially, since most therapists change jobs several times over a professional career, besides dividing their work into several concurrent part-time sections.

Conditions in Managed Care Clinics and Public Mental Health Services

We turn first to public clinical options.

Managed Health Care and Depth Therapy

Where do new doctoral psychologists and other psychotherapists find work? Many graduate students hope to set up private practices; within this group many hope to have as clients primarily individual, garden-variety neurotic clients who want to improve their quality of life. Students of Jung further wish to work with their clients toward individuation, by way of Jungian techniques such as dream analysis in long-term treatment.

Relatively few psychotherapy graduates will ever have the opportunity for full-time practice of this sort, certainly not at the beginning of their professional careers. It becomes a bit more likely if an individual can first set up effective referral networks and become certified as a Jungian analyst.

But what can you do while still in supervision, or if you are not ready, able, or willing to undergo analytical training? Even as an analyst trainee you must find clients to serve as subjects of your early analyses.

Opportunities for Short-Term Therapy

Most new clinicians hold positions in health maintenance organizations (HMOs) or state, county, or private clinics. Some work as human resource counselors in large corporations or as prison therapists. Some individuals find assistantships with private practitioners. Discussions at meetings of professional organizations such as the National Council of Schools and Programs of Professional Psychology (NCSPP) suggest that psychologists in particular are replacing their clinical work with more managerial and supervisory roles.

In such jobs, will you be doing long-term therapy with individual clients? Not likely. Most HMOs and public clinics allow only short-term therapy, with selected clients. "Short-term" therapy can be anything from just one emergency session to a total of 10 or 20 hours of therapy once or twice a week. This does not mean one or more sessions a week for a number of years, like Jungian therapy, let alone sessions five times a week for ten years or more, as is usual in formal Freudian psychoanalysis. Those modalities are almost entirely confined to private practice.

Employers, insurance companies, clinics, and HMOs often screen potential mental health clients for their psychological accessibility. Those with severe emotional disturbances of long standing are excluded from many insurance policies, and after diagnosis and crisis intervention are referred away from outpatient clinics to dwindling alternative community resources.

GROUP THERAPY. Group work is advocated for problems of addiction or any other widespread difficulty such as child abuse or marital discord where a group can focus on a single theme. Adolescent groups, parent groups, and child groups are all on the increase. Therapeutic groups are often more effective than individual appointments in producing rapid attitude and behavior change. Both child and adult clients sometimes learn faster from their peers in a group than from hearing the input from just one therapist alone with them in a room.

There are some real advantages to all of these policies. Many people want (and may only tolerate) short-term, problem-oriented therapy, rather than an extended and painful probe of their innermost feelings. Short therapy can also "process" many people in a brief period. It can ameliorate symptoms, resolve crises, and reduce wait lists, minimally disrupting clients' work and home lives. Perhaps most important to the health care industry, it is less expensive than long-term therapy for everyone involved, at least in the short run.

WHY DO LONG-TERM THERAPY, ANYWAY? Why do some mental health professionals wring their hands over these developments? Are we just greedy people who want to keep clients interminably for the sake of the money they provide? We have been hearing for years that long-term, individual psychotherapy is a self-indulgent "frill" for the rich. The Jungian reply has traditionally been that after all, only individuals are capable of change; the collective cannot change on its own. Each step that one individual takes toward becoming a more evolved person adds a bit to the collective consciousness. Even large-scale social and political changes depend on how individuals in power define and pursue personal goals.

Some social activists call such reflections unrealistic and elitist. They ask, "What of the children witnessing, even dying in, gang wars in the inner city? What about poor people, illiterate people, people with AIDS?" These populations have few opportunities for introspective therapy. Even if they did, would they want it? And who would pay for it?

Most of us, whether clinicians or clients, not being saints, must have a place to live, something to eat, and a decent education before we can turn to saving our souls (or anyone else's). Poverty is demoralizing, and Abraham Maslow's (1962) hierarchy of needs applies to the less fortunate even more strongly than to the middle-income person. In spite of such obstacles, we should not write off the potential for personal development among the disadvantaged.

On the other hand, we already see long lines at the mental health clinics and crowded waiting rooms filled with "urgent care" clients facing desperate problems. Most can only get half-hour appointments with a different stranger at each visit to the emergency room. "Chronic" patients receive a series of referrals from one overburdened agency to the next. How can anonymous, dehumanizing "treatment" like that heal anything? Too many people drop out of sight and end up on the streets as criminals, panhandlers, and the mentally disordered homeless.

DYNAMIC PRINCIPLES APPLY ACROSS THE BOARD. Let me add that the principles of dynamic psychotherapy can be most helpful in shorter-term interventions. Not every client that you meet needs a full-blown analysis, or perhaps more than a little skilled help in problem solving. But no matter what problems are presented, they all stem from similar principles operating in the human psyche. A thorough knowledge of the origins, relationships, and processes of psychic functioning can illuminate even the most fleeting therapeutic encounter. It never hurts to understand a client.

THE SPECTER OF MANAGED CARE.   In faculty meetings at clinical departments of universities, at professional schools of psychology, in professional journals, at HMOs, and in the media we hear that "managed care" must inevitably and increasingly drive the provision of mental health services. In this mode, the therapist becomes "the provider," who is paid a salary or flat fee for a stated number of "contact hours" and allowed to see only clients carrying certain diagnoses for a specified number of appointments.

County agencies, short on money, with bursting wait lists, want to hire psychologists (or less-costly practitioners) better trained in case management and crisis intervention. We are told that these will compose most of these professionals' workload. (Psychiatrists' time is reserved for prescribing medication.)

Daily Life at the Clinic

This section provides a cautionary note about what you can expect from life in the crowded halls of the current mental health job market. It may even be a bit outdated and rosy by the time it reaches you. Therapists are a hard-working and hard-worked lot, on the whole—but the rewards can be worth the aggravation.

HEALTH MAINTENANCE ORGANIZATIONS.   HMOs often include mental health coverage. The client pays the HMO a fixed amount each year, usually through an employer, and is covered for many medical and mental problems.

In a typical large HMO providing typical mental health coverage, clients are limited to between 5 and 20 sessions for any problem, and persons suffering from long-term emotional ailments are specifically excluded. As a full-time predoctoral intern or licensed practitioner, you will typically have six or seven hour-long appointments every day. You may see families or groups; sometimes these group appointments last an hour and a half.

Therapists are often on call for a week or more of each year. This means that you will receive calls at home from the hospital emergency rooms or from clients in crisis, and may be required to go into the hospital in the middle of the night or over the weekend. Being on call does not affect the schedule of regular appointments, so you may be very tired indeed at the end of a tour of on-call duty.

Patients at HMOs do not have the luxury of working on entrenched neuroses, character problems, or serious psychotic processes. Their treatment is directed at problem solving and crisis intervention. Therapists tend to describe the process to the client as if the mental problem were an old car: "In these sessions we will work to fix the part of your life that has broken down; you can return later if a different part needs adjustment."

The inpatient mental wards of HMO hospitals have revolving doors. When you encounter suicidal patients (or patients suffering a psychotic break), you are expected to evaluate, admit, and medicate them. You will see them once a week in group therapy until they are "stabilized" and then discharge them to complete an alloted number of outpatient appointments. When those run out, or the client gets worse and returns to the hospital, you may not readmit the client but must refer him or her to a public health clinic, since most HMOs do not cover "chronic" conditions. Even brief subsequent HMO hospitalizations for emotional reasons may no longer be covered.

PUBLIC MENTAL HEALTH CLINICS. The drying up of public money has forced clinics to rely on "case management" rather than individual or family therapy to handle the enormous numbers of distressed, abused, and psychologically overburdened clients who exist in this country. A typical caseload for a therapist at a county clinic will consist of crisis interventions, intake evaluations, and a few short-term therapy sessions. It is clear that you will not be conducting depth therapy under these circumstances. Since conditions are even less flexible in most public clinics than in HMOs, I will not spell out more details here.

Possible Alternatives

How do we situate Jungian analysis in this "marketplace"? Practitioners agree that emergency services are vital but are dismayed at the prospect that every other kind of treatment could be squeezed out of existence.

Is it possible that government officials might be brought to realize that in this country of individual ideals, individual growth therapy may have a place? Just as our talented children are neglected in public schools, so are talented but tormented individuals neglected in our public mental health programs. Individual scientists make important scientific advances; individuals create our works of art. The collective ideal is necessary, but change and creativity come from the heart of an individual, not from the thoughtless reflection of popular culture.

Individual therapy is the only modality short of Prozac/that can change personality. People who are successful in business or the arts, but suffer from feelings of emptiness and depression, can find inner strength through psychotherapy without dulling their creative edge—as happens with chemical therapy.

Unfortunately, unless one has personally undergone such a process, it is almost impossible to believe or understand the potential results. We need more good outcome research on analytical psychology to supplement the numerous anecdotal reports of its usefulness.

This book can only skim the surface of such issues. It is my personal conviction that longer-term analysis of character problems is a vital part of psychotherapy. Perhaps we can only allot 10% of our resources to it, but it needs its own small corner of the public sector.

Am I suggesting that psychotherapists become missionaries for mental health? Perhaps. We are all supposed to donate some of our time "pro bono," under our ethical principles. Some of that time could go to children and others in the inner city, on the basis of need.

SANDNER'S ALTERNATIVE. Sandner (1994) takes a novel stance. He believes that long-term, intensive psychotherapy using transference/countertransference must be differentiated from medicine, psychology, social work, and theology. He believes that the central task of analytical therapy is to make darkness conscious, and that this powerful, intense experience of inner nature can only be done within the dynamism of the transference and countertransference.

This is Shadow work. Sandner (1994) says that in this Shadow work, Freud dealt with sex, Fairbairn with hatred, and Jung with the shadow of God. The experience of analytical therapy is a possibility, not a right or privilege; as with an advanced education, the person must go get it for himself or herself. The client must make a sacrifice of money and time to achieve it—and Sandner, with others, believes it is worth it.

Analysis is also moving away from the medical model, and Sandner hopes it will renew itself as a completely separate discipline. If private practitioners' work is not supported by insurance or public money, they will have to reduce their hourly fees and do a fair amount of pro bono work to reach even the members of the middle class.

PERSONAL SHADOW OR PUBLIC SHADOW? My own hope for some public support is perhaps unrealistic. We need not expect that the government will pay for all our personal needs. The middle-income person suffering psychic pain can divert some funds from new clothes or a vacation trip to the care of his or her soul, if it seems important enough—even though it may widen the split between rich and poor to expect the solvent to buy services unavailable to the poor.

These are moral and practical reasons to provide a small percentage of support, including financial, political, and emotional, for an individual's quest for the Shadow, regardless of finances, color, creed, or national origin.

The bulk of support will inevitably go to deal with the results of the Shadow of society as a whole—for short-term therapy and crisis intervention to deal with violence, abuse, addiction, and related problems. It might nevertheless be possible to reserve 5% or 10% of our national mental health resources for long-term, individual psychotherapy.

As psychotherapists, we can spend some time with the psyche. Casework is desperately important, but it need not comprise the total workload of all psychotherapy professionals.

This book has delineated one of several methods that may be used for individual, long-term treatment. The Jungian approach can also be used with couples, and to some extent with groups. It is valuable. It works. Over the long run, it has already made a difference, and it will make more of one. This section is a plea for students to keep alive the effort to retain a small part of our plans and resources for the survival of such therapy.

Coping with the Crunch

Does all this mean that nobody does long-term analytical therapy any more? Of course not. Readers who have already had some Jungian therapy know that private practitioners are still available. Some analytical institutes have a sliding-fee clinic, where clients are treated by analysts in training, interns, and certified senior analysts.

A few hardy souls maintain a practice with long-term clients independent of formal affiliation with any organization. With luck, dedication, and perseverance you too can join the ranks of therapists making treatment decisions based on what the client needs and the therapist respects, rather than focusing on what insurance executives are willing to pay for. How can a budding therapist arrange such a happy outcome?

Striking Out on Your Own

Many therapists keep a corner of their heart reserved for the dream of establishing their own independent practice. It isn't easily achieved, but it can be done.

Once you, the new practitioner, have served some time in an HMO, public mental health clinic, or hospital, you will have accumulated both experience and a list of contacts in the community, perhaps in the specialty that attracts you most. Now you have some hope of creating a private practice on your own terms that will still pay the bills. Let's start with the organized and lucky ones who land a private assistantship.

Working as an Assistant in Private Practice

Most private practitioners rely heavily on insurance payments to make their services affordable to clients. Whether private, or public like Medicare, insurance providers still "manage" the care their clients receive.

The licensed therapist who has more clients than she or he can handle may choose to pass some of them on to an assistant. Each state regulates such arrangements and requires ongoing paperwork and supervision.

In general practice, it is likely that you will be seeing the least-challenging clients; as a new therapist you are not yet considered skilled enough to take on the really "interesting" cases, meaning the ones who are complex, difficult, but still making progress.

Relatively few private practitioners do much long-term therapy. Most are involved with third-party payments, as mentioned above. Typically, the insurance company will pay only part of a "full" fee and only cover a set number of sessions. Medi-Cal, Champus, and other insurance companies all have complex regulations as to who can be seen, and for how long, for what problems. Too often your job as an assistant may consist substantially of the paperwork of case reviews and diagnostic summaries beyond the capability of a secretary to complete.

More fortunate assistants help the licensed therapist conduct intake screenings and triage, which may include psychological assessment. You might pick up some appointments with family members of the identified patient (IP) and work as a second therapist with families or groups.

In short, unless the primary therapist is unusually dedicated to training new therapists, the assistant will truly "assist," and do the chores the licensed therapist is less interested in or needs help with. This seldom provides the opportunity to work on a long-term basis with individual neurotic clients.

For Jungians, the picture is brighter. If you like Jungian theory and have some relevant training plus personal analysis, you should of course apply as an assistant to a Jungian practitioner. If you are accepted, your work may be more satisfying than the kind delineated above. Jungians in private practice tend to shun the inner reaches of bureaucracy, keep paperwork to a minimum, and by profession are committed to the value of longer-term therapy.

Springboards to Independent Private Practice

If possible, as a neophyte Jungian choose jobs that promise some professional development. Look for supervisors who are Jungian analysts and for in-house training presented from a Jungian viewpoint. Attend Jungian seminars, continue your analysis, join an Analytical Club. Find some friends among members of the Jungian community. Get a license to practice in your state.

Then, while still working at any clinic or other group setting, you can gradually decrease your hours as private clients start to appear. To generate new clients you can give talks to parent or religious groups and otherwise make yourself visible locally. (Several good books have been written on how to build a private practice.)

When you feel ready to branch out, gradually pick up a few more private clients. Pay for consultations with an established Jungian practitioner. Find someone with a private office to share until your practice develops, rather than undertaking a high rent alone. If all goes well, in a year or two you may be able to quit your salaried job—but hang on to it until your practice has grown.

This is the latest point at which you should start analytical training. A personal analysis is an integral part of this training. Many analysts begin their own analyses much earlier in their lives; the experience of an effective personal analysis often intensifies the determination to make Jungian analytical psychology a life work. The next section touches on some procedures for obtaining Jungian training, informally or as an analyst trainee.

The Beginning Clinician and Jungian Training

If you are reading this book as part of a survey course on psychological theory, and have no interest in a career as a Jungian therapist, this section may not be for you—unless you are curious about other life forms. It takes a look at some of the general pros and cons of a career in analytical psychology. It cannot be overemphasized that analytical psychology is not something one can do by reading about it; it requires years of training and supervised practice.

Personal Considerations

There are personal decisions to make if you want to do Jungian therapy. Are you temperamentally suited to the Jungian style? Are there good training opportunities nearby, or can you move to a place where they exist? Can you support yourself while you are an analytical candidate? We consider some of these issues below.

JUNGIAN ANALYSIS AND JUNGIAN THERAPY. Many therapists who base their work on Jungian theory are not analysts, and some analysts work with clients in modalities other than analysis. In the field of Jungian psychotherapy, *analysts* are those who have graduated from a training program of a Jung Institute. Jungian *therapists* are professionals who know Jungian theory and have usually undergone Jungian analysis but are not certified as analysts. A Jungian *analysis* seeks to unravel the knots tied in your psyche by a lifetime of faulty perceptions and actions, and to enable you to achieve your personality's full potential. You can find Jungian-oriented therapists for children, couples, and groups, in low-cost clinics, and in short-term, problem-oriented therapeutic work. Jungians also do Sandplay, art therapy, and dance therapy, all of which may accompany "talking" therapy or proceed independently and are suited to all ages.

Analytical therapy can be accomplished in less time than a complete analysis. Even so, it will usually take months or years, rather than weeks, for Jungian therapy to produce a perceptible change in character or personality.

A formal Jungian analysis, in contrast, is long-term therapy, and once started may continue with interruptions of various lengths for a lifetime. This holds whether you are the client or the therapist. If you do become an analyst you make a major commitment of interest and time to your clients. Analytical practice also requires a fair amount of geographical stability, since you should stick around in one place long enough for your analysands to see you as long as they need to.

That being said, Jungian analysands do not necessarily stay for all of their treatment with one analyst. Some theorists consider it useful for them to experience working with therapists of both genders and perhaps of different styles or ages.

THE NEED FOR PERSONAL ANALYTICAL PSYCHOTHERAPY. Even practitioners who decide to forgo the analytical certificate still need to go through a personal analysis to be competent Jungian psychotherapists. Your psyche is always involved in the work, and you need to be familiar with its little ways.

Jungian analysts go through rigorous training programs and must undergo many hours of personal analysis before being certified. All of this requires a substantial commitment of time and money from the very beginning. Typically, an analyst will continue to seek consultation, training, and personal therapy for all of his or her life.

THE THERAPIST'S SHADOW. During long-term, intensive therapy, both the client and the therapist divest themselves of the Persona and get down to a primitive identity with one another (Sandner, 1994). This brings up the Shadow in both parties and is a major reason why therapists need analysis.

In any long analysis the client is bound to become a positive or negative *personal* problem. Perhaps a client tearfully begs you to telephone him when you are on vacation or "accidentally" shows up repeatedly at your favorite grocery store, or maybe on weekends you find yourself daydreaming about another special client.

In any transference relationship, the client *wants* to get a personal reaction somehow. Unfortunately, such a personal connection breaks the symbolic family taboo: It is *always* incestuous—and the prohibition against incest is nearly universal, both across cultures and within psychotherapy.

Any kind of incest, physical or "just" symbolic, creates a wounding of sexuality and destabilization of personality. When the impulse is thwarted, as it must be in therapy, the acute frustration of that prohibition leads to either a breakdown of the relationship or a useful turning in of libido, activating the deeper psyche (Sandner, 1994).

The transference yearning may badly inflate part of the therapist. The transference becomes the psyche, and the therapist becomes mythical or godlike. In Chapter 7 this phenomenon is called "archetypal transference" because it goes beyond human expectations.

Archetypal transference can become a *big* problem in therapy. When evoked by a charismatic leader, it doesn't turn away from sacrifice and death; the tragedies at Waco and Jonestown were good examples. This is the Shadow side of transference—the position of power in which the analyst, teacher, or other leader is placed. To stay out of trouble when in that position, you must be aware of your countertransference (Sandner, 1994). To become aware, you need personal analysis.

ROOM FOR THE SOUL. Whether doing analysis or "just" therapy, Jungians must be attracted to and comfortable with a theory that is soul-oriented, rather than dedicated to clockwork scientific principles. You probably realize by now that "soul" does not mean a transparent ghost that resides after death in some sectarian afterlife. That notion is not totally ruled out, but you do not have to subscribe to it to deal with the concept of soul.

The Jungian theoretical view incorporates aspects of the transpersonal and a willingness to assume that as limited humans, we will never have all the answers to the Great Questions of life. Most Jungian practitioners espouse some aspects of that outlook.

Informal Jungian Training

Assuming your mind is made up in favor of the Jungian approach, how do you start to acquire training? C. G. Jung Institutes are your first choice. They serve as educational and social centers for analysts, candidates, trainees, and members of the community who attend their public programs.

Many Jung Institutes allow access to their libraries and to the Archive(s) for Research in Archetypal Symbolism (ARAS) containing thousands of annotated photographic slides and prints of symbolic subjects, as well as collections of books on archetypal symbolism.

Students and seasoned therapists alike find ARAS fascinating to consult. It can be salutary to look up elements from your dreams, fantasies, or Sandplay scenes. Since no two symbol descriptions agree, you are compelled to pick and choose among them and are reminded that symbol interpretation is a personal and paradoxical matter. The art collections of public libraries are also often surprisingly well equipped for such research.

If you live close enough to a Jung Institute, you may apply to be an intern predoctorally, or a candidate later; details follow this section on informal training. If you are not ready to apply for certification at a Jung Institute but live near one, you can attend public and professional educational programs to enlarge your acquaintance with Jungian issues.

SEMINARS. If you are close enough to travel to the nearest institute, ask to be put on a mailing list for educational activities available to the general public and to professional therapists. Attending such classes and workshops provides personal familiarity with Jung's theory as conveyed by modern Jungians, and often some minor in-class consultation on your current cases.

Sometimes dream discussion groups or other activities are available in the community at large. These may be good places to develop a network of acquaintances who are interested in Jungian practice and who will refer clients to you once they know you are competent.

SUPERVISION/CONSULTATION. Both Jungian therapists and those merely interested in finding out more about the field before making a commitment can seek case supervision and consultation by an analytically trained Jungian. The fee is comparable to that for individual therapy, and the number of sessions is negotiable.

With good luck and good management, you may find, financially and psychologically, that you next can afford formal analytical training.

Formal Jungian Training

Jung himself trained the first cadre of Jungian practitioners, and for a long time the process continued to be relatively casual. After World War II, interest in Jungian therapy mushroomed, candidates were no longer so personally known to senior analysts, and Jungian groups adopted more codified rules and training practices. Nowadays, Jungian analysts go through an extensive training program to become certified and are then eligible to join the International Association for Analytical Psychology (IAAP), the global society of Jungian analysts.

The number of Jungian analysts is fast increasing. There were only about 40 when the IAAP was founded in 1955, six years before Jung's death. One hundred and fifty-eight members attended the first International Congress in 1958, and at the 1992 meeting there were 2000 Jungian analysts in various member groups (Mattoon, 1993, p. 5). The number of Jung Institutes in the United States increased from 3 to 11 between the 1970s and the 1990s (Tresan, 1994). About one-quarter of all present Jungian analysts live in the United States.

JUNGIAN ANALYSTS. The Jungian analysts trained by Jung were often medical doctors, although other professionals were represented. Post-Jungian analysts come from a wide assortment of occupations, entering analytical training from psychology, social work, family counseling, pastoral counseling, or other specialties. Not surprisingly, although analysts have widely differing backgrounds, they have similar outlooks on such general subjects as the usefulness of dreams in therapy (Roth, 1994).

INTERNSHIPS. Several Jung Institutes offer predoctoral internships to qualified applicants. The internship program is entirely separate from the procedure for being admitted as an analytical candidate. Internships offer a chance to explore the profession and to make friends in the Jungian community.

Internship training includes seminars, supervision, and practice in Jungian therapy with actual clients. The James Goodrich Whitney Clinic at the San Francisco C. G. Jung Institute is one of several outpatient clinics in this country attached to an institute. Analysts in training and a few senior analysts see clinic clients in this setting. In San Francisco, interns may also see clients through the clinic and receive training and supervision from institute staff. As a client or trainee this is a convenient, low-cost way to obtain Jungian therapy; however, if you want to be an analyst or even an intern, only therapy hours with one of the certified analysts will count for admission to the program. The certified clinic analysts have waiting lists, so it would be wise to apply as soon as you think you might want this option.

Opportunities are few, but Jungian internship is an excellent way to build up your knowledge of analytical psychology, as well as a practice, a referral network, and possibly a foundation for later admission as an analyst in training.

BECOMING A JUNGIAN ANALYST. As the popularity of Jungian analysis has increased, the number of applicants for training has risen sharply. It is impossible for admissions committees to make entirely personal discriminations among dozens of applicants, and so the requirements for admission have become more bureaucratized.

To become a certified Jungian analyst, you must be accepted to candidacy at one of the training institutes here or abroad. Although candidates can be drawn from nonclinical fields like comparative religion or philosophy, you must usually be established in a career that includes some ongoing clients on whom to start practicing your new Jungian skills. You may be able to expand your private clientele with referrals from the institute.

The number of training years and other requirements differ from one institute to the next, but the requirements always include ongoing analysis for yourself.

Generally speaking, analytical training proceeds through several stages. To apply, you must have had about 200 hours of individual analysis from a Jungian analyst. The application forms are likely to be extensive. You may be asked to write essays on personal subjects, provide an autobiographical summary, and demonstrate your ability to discuss concepts from books by and about Jung.

After surviving the preliminary screening, you will go for one or more evaluative interviews with training analysts. If your first application is not successful, you are usually allowed to try again after a specified time period.

Analytical education consists of formal seminars, supervisory and continued therapy hours, and usually the submission of one or more papers. This stage takes about four years, culminating in a major examination on all aspects of clinical practice in analytical psychology (known as the *propaedeuticum examination*).

Once formally advanced to *candidacy*, the candidate conducts one or more analyses under the direct supervision of a senior analyst; these are called *training analyses*. Often the final hurdles before certification include written and oral presentations of a case to a panel of examiners. The whole process typically takes six to eight years.

Summary

In this book you have read about the origins and basic concepts of Jungian theory, mapped personality development, learned some applications, and discovered some of Jung's limitations. You have also taken a brief tour of some employment and training options. This section summarizes what I consider to be the most important contributions of Jungian theory to contemporary psychology.

Transformation

Jungian theory deals with the growth and transformation of personality. Energy for this process arises from the tension of opposites within the Self, which tends to reduce the tension by a transcendent movement toward balanced development. Although bringing one's Shadow to consciousness is arduous, the nonlinear movement of transformation is due more to "grace" than to hard work. The most one can do consciously is to accept the possibility of such kaleidoscopic shifts. This hope for transformation leads to a low-key but persistent optimism among Jungians, since it is never too late for a transformative experience (see Tresan, 1994, pp. 25–26).

Initiation

Becoming a Jungian requires much more than book learning and the practice of techniques. You need to undergo an extensive experience of, and initiation into, the Jungian approach to the psyche. Formally or informally, a Jungian therapist has joined a group of people who share a worldview. Although this can be like discovering one's natural home, it invariably requires a painful process of sacrifice, growth, and change.

Twelve Basic Principles of Jungian Psychology

In my experience, most Jungians agree on the following principles:

1. The psyche is real. It is as real as love, diabetes, or the pi meson. It encompasses both conscious and unconscious processes.

2. Unconscious processes include both positive and negative personal, cultural, and collective elements, rather than merely providing asylum for unacceptable conscious impulses.

3. The Self guides each person toward individuation. The purpose of individuation is to balance the distribution of personality. This work

is often interior; it develops over a lifetime and its results are unpredictable.

4. Each conscious element of our personality has an equal and opposite balancing reaction in the unconscious. Carrying one aspect of any of these bipolar issues to an extreme leads to *enantiodromia:* The element assumes its opposite aspect.

5. Psychic energy (libido) arises from tension between the many pairs of archetypal opposites in the psyche, rather than being derived solely from the generative (sexual) instinct.

6. Dreams and other symbolic idioms express the compensatory movements of unconscious energy that balance our conscious preoccupations.

7. Jung's typology provides a useful explanation of how our energy is distributed. Energy may be directed inward or outward; introversion does not correspond to pathological narcissism. The irrational personality elements are of equal importance to the rational.

8. Archetypes exist as slowly evolved and inherited psychoid tendencies to organize the perception of our experiences into typically human patterns.

9. The universe of matter is a *unus mundus,* interconnected at all levels of meaning.

10. In addition to the material universe as we know it, there is a region beyond time and space, of which we can know very little, that affects all aspects of the material world. We occupy the field of tension between the visible and invisible worlds.

11. The principles of Jungian psychology add up to *paradox:* Every event or symbol contains the possibility of its own contradiction and shifts meaning according to context.

12. There are no hard-and-fast rules in Jungian psychology.

Six Comparisons Between Jung and Freud

The identities of Jung and Freud are often mixed up with each other, and so are their theories. This short list of differences may help you to tell the theories apart.

1. Jung focused on empirical data derived from personal observation. Freud constructed a theoretical system.

2. Jung saw the ego as a complex in the psyche, engaged in continual dialectic with the Self and other complexes. Freud saw the ego as separate from, and opposed to, unconscious parts of the personality.

3. Jung promoted adaptation to the inner world over adaptation to the collective. Freud emphasized adaptation to the outer world.

4. Jung saw psychological, psychosomatic, and even some physical symptoms as indicators from the Self of psychic imbalance and a need for change. Freud saw symptoms as evidence of pathology.

5. Jung saw symbols in myth, dream, and fantasy as pointing to multiply determined meanings, ultimately beyond our knowledge. Freud saw symbols as disguising specific repressed generative (sexual) contents—as "signs," not true symbols.

6. Jung's theory was mostly teleological. Freud's was mostly reductive.

Caution and Valediction

The lists above are neither credos nor exhaustive rosters of principles, but are intended to provide a review of some basic precepts drawn from various writers. Not every Jungian practitioner will agree with all the items on the lists, and few, if any, would define them in exactly the same way.

Nevertheless, if these lists make your skin creep, you are unlikely to feel attracted to Jungian psychology (although who knows what the years may bring?). To those who are stimulated and charmed by these Jungian principles: Welcome to the group!

READINGS

Hall, J. A. (1986). *The Jungian experience: Analysis and individuation*. Toronto: Inner City Books.

Stein, M. (Ed.). (1995). *Jungian analysis* (2nd ed.). La Salle, IL: Open Court.

References

Albert, D. Z. (1994, May). Bohm's alternative to quantum mechanics. *Scientific American* 270(5), 65–66.

Allan, J. (1988). *Inscapes of the child's world: Jungian counseling in schools and clinics.* Dallas, TX: Spring Publications.

American Psychiatric Association. (1987). *Diagnostic and statistical manual of mental disorders* (3rd ed., rev.). Washington, DC: American Psychiatric Association.

Ammann, R. (1991). *Healing and transformation in sandplay: Creative processes become visible.* La Salle, IL: Open Court.

Auden, W. H. (1975). Numbers and faces. In *Collected shorter poems, 1927–1957* (pp. 319–320). New York: Random House.

Avens, R. (1980). *Imagination is reality: Western Nirvana in Jung, Hillman, Barfield, and Cassirer.* Dallas, TX: Spring Publications.

Baker, B., & Wheelwright, J. (In 1982 ed.). Analysis with the aged. In M. Stein (Ed.), *Jungian analysis* (pp. 256–274). La Salle, IL: Open Court.

Bateson, M. C. (1989). *Composing a life.* New York: Penguin/Plume.

Beebe, J. (Speaker). (1984a). *Basic concepts of Jungian psychology reviewed and renewed* [Two tapes]. San Francisco: C. G. Jung Institute.

Beebe, J. (1984b) Psychological types in transference, countertransference, and the therapeutic interaction. In *Transference/Countertransference* (pp. 147–161). Wilmette, IL: Chiron.

Beebe, J. (Speaker). (1986). *Basic concepts of Jungian psychology: Psychological types* [Two tapes]. San Francisco: C. G. Jung Institute.

Beebe, J. (Speaker). (1988a). *More about types* [Two tapes]. San Francisco: C. G. Jung Institute.

Beebe, J. (1988b). Primary ambivalence toward the Self: Its nature and treatment. *The borderline personality in analysis* (pp. 97–127). Wilmette, IL: Chiron.

Beebe, J. (1991, August). *Jung's personality types*. Albert Einstein Cape Cod Seminars.

Beebe, J. (1992). Identifying the American shadow. *Psychological Perspectives, 27*, 135–139.

Beebe, J. (Speaker). (1993a). *Homosexuality and the renewal of gender* (Audiotape No. 529). Talk given at a conference titled "Who do we think we are? The mystery and muddle of gender," C. G. Jung Institute of Chicago, Evanston, IL.

Beebe, J. (1993b, October). *A Jungian analysis of character*. Paper presented at the National Meeting of Jungian Analysts, Cambridge, MA. (No. 14347) San Francisco: C. G. Jung Institute.

Beebe, J. (1993c). *Jung's typology*. Lectures at the California School of Professional Psychology, Alameda.

Belenky, M. F., Clinchy, B. M., Goldberger, N. R., & Tarule, J. M. (1986). *Women's ways of knowing: The development of self, voice, and mind*. New York: Basic Books.

Bell, J. S. (1988). Nonlocality in physics and psychology: An interview with John Stewart Bell. *Psychological Perspectives, 19*(2), 294–312.

Bellak, L. (1993). *The Thematic Apperception Test, The Children's Apperception Test, and the Senior Apperception Technique in clinical use* (5th ed.). Revised with the collaboration of D. M. Abrams. Boston: Allyn & Bacon.

Bentz, L. T. (1992). Seasoned reflections on midlife transition: A *Quadrant* interview with Aryeh Maidenbaum and Daniel Levinson. *Quadrant, 25*(1), 9–19.

Berne, E. (1964). *Games people play*. New York: Grove Press.

Bohm, D. (1980). *Wholeness and the implicate order*. London: Routledge & Kegan Paul.

Bolen, J. S. (1984). *Goddesses in everywoman*. New York: Harper & Row.

Booth, T. Y. (1990). A suggested analogy for the elusive Self. *Journal of Analytical Psychology, 35*(3), 335–337.

Bradway, K. (1985). *Sandplay bridges and the transcendent function*. San Francisco: C. G. Jung Institute.

Bradway, K., Signell, K. A., Spare, G. S., Stewart, C. S., Stewart, L. H., & Thompson, C. (1990). *Sandplay studies: Origins, theory, and practice*. Boston, Sigo Press.

Brewi, J., & Brennan, A. (1992). Midlife and the spirituality of the child. *Quadrant, 25*(1), 59–71.

Brien, D. E. (Ed.). Quakers & Jung: A fiftieth anniversary. (1993, November–December). *Round Table Review, 1*(2), 10–11, 14.

Butler, T. (1992). Desperation. *Quadrant, 25*(1), 87–99.

Campbell, J. (1976). *The masks of God* (Vols. 1–4). New York: Penguin Books.

Campbell, J. (1988). *The power of myth* [Film series of six programs]. New York: Mystic Fire Video.

Carotenuto, A. (1982). *A secret symmetry*. New York: Random House.

Castaneda, C. (1984). *The fire from within*. New York: Simon & Schuster.

Chess, S., Thomas, A., & Birch, H. (1965). *Your child is a person.* New York: Viking Press.

Chinen, A. B. (1989). *In the ever after: Fairy tales and the second half of life.* Wilmette, IL: Chiron.

Chodorow, J. (1991). *Dance therapy and depth psychology: The moving imagination.* London: Routledge.

Chodorow, N. (1978). *The reproduction of mothering.* Berkeley: University of California Press.

Chomsky, N. (1957). *Syntactic structures.* The Hague, the Netherlands: Mouton.

Chomsky, N. (1986). *Knowledge of language: Its nature, origin, and use.* New York: Greenwood Press.

Clarke, J. J. (1992). *In search of Jung.* New York: Routledge.

Coleman, R. M. (1986). *Wide awake at 3:00 A.M.* New York: Freeman.

Conforti, M. (1994). Morphogenetic dynamics in the analytic relationship. *Psychological Perspectives, 30,* 12–21.

Cooper, J. C. (1978). *An illustrated encyclopedia of traditional symbols.* London: Thames & Hudson.

Crick, F. (1994). *The astonishing hypothesis: The scientific search for the soul.* New York: Charles Scribner's Sons.

DeAngeles, T. (1994). Jung's theories keep pace and remain popular. *APA Monitor,* p. 41.

Dement, W. C. (1972). *Some must watch while some must sleep.* The Portable Stanford, Stanford, CA: Stanford Alumni Association.

Dimen, M. (1994). Money, love, and hate. *Psychoanalytic Dialogues,* 4(1), 69–100.

Ditto, W. L., & Pecora, L. M. (1993, August). Mastering chaos. *Scientific American,* 269(2), 78–84.

Dudai, Y. (1989). *The neurobiology of memory: Concepts, findings, trends.* New York: Oxford University Press.

Eccles, J. C. (1989). *Evolution of the brain: Creation of the self.* New York: Routledge.

Edelman, G. M. (1990). *The remembered present: A biological theory of consciousness.* New York: Basic Books.

Edelman, G. M. (1992). *Bright air, brilliant fire.* New York: Basic Books.

Edinger, E. (1972). *Ego and archetype: Individuation and the religious function of the psyche.* New York: Putnam.

Edinger, E. (Speaker). (1977). *The opus of alchemy* [cassette recording]. San Francisco C. G. Jung Institute.

Edinger, E. (1985). *Anatomy of the psyche.* La Salle, IL: Open Court.

Ehlers, L. (1992). The alchemical Nigredo, Albedo, Citrinitas, and Rubedo: Stages of transformation: A case study. (Doctoral dissertation, California School of Professional Psychology, Alameda, 1992). *Dissertation Abstracts International, 50.* (University Microfilms No. 03B93-12783)

Eliot, T. S. (1988). Burnt Norton. In *Four quartets* (p. 13). New York: Harcourt Brace Jovanovich. (Original work published 1943)

Erikson, E. H. (1963). *Childhood and society* (2nd ed.). New York: Norton.

Estés, C. P. (1992). *Women who run with the wolves.* New York: Ballantine Books.

Exner, J. E. (1986). *The Rorschach: A comprehensive system.* New York: Wiley.

Eysenck, H. J. (1947). *Dimensions of personality.* London: Routledge & Kegan Paul.

Fordham, M. (1957). *New developments in analytical psychology.* London: Routledge & Kegan Paul.

Fordham, M. (1961). Comment on the theory of the original self. *Journal of Analytical Psychology, 6*(1), 78–79.

Fordham, M. (1963). The empirical foundation and theories of the self in Jung's works. *Journal of Analytical Psychology, 8*(1), 1–24.

Fordham, M. (1967). Active imagination—Deintegration or disintegration? *Journal of Analytical Psychology, 12*(1), 51–66.

Fordham M. (1978). Transference and countertransference. In M. Fordham (Ed.), *Jungian psychotherapy* (pp. 80–96). New York: Wiley.

Fosshage, J. L. (1983). The psychological function of dreams: A revised psychoanalytic perspective. *Psychoanalysis and Contemporary Thought, 6*(4), 67.

Freud, S. (1938). *The basic writings of Sigmund Freud.* (A. A. Brill, Ed.). New York: Random House.

Freud, S. (1959). Some psychological consequences of the anatomical distinction between the sexes. In J. Strachey (Ed. and Trans.), *The standard edition of the complete psychological works of Sigmund Freud* (Vol. 20, pp. 257–258). London: Hogarth Press. (Original work published 1925)

Freud, S. (1961). Civilization and its discontents. In J. Strachey (Ed. and Trans.), *The standard edition of the complete psychological works of Sigmund Freud* (Vol. 12, pp. 159–176). London: Hogarth Press. (Original work published 1930)

Friedan, B. (1993). *The fountain of age.* New York: Simon & Schuster.

Gabbard, G. O. (1994). Commentary on papers by Tansey, Hirsch, and Davies. *Psychoanalytic Dialogues, 4*(2), 203–213.

Gates, L. (1992). The death and rebirth of values at midlife. *Quadrant, 25*(1), 111–121.

Gilligan, C. (1982). *In a different voice: Psychological theory and women's development.* Cambridge, MA: Harvard University Press.

Gleick, J. (1987). *Chaos: Making a new science.* New York: Viking Penguin.

Goldberg, A. (1980). Introduction. In A. Goldberg (Ed.), *Advances in self psychology.* New York: International Universities Press.

Goldberger, A. L., Rigney, D. R., & West, B. J. (1990, February). Chaos and fractals in human physiology. *Scientific American, 262*(2), 42–49.

Gray, E. (1970). *A complete guide to the Tarot.* New York: Bantam Books.

Groesbeck, C. J. (1989). C. G. Jung and the shaman's vision. *Journal of Analytical Psychology, 34*, 255–275.

Hall, J. A. (1986). *The Jungian experience: Analysis and individuation.* Toronto: Inner City Books.

Hamilton, E. (1969). *Mythology: Timeless tales of gods and heroes.* New York: Mentor Books. (Original work published 1942)

Hannah, B. (1976). *Jung: His life and work—A biographical memoir.* New York: Putnam.

Hannah, B. (1981). *Encounters with the soul: Active imagination as developed by C. G. Jung.* Boston: Sigo Press.

Harding, M. E. (1952). Anima and animus: A curtain lecture. *Spring,* 25–43.

Harris, A. S. (1988). *Dream record protocol.* Unpublished manuscript. California School of Clinical Psychology, Alameda.

Henderson, J. L. (1964). The archetype of culture. In A. Guggenbühl-Craig (Ed.), *Proceedings of the Second International Congress for Analytical Psychology* (pp. 3–14). Basel: Karger.

Henderson, J. L. (1984). *Cultural attitudes in psychological perspective.* Toronto: Inner City Books.

Henderson, J. L. (1990a). The cultural unconscious. In *Shadow and Self: Selected papers in analytical psychology* (pp. 103–113). Wilmette, IL: Chiron.

Henderson, J. L. (1990b). The origins of a theory of cultural attitudes. In *Shadow and Self: Selected papers in analytical psychology* (pp. 114–123). Wilmette, IL: Chiron.

Henderson, J. L. (1990c). *Shadow and Self: Selected papers in analytical psychology.* Wilmette, IL: Chiron.

Herbert, N. (1988). How Bell proved reality cannot be local. *Psychological Perspectives, 19*(2), 313–319.

Herron, W. G., & Welt, S. R. (1992). *Money matters.* New York: Guilford Press.

Hill, G. (1992). *Masculine and feminine: The natural flow of opposites in the psyche.* Boston: Shambhala.

Hillman, J. (1972). *The myth of analysis: Three essays in archetypal psychology.* Evanston, IL: Northwestern University Press.

Hillman, J. (1979). Senex and Puer. In J. Hillman, H. A. Murray, T. Moore, J. Baird, T. Cowan, & R. Severson (Eds.), *Puer Papers* (pp. 3–53). Dallas, TX: Spring Publications.

Hillman, J. (1980). Silver and the White Earth: Pt. I. *Spring,* 21–48.

Hillman, J. (1981). Silver and the White Earth: Pt. II. *Spring, 1,* 21–66.

Hillman, J. (1982). Salt: A chapter in alchemical psychology. In J. Stroud & G. Thomas (Eds.), *Images of the untouched* (pp. 111–138). Pegasus Foundation Series I. Dallas TX: Spring Publications.

Hillman, J. (1985). *Anima: An anatomy of a personified notion.* Dallas, TX: Spring Publications.

Hillman, J. (1991). The yellowing of the work. *Proceedings of the 11th International Congress for Analytical Psychology, Paris, 1989* (pp. 77–96). Einsedeln, Switzerland: Daimon-Verlag.

Hobson, J. A. (1977). *The dreaming brain.* New York: Basic Books.

Hoffman, I. Z. (1991). Discussion: Toward a social-constructionist view of the psychoanalytic situation. *Psychoanalytic Dialogues, 1,* 74–105.

Hoffman, I. Z. (1992). Some practical implications of a social-constructivist view of the psychoanalytic situation. *Psychoanalytic Dialogues, 2*(3), 287–304.

Hopcke, R. H. (1992). Midlife, gay men, and the AIDS epidemic. *Quadrant, 25*(1), 101–109.

Hopcke, R. H., Carrington, K. L., & Wirth, S. (Eds.). (1993). *Same-sex love and the path to wholeness.* Boston: Shambhala.

Howard, M. (1994). The Jungian reading of Gnosticism—An interview with Robert Segal. *San Francisco Jung Institute Library Journal, 13*(2), 51–65.

Hume, D. (1965). *An enquiry concerning human understanding.* New York: Bantam Books. (Original work published 1777)

Jaffe, L. W. (1990). *Liberating the heart: Spirituality and Jungian psychology.* Toronto: Inner City Books.

James, W. (1902). *Varieties of religious experience.* Cambridge, MA: Riverside Press.

James, W. (1950). *Principles of psychology.* New York: Dover. (Original work published 1890)

Jobes, G. (1962). *Dictionary of mythology, folklore, and symbols.* New York: Scarecrow Press.

Jordan, J., Kaplan, A., Miller, J., Stiver, I., & Surrey, J. (1991). *Women's growth in connection: Writings from the Stone Center.* New York: Guilford Press.

Jung, C. G. (1933). *Modern man in search of a soul.* New York: Harcourt Brace Jovanovich.

Jung, C. G. (1950). *CW 18: The symbolic life (miscellaneous writings).* Bollingen Series XX. Princeton, NJ: Princeton University Press.

Jung, C. G. (1954). The development of personality. In *CW 17: The development of personality* (para. 284–323, pp. 167–186). Bollingen Series XX. Princeton, NJ: Princeton University Press. (Original work published 1934)

Jung, C. G. (1961a). *Memories, dreams, reflections* (A. Jaffé, Ed.). New York: Random House.

Jung, C. G. (1961b). The theory of psychoanalysis. In *CW 4: Freud and psychoanalysis* (para. 203–522, pp. 84–226). Bollingen Series XX. Princeton, NJ: Princeton University Press.

Jung, C. G. (1966a). Anima and Animus. In *CW 7: Two essays on analytical psychology* (2nd ed., para. 296–340, pp. 198–223). Bollingen Series XX. Princeton, NJ: Princeton University Press.

Jung, C. G. (1966b). On the psychology of the unconscious. In *CW 7: Two essays on analytical psychology* (2nd ed., para. 1–201, pp. 3–119). Bollingen Series XX. Princeton, NJ: Princeton University Press.

Jung, C. G. (1966c). On the relation of analytical psychology to poetry. In *CW 15: The spirit in man, art, and literature* (para. 97–132, pp. 65–83). Princeton, NJ: Princeton University Press.

Jung, C. G. (1966d). The aims of psychotherapy. In *CW 16: The practice of psychotherapy* (2nd ed., para. 66–113, pp. 36–52). Princeton, NJ: Princeton University Press.

Jung, C. G. (1966e). The psychology of the transference. In *CW 16: The practice of psychotherapy* (2nd ed., para. 353–539, pp. 163–323). Princeton, NJ: Princeton University Press.

Jung, C. G. (1967a). *CW* 5: *Symbols of transformation* (2nd ed.). Bollingen Series XX. Princeton, NJ: Princeton University Press.

Jung, C. G. (1967b). *CW* 13: *Alchemical studies*. Bollingen Series XX. Princeton, NJ: Princeton University Press.

Jung, C. G. (1967c). Foreword. In *The I Ching or Book of Changes* (3rd ed., pp. xxi–xxxix) (R. Wilhelm & C. Baynes, Trans.). Princeton, NJ: Princeton University Press. (Also in *CW* 11, para. 964–1018)

Jung, C. G. (1967d). *Septem sermones ad mortuos* [Seven sermons to the dead] (2nd ed., H. G. Baynes, Trans.). London: Watkins.

Jung, C. G. (1968). *CW* 12: *Psychology and alchemy* (2nd ed.). Bollingen Series XX. Princeton, NJ: Princeton University Press.

Jung, C. G. (1969a). General aspects of dream psychology. In *CW* 8: *The structure and dynamics of the Psyche* (2nd ed., para. 443–529, pp. 237–280). Bollingen Series XX. Princeton, NJ: Princeton University Press.

Jung, C. G. (1969b). On the nature of the psyche. In *CW* 8: *The structure and dynamics of the psyche* (2nd ed., para. 343–442, pp. 159–234). Bollingen Series XX. Princeton, NJ: Princeton University Press.

Jung, C. G. (1969c). Synchronicity: An acausal connecting principle. In *CW* 8: *The structure and dynamics of the psyche* (2nd ed, para. 815–997, pp. 417–531). Bollingen Series XX. Princeton, NJ: Princeton University Press.

Jung, C. G. (1969d). *CW* 9i: *The archetypes and the collective unconscious* (2nd ed.). Bollingen Series XX. Princeton, NJ: Princeton University Press.

Jung, C. G. (1969e). *CW* 9ii: *Aion* (2nd ed.). Bollingen Series XX. Princeton, NJ: Princeton University Press.

Jung, C. G. (1969f) Answer to Job. In *CW* 11: *Psychology and religion: West and East* (2nd ed., para. 553–758, pp. 355–470). Bollingen Series XX. Princeton, NJ: Princeton University Press.

Jung, C. G. (1969g). Psychological commentary on the "Tibetan Book of the Dead." In *CW* 11: *Psychology and religion: West and East* (2nd ed., para. 831–858). Bollingen Series XX. Princeton, NJ: Princeton University Press.

Jung, C. G. (1970b). The fight with the Shadow. In *CW* 10: *Civilization in transition* (2nd ed., para. 444–457, pp. 218–226). Bollingen Series XX. Princeton, NJ: Princeton University Press.

Jung, C. G. (1970c). Flying saucers: A modern myth. In *CW* 10: *Civilization in transition* (2nd ed., para. 589–824, pp. 309–433). Bollingen Series XX. Princeton, NJ: Princeton University Press.

Jung, C. G. (1970d). Religion as the counterbalance to mass-mindedness. In *CW* 10: *Civilization in transition* (2nd ed., para. 505–516, pp. 256–262). Bollingen Series XX. Princeton/Bollingen Paperback: Princeton University Press.

Jung, C. G. (1970e). The undiscovered self (present and future). In *CW* 10: *Civilization in transition* (2nd ed., para. 488–588, pp. 245–305). Bollingen Series XX. Princeton, NJ: Princeton University Press.

Jung, C. G. (1970f). The conjunction. In *CW 14: Mysterium Coniunctionis* (2nd ed.). Bollingen Series XX. Princeton, NJ: Princeton University Press.

Jung, C. G. (1970g). *CW 14: Mysterium Coniunctionis: An inquiry into the separation and synthesis of psychic opposites in alchemy* (2nd ed.). Princeton, NJ: Princeton University Press.

Jung, C. G. (1971). Definitions. In *CW 6: Psychological types* (para. 672–857, pp. 408–495). Bollingen Series XX. Princeton, NJ: Princeton University Press.

Jung, C. G. (1973a). *CW 2: Experimental researches.* Bollingen Series XX. Princeton, NJ: Princeton University Press.

Jung, C. G. (1973b). *Letters* (Vol. I: 1906–1950) (G. Adler & A. Jaffé, Eds.; Trans. R. F. C. Hull). London, Routledge.

Jung, C. G. (1994). *Collected works* (2nd ed., 20 vols.) (H. Read, M. Fordham, G. Adler, & W. McGuire, Eds.). Bollingen Series XX. Princeton, NJ: Princeton University Press.

Jung, E., & von Franz, M.-L. (1970). *The grail legend.* New York: Putnam.

Kalff, D. M. (1981). *Sandplay: A psychotherapeutic approach to the psyche* (2nd ed.). Boston: Sigo Press.

Kandel, E. R., & Hawkins, R. D. (1992, September). The biological basis of learning and individuality. *Scientific American, 267*(3), 78–86.

Kelpius, J. (1951). In E. Gordon Alderfer (Ed.), *A method of prayer.* New York: Harper & Brothers.

Kerr, J. (1993). *A most dangerous method: The story of Freud, Jung, and Sabina Spielrein.* New York: Knopf.

Kirsch, T. B. (1994). Difficulty at the beginning [Review of *A Most Dangerous Method: The Story of Freud, Jung, and Sabina Spielrein*]. *San Francisco Jung Institute Library Journal, 11*(3), 37–41.

Klein, M. (1953). With J. Rivière. *Love, hate, and reparation.* London: Hogarth Press.

Klein, M. (1975). *Envy and gratitude and other works, 1946–1963.* New York: Delacorte Press.

Kluckhohn, C., & Morgan, W. (1951). Some notes on Navaho dreams. In G. B. Wilbur & W. Muensterberger (Eds.), *Psychoanalysis and culture.* New York: International University Press.

Kohlberg, L. (1969). *Stages in the development of moral thought and action.* New York: Holt, Rinehart & Winston.

Kohut, H. (1971). *The analysis of the self.* New York: International Universities Press.

Kreinheder, A. (1979). *The healing power of illness.* Paper presented at the C. G. Jung Institute, Los Angeles.

Lauwerier, H. (1991). *Fractals: Endlessly repeated geometrical figures.* Princeton, NJ: Princeton University Press.

LeDoux, J. E. (1994, June). Emotion, memory, and the brain. *Scientific American, 270*(6), 32–39.

Lewis, R. (1970). *The way of silence: The prose and poetry of Basho.* New York: Dial Press.

Lockhart, R. A., Hillman, J., Vasavada, A., Perry, J. W., Covitz, J., & Guggenbühl-Craig, A. (1982). *Soul and money.* Dallas, TX: Spring Publications.

Loevinger, J. (1976). *Ego development: Conceptions and theories*. San Francisco: Jossey-Bass.

Machtiger, H. G. (1982). Countertransference-transference. In M. Stein (Ed.), *Jungian analysis* (pp. 86–110). La Salle, IL: Open Court.

Maduro, R. J., & Wheelwright, J. B. (1983). Analytical psychology. In Corsini, R. J., & A. J. Marsella (Eds.), *Personality theories, research, and assessment* (pp. 125–188). Itasca, IL: Peacock Press.

Mahler, M. (1975). *The psychological birth of the human infant*. New York: Bantam Books.

Maidenbaum, A., & Martin, S. A. (1991). *Lingering shadows: Jungians, Freudians, and anti-Semitism*. Boston: Shambhala.

Martin, G. (1994, May 29). The hand of Dog. "This World" section of *San Francisco Chronicle*, p. 12.

Maslow, A. (1962). *Toward a psychology of being*. Princeton, NJ: Van Nostrand.

Maslow, A. (1968). *The farther reaches of human nature* (Rev. ed.). Harmondsworth, Middlesex, England: Penguin.

Matthews, J. (1985, February). Talk given at a sandtray study group. Palo Alto, CA.

Mattoon, M. A. (1984). *Understanding dreams*. Dallas, TX: Spring Publications.

Mattoon, M. A. (1993). Jungian psychology after Jung. *Round Table Review of Contemporary Contributions to Jungian Psychology, 1*(2), 1, 4–7.

Maugham, W. S. (1915). *Of human bondage*. NY: Doubleday, Doran.

May, J., & Groder, M. (1989). Jungian thought and dynamical systems: A new science of archetypal psychology. *Parabola, 20*(1), 142–155.

McAdams, D. P. (1988). *Power, intimacy, and the life story*. New York: Guilford Press.

McCully, R. (1971). *Rorschach theory and symbolism: A Jungian approach to clinical material*. Baltimore: Williams & Wilkins.

McGuire, W. (Ed.). (1974). *The Freud/Jung letters*. Princeton, NJ: Princeton University Press.

Meador, B. DeS. (1992). *Uncursing the dark: Treasures from the underworld*. Wilmette, IL: Chiron.

Mercer, R. T., Nichols, E. G., & Doyle, G. C. (1989). *Transitions in a woman's life: Major life events in developmental context*. New York: Springer.

Miller, A. (1981). *Prisoners of childhood*. New York: Basic books.

Miller, J. B. (1976). *Toward a new psychology of women*. Boston: Beacon Press.

Milner, M. (1957). *On not being able to paint* (2nd ed.). New York: International Universities Press.

Monick, E. (1987). *Phallos: Sacred image of the masculine*. Toronto: Inner City Books.

Morgan, W. (1932). Navaho dreams. *American Anthropologist, 34*, 390–405.

Mullett, G. M. (1991). Spider Woman stories: Legends of the Hopi Indians. Tucson: University of Arizona Press.

Murray, H. A., & Kluckhohn, C. (1951). Personality formation: The determinants. In C. Kluckhohn & H. A. Murray (Eds.), *Personality in nature, society, and culture* (pp. 35–51). New York: Knopf.

Myers, J. B., & McCaulley, M. H. (1985). *Manual: A guide to the development and use of the Myers-Briggs Type Indicator.* Palo Alto, CA: Consulting Psychologists Press.

Napier, A. D. (1986). *Masks, transformation, and paradox.* Berkeley: University of California Press.

Neumann, E. (1954a). On the moon and matriarchal consciousness. *Spring,* 83–100.

Neumann, E. (1954b). *The origins and history of consciousness.* Bollingen Series XLII. Princeton, NJ: Princeton University Press.

Neumann, E. (1973). *The child: Structure and dynamics of the nascent psyche.* New York: Pantheon Books.

Noll, R. (1992). Jung the leontocephalus. *Spring, 53,* 12–60.

Noll, R. (1993). Multiple personality and the complex theory: A correction and a rejection of C. G. Jung's "collective unconscious." *Journal of Analytical Psychology, 38,* 321–323.

Noll, R. (1994). *The Jung cult: Origins of a charismatic movement.* Princeton, NJ: Princeton University Press.

Peat, F. D. (1987). *Synchronicity: The bridge between matter and mind.* New York: Bantam Books.

Peat, F. D. (1994, August). *Codes, structures, and repetition in the natural world.* Assisi Seminar, Assisi, Italy. (Tape available from Assisi Seminars, Box 6033, Brattleboro, VT 05302)

Perera, S. B. (1981). *Descent to the goddess.* Toronto: Inner City Books.

Perera, S. B. (1986). *The scapegoat complex: Towards a mythology of shadow and guilt.* Toronto: Inner City Books.

Perry, J. W. (1970). Emotion and object relations. *Journal of Analytic Psychology, 15(1),* 1–12.

Perry, J. W. (1987). *The self in psychotic process* (Rev. ed.). Dallas, TX: Spring Publications.

Peterson, C. (1989). [Review of the book *Jung: A biography*]. *Journal of Analytic Psychology, 34,* 301–303.

Piaget, J. (1954). *The construction of reality in the child.* New York: Basic Books.

Plaut, F. (1993). *Analysis analyzed.* London: Routledge.

Pribram, K. (1971). *Languages of the brain.* Englewood Cliffs, NJ: Prentice-Hall.

Quenk, A. T., & Quenk, N. L. (1982). The use of psychological typology in analysis. In M. Stein (Ed.), *Jungian analysis* (pp. 157–172). La Salle, IL: Open Court.

Quispel, G. (1994). How Jung became a Gnostic [Review of the book *The Gnostic Jung*]. *San Francisco Jung Institute Library Journal, 13(2),* 47–65.

Radin, P. (1936). Ojibwa and Ottawa puberty dreams. In *Essays in anthropology, presented to A. L. Kroeber.* Berkeley: University of California Press (pp. 233–264).

Riesman, D. (1961). *The lonely crowd.* New Haven, CT: Yale University Press.

Rilke, R. M. (1984). Orpheus, Eurydice, Hermes. In *New poems* (E. Snow, Trans.). San Francisco: North Point Press. (Original work published 1907)

Rorschach, H. (1971). The Rorschach Psychodiagnostic Inkblot Test.

Rossi, E. (1992). What is life? From Quantum Flux to the Self. *Psychological Perspectives 26,* 6–22.

Roth, C. (1994). *The clinical uses of the initial dream in Jungian analysis: Clinical practice compared with the psychoanalytic and Jungian initial dream literature.* (Doctoral dissertation, California School of Professional Psychology, Alameda, 1994). *Dissertation Abstracts International, 55.* (University Microfilms No. 11B9510939)

Rovner, S. (1992). *The clinical use of the initial dream among Freudian psychoanalysts.* (Doctoral dissertation, California School of Clinical Psychology, Alameda, 1992). *Dissertation Abstracts International, 53.* (University Microfilms No. 09B93-03628)

Ruskin, A. (1994, February). Lecture at California School of Professional Psychology, Alameda.

Rutter, R. (1989). A phenomenological study of somatic countertransference and therapist type. (Doctoral dissertation, California School of Professional Psychology, Alameda, 1989). *Dissertation Abstracts International, 50.* (University Microfilms No. 08B89-26370)

Ryce-Menuhin, J. (1992). *Jungian sandplay.* New York: Routledge.

Samuels, A. (1985a). Countertransference, the "Mundus Imaginalis," and a research project. *Journal of Analytic Psychology, 30,* 47–71.

Samuels, A. (1985b). *Jung and the post-Jungians.* London: Routledge & Kegan Paul.

Samuels, A. (1989). *The plural psyche: Personality, morality, and the father.* London: Routledge.

Samuels, A. (1992a). National psychology, national socialism, and analytical psychology: Reflections on Jung and anti-Semitism: Pt. I. *Journal of Analytical Psychology, 37*(1), 3–28.

Samuels, A. (1992b). National psychology, national socialism, and analytical psychology: Reflections on Jung and anti-Semitism: Pt. II. *Journal of Analytical Psychology, 37*(2), 127–147.

Samuels, A., Shorter, B., & Plaut, F. (1986). *A critical dictionary of Jungian analysis.* London: Routledge.

Sandner, D. (1993). The role of Anima in same-sex love between men. In R. H. Hopcke, K. L. Carrington, & S. Wirth (Eds.), *Same-sex love and the path to wholeness* (pp. 219–230). Boston: Shambhala.

Sandner, D. (1994, February). Lecture at California School of Professional Psychology, Alameda.

Sandner, D., & Beebe, J. (1995). Psychopathology and analysis. In M. Stein (ed.) *Jungian analysis* (2nd ed.). 297–348. La Salle, IL: Open Court.

Satinover, J. B., & Bentz, L. T. (1992). Aching in the places where we used to play: A Jungian approach to midlife change. *Quadrant, 25*(1), 21–57.

Scholem, G. (1974). *Kabbalah.* New York: Dorset Press.

Schwartz-Salant, N. (1982). *Narcissism and character transformation.* Toronto: Inner City Books.

Schwartz-Salant, N. (1989). *The borderline personality: Vision and healing.* Wilmette, IL: Chiron.

Schwartz-Salant, N., & Stein, M. (Eds.). (1992). *Chiron: Gender and soul in psychotherapy.* Wilmette, IL: Chiron.

Searle, J. R. (1990, February). Is the brain's mind a computer program? *Scientific American, 262*(2), 26–31.

Segal, R. A. (1992). *The Gnostic Jung.* Princeton, NJ: Princeton University Press.

Shah, I. (1971). *The pleasantries of the incredible Mulla Nasrudin.* New York: Dutton.

Sheldrake, R. (1981). *A new science of life: The hypothesis of formative causation.* Los Angeles: Tarcher.

Shelley, P. B. (1925). Adonais. In T. Hutchinson (Ed.), *The complete poetical works of Percy Bysshe Shelley* (p. 438). London: Oxford University Press.

Shepherd, L. J. (1993). *Lifting the veil: The feminine face of science.* Boston: Shambhala.

Sherry, J. (1989). "Lingering shadows: Jungians, Freudians, and anti-Semitism." Proceedings of a conference at the New School, New York. *San Francisco Jung Institute Library Journal, 8*(4), 28–42.

Sidoli, M. (1989). *The unfolding self.* Boston: Sigo Press.

Singer, J. (1991). *Seeing through the visible world: Jung, Gnosis, and Chaos.* New York: Harper-Collins.

Singer, J., & Loomis, M. (1984). *The Singer-Loomis Inventory of Personality (SLIP).* Palo Alto, CA: Consulting Psychologists Press.

Singer, R. D., & Singer, A. (1969). *Psychological development in children.* Philadelphia: Saunders.

Smoot, G., & Davidson, K. (1993). *Wrinkles in time.* New York: Morrow.

Solomon, H. M. (1991). Archetypal psychology and object relations psychology: History and communalities. *Journal of Analytical Psychology, 36*(3), 307–330.

Spencer, D. M. (1988). [Review of the book *Synchronicity: The bridge between matter and mind*]. *Psychological Perspectives, 19*(1), 153–158.

Sperry, R. (1983). *Science and moral priority.* Oxford, England: Blackwell.

Spielrein, S. (1994). Destruction as the cause of coming into being. *Journal of Analytical Psychology, 39*(2), 155–186.

Stein, M. (1983). *In midlife.* Ann Arbor, MI: Spring Publications.

Stein, M. (Ed.). (1982). *Jungian analysis.* La Salle, IL: Open Court.

Stein, M. (Ed.). (1995). *Jungian analysis.* (2nd ed.). La Salle, IL: Open Court.

Storr, A. (1960). *The integrity of the personality.* London.

Storr, A. (1983). *The essential Jung.* Princeton, NJ: Princeton University Press.

Storr, A. (1988). *Solitude: A return to the self.* New York: Free Press.

Sullivan, B. S. (1989). *Psychotherapy grounded in the feminine principle.* Wilmette, IL: Chiron.

Sullwold, E. (1982). Treatment of children in analytical psychology. In M. Stein (Ed.), *Jungian analysis* (pp. 237–239). La Salle, IL: Open Court.

Tansey, M. J. (1994). Sexual attraction and phobic dread in the countertransference. *Psychoanalytic Dialogues, 4*(2), 139–152.

Tecau, P. (1994). Speaking its name [Review of the book *Same-sex love and the path to wholeness*]. *San Francisco Jung Institute Library Journal, 12*(4), 5–12.

Thomas, A., Chess, S., & Birch, H. G. (1968). *Temperament and behavior disorders in children.* New York: New York University Press.

Tresan, D. I. (1992). The anima of the analyst. In N. Schwartz-Salant & M. Stein (Eds.), *Gender and soul in psychotherapy* (pp. 73–110). Wilmette, IL: Chiron.

Tresan, D. I. (1994). *Training*. Unpublished manuscript on Jungian analytic training.

Ulman, E., & Dachinger, P. (Eds). (1975). *Art therapy in theory and practice*. New York: Schocken Books.

van den Daele, L. (1991). Lecture at California School of Professional Psychology, Alameda.

van Eenwyk, J. R. (1991a). The analysis of defences. *Journal of Analytical Psychology, 36*(2), 141–163.

van Eenwyk, J. R. (1991b). Archetypes, the strange attractors of the psyche. *Journal of Analytical Psychology, 36*(1),1–25.

von Franz, M.-L. (1970). *Puer aeternus* (2nd ed.). Santa Monica, CA: Sigo Press.

von Franz, M.-L. (1980). *On divination and synchronicity*. Toronto: Inner City Books.

von Franz, M.-L. (1988). *Some historical aspects of C. G. Jung's synchronicity hypothesis, psyche, and matter*. Boston: Shambhala.

von Franz, M.-L. (with Hillman, J.). (1971). *Lectures on Jung's typology*. Dallas, TX: Spring Publications.

Walker, B. G. (1983). *The woman's encyclopedia of myths and secrets*. New York: Harper & Row.

Wehr, G. (1987). *Jung: A biography*. Boston: Shambhala.

Weinrib, E. (1983). *Images of the Self: The sandplay therapy process*. Boston: Sigo Press.

Welwood, J. (1982). The holographic paradigm and the structure of experience. In K. Wilber (Ed.), *The holographic paradigm and other paradoxes*. London: Shambhala.

Wheelwright, J. B., Wheelwright, J. H., & Buehler, H. A. (1964). *Jungian Type Survey: The Gray Wheelwrights Test* (18th rev.). San Francisco: Society of Jungian Analysts of Northern California.

Wheelwright, J. H. (1981). *The death of a woman*. New York: St. Martin's Press.

Wheelwright, J. H. (1984). *For women growing older*. Houston, TX: C. G. Jung Educational Center.

Whitehead, A. N. (1967). *Science and the modern world*. New York: Free Press.

Whitmont, E. C. (1969). *The symbolic quest*. Princeton, NJ: Princeton University Press.

Whitmont, E. C., & Perera, S. B. (1989). *Dreams: A portal to the source*. New York: Routledge.

Who do we think we are? The mystery and muddle of gender. [Audiotapes of conference]. (1993, October). Evanston, IL: C. G. Jung Institute of Chicago.

Wickes, F. (1927). *The inner world of childhood*. New York: Appleton.

Willshaw, D. (1981). Holography, associative memory, inductive generalization. In G. E. Hinton & J. A. Anderson (Eds.), *Parallel models of associative memory* (pp. 83–104). Hillsdale, NJ: Erlbaum.

Winnicott, D. W. (1951). Transitional objects and transitional phenomena. In *Through paediatrics to psycho-analysis* (pp. 229–242). New York: Basic Books.

Winnicott, D. W. (1969). The capacity to be alone. *The maturational processes and the facilitating environment* (pp. 29–36). New York: International Universities Press.

Wolf, F. A. (1989). *Taking the quantum leap: The new physics for non-scientists* (Rev. ed.). San Francisco: Harper & Row.

Wolf, F. A. (1994). *The dreaming universe: A mind-expanding journey into the realm where psyche and physics meet.* New York: Simon & Schuster.

Yandell, J. (1977). *The imitation of Jung: An exploration of the meaning of Jungian.* Adaptation of a presentation at the Joint Conference, United States Societies of Jungian analysts, Palm Desert, CA. St.Louis, MO: Centerpoint Foundation.

Yandell, J. (1993, October). Lecture at California School of Professional Psychology, Alameda.

Young-Eisendrath, P. (1992). *Hags and heroes: A feminist approach to Jungian psychotherapy with couples.* Toronto: Inner City Books.

Young-Eisendrath, P., & Wiedeman, F. L. (1987). *Female authority: Empowering women through psychotherapy.* New York: Guilford Press.

Zinkin, L. (1987). The hologram as a model for analytic psychology. *Journal of Analytic Psychology, 32,* 1–21.

Index

TO THE OWNER OF THIS BOOK:

I hope that you have enjoyed *Living with Paradox*, as much as I have enjoyed writing it. I'd like to know as much about your experiences with the book as you care to offer. Only through your comments and the comments of others can I learn how to make *Living with Paradox* a better book for future readers.

School: _____

Your instructor's name: _____

1. What I like most about this book is: _____

_____

_____

2. What I like least about this book is: _____

_____

_____

_____

3. The name of the course in which I used this book is: _____

_____

_____

4. Were all of the chapters of the book assigned for you to read? _____

 If not, which ones weren't? _____

_____

5. In the space below, or on a separate sheet of paper, please write specific suggestions for improving this book and anything else you'd care to share about your experience in using the book.

_____

_____

_____

_____

_____

Optional:

Your name: _____ Date: _____

May Brooks/Cole quote you, either in promotion for *Living with Paradox* or in future publishing ventures?

Yes: _____ No: _____

Sincerely,

Anne Singer Harris

Brooks/Cole is dedicated to publishing quality publications for education in the human services fields. If you are interested in learning more about our publications, please fill in your name and address and request our latest catalogue, using ths prepaid mailer.

Name: _____

Street Address: _____

City, State, and Zip: _____

FOLD HERE

FOLD HERE